WARCRAFT III
THE FROZEN THRONE

EXPANSION SET
OFFICIAL STRATEGY GUIDE
BY BART G. FARKAS

WARCRAFT® THE FROZEN THRONE™
OFFICIAL STRATEGY GUIDE
©2003 PEARSON EDUCATION

BradyGAMES is a registered trade-
mark of Pearson Education, Inc.

BradyGAMES®

An Imprint of Pearson Education
201 West 103rd Street
Indianapolis, Indiana 46290

ISBN: 0-7440-0262-1

Library of Congress No.: 2003107523

Printing Code: The rightmost double-digit number is the year of the book's printing; the
rightmost single-digit number is the number of the book's printing. For example, 03-1
shows that the first printing of the book occurred in 2003.

06 05 04 03   4 3 2 1

Manufactured in the United States of America.

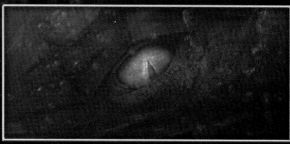

BradyGAMES Staff

Publisher
David Waybright

Editor-In-Chief
H. Leigh Davis

Marketing Manager
Janet Eshenour

Creative Director
Robin Lasek

Licensing Manager
Mike Degler

Assistant Marketing Manager
Susie Nieman

Credits

Senior Project Editor
David B. Bartley

Screenshot Editor
Michael Owen

Production Designer
Tracy Wehmeyer

Lead Designer
Dan Caparo

Design Team
Tim Amrhein
Ann-Marie Deets
Doug Wilkins

BradyGAMES Acknowledgements

Special thanks to Lisa Pearce and Elaine Di Iorio for always making sure we got what we needed and expertly managing the approval process. Thanks also to Frank Gilson for providing us with the myriad item icons that populate this guide. Finally, a Meat Wagon-full of gratitude must be expressed to Kelly Chun, Jason Hutchins, and Nick Carpenter, as well as Evelyn Smith, Zach Callanan, Susan Bronwell, and the entire Blizzard QA staff for lending their time and expertise to this project.

ACKNOWLEDGEMENTS

As always, the people behind the scenes at Brady are responsible for much of the book, and it starts with David Bartley, the editor extraordinaire. Thanks also to Leigh Davis, David Waybright, and the masterful design staff who turn the pages into works of art. As for the folks at Blizzard Entertainment, they (as usual) were spectacular to work with! A big thanks to Elaine Di Iorio, Ian Welke, John Lagrave, Eric Dodds, Paul Sams, Mark Kern, and Chris Sigaty (the producer of this game). For Brian Love in QA, a special credit as the Dunsel supervisor. I am also very grateful to the crew that works on the Warcraft III website, including Geoff Fraizer. As for the many people in QA and all of Blizzard that helped me out, I want to thank them for both their help and for putting up with me! Those folks are:

Zach Allen

Zach Callanan

Frank Gilson

Ray 'you can call me Ray' Laubach

Craig Steele

Dave 'I'm Dave, not Ray' Elliasberg

Justin 'Hair is meant to be orange' Parker

Jonas Laster

Manuel T. Gonzales

Kenny 'Doger Dog' Zigler

Mike Nguyen

Mike 'Burn Man' Kramer

Suzie Brownell

Michelle Elbert

Andrew Brownell

Ron Frybarger

Derek 'the Kurgan' Simmons (who's actually the Producer of Battle.net)

Mark Moser

Rob Pardo

John Yoo

Emilio Segura

…And anyone else that I've forgotten (which I always do)

An extra-special, super-duper thanks to Sean McCrea because I left him out of the last book, and my hope is that this mention will quell his exquisite inner pain.

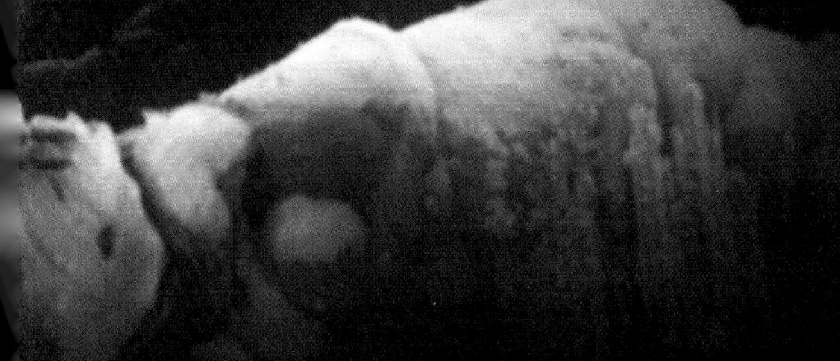

DEDICATION

For Cori 'The Glue' LaCoste

CONTENTS

INTRODUCTION

Warcraft® III: The Frozen Throne™ really isn't an expansion. In my opinion, this is an awesome, stand-alone game that is every bit as complex and rich as Warcraft III was. In fact, the inclusion of the innovative Bonus Campaign, which incorporates many elements from *Diablo® II* into the Warcraft universe, is a stroke of genius that will ensure this game reigns for many years to come as the best RTS on the market.

Because Warcraft III is such a complex realm, and there are so many variants within each mission (not to mention multiplayer), it is impossible to definitively explore each and every permutation and combination of strategy for each mission. In this book, however, we have covered each mission in detail, suggesting one or two guaranteed strategies for accomplishing the tasks set before you. Since The Frozen Throne has many more items, and the missions have a large number of secret power-ups strewn throughout the maps, we have taken great pains to create accurate color maps that show you exactly where you need to go to get these myriad items. In this way, you can make gameplay decisions as to whether or not it's worth going after the loot in question.

Perhaps the best way to use this book is to open the page to the map of each mission, then read the detailed strategy we've provided if you run into any trouble. This method avoids 'ruining' the surprise of the missions, but allows you to have the map right there as an excellent reference.

This game is not only a triumph in the genre of real time strategy, it's a triumph in the history of computer gaming, and we're sure you'll enjoy it as much as we enjoyed putting together this guide.

USING THIS GUIDE

Here's a description of the various elements and layers of information we've provided for the single-player strategy. Familiarize yourself with these conventions to get the most out of this guide.

Our Map Secrets Legend lists all of the items available in each mission. These item icons appear on our map in their secret locations.

Required and Optional Quests are presented upfront so you can plan your strategy.

Creeps and wandering enemy units are identified in small ovals. This indicates a general vicinity and not a precise location, so be on the lookout for these foes when exploring these areas.

Other unique objects on the map appear as text inside rectangular boxes.

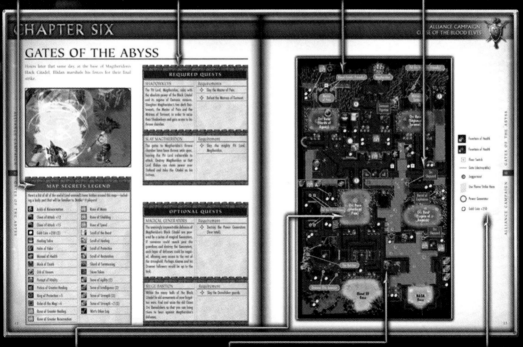

The location and territorial sprawl of each friendly base and enemy camp is clearly identified with a transparent, colorized watermark.

Item icons show you where to find all of the useful power-ups on the map.

Most maps also include a custom legend to provide a library of symbols for neutral buildings, enemy attack paths, preferred routes, and other special features.

BASICS AND MULTIPLAYER TACTICS

WHAT'S NEW

As with all Blizzard expansion games, the Frozen Throne is loaded with great advances, additions, and overall gameplay changes that make it even better than its predecessor. Here's a breakdown of what's new:

- There are many new units, each equipped with new abilities and spells. Every race has several new additions, but there are also new neutral units, as well.
- There is one new Hero per race, including Heroes for the Draenei and the Naga—races that you control in the single-player game.
- Player-built shops are now available, allowing anyone to build their own item shop in their base. Players must no longer go searching for Goblin Merchants; the goodies can be available for purchase right in the center of the base!
- More neutral buildings have been added to the game, giving gamers more items, mercenaries, Heroes, and abilities to purchase.
- There's a host of new multiplayer maps and features.
- Many new Creeps and Critters are unique to the Frozen Throne.
- There are now Neutral Heroes! They are very powerful (just like the Heroes from each race), featuring their own special abilities and powers.

THE BASICS

With such a complex game, there's a great deal of ground that needs to be covered. Fortunately, there's the in-game tutorial, the game's manual, and the excellent Mojo Stormstout's strategy guide on Blizzard's own website. Even with those awesome resources, there are a few key things we think you need to know before moving on.

MANAGING IT ALL

Perhaps the most important aspect of gameplay for first-time Warcraft III gamers to master is using the various shortcuts, hotkeys, and management tricks. These tactics make the gaming experience flow without a hitch. We'll talk a little about the key (pun intended) things to remember here.

CONTROL GROUPS

Using control groups is essential to victory, in both multiplayer and single-player action. Press the CTRL key along with numbers 0-9 to set up 10 distinct control groups. Once assigned as a control group, you can jump to those units simply by hitting the assigned number key.

These groups can be individual units, groups of units, or even Town Halls (so that you can quickly return to your home base). Control groups can even overlap between each other, so that several units can be controlled by two groups. The uses for something like this are limited, but it shows how much flexibility there is in the control group system.

SUB-GROUPS

When units are in a group, they are automatically sorted into sub-groups by type. This means that all the Archers in a group stand out together when you press the TAB key. By using sub-groups, you can efficiently use the spells of a specific unit while remaining within the framework of the main group.

FOLLOW

You can command one unit (or a group of units) to follow another unit by right-clicking on the unit you want it (them) to follow. In this way, you can have several full control groups of units all move together, following the 'lead' control group. Follow is an important ability for protecting key units and for leading large forces into battle.

NEUTRAL BUILDINGS

There are a few new neutral buildings in Warcraft III: The Frozen Throne that add to the rich complexity of the gaming experience. The following section covers these structures and what they contain.

GOBLIN MERCHANT

The Goblin Merchant is a holdover from the original Warcraft III. It allows your Heroes to buy key items that aid them in battle. Here's a list of the items available at the Goblin Merchant and how much they cost.

- Boots of Speed (150 Gold)
- Circlet of Nobility (175 Gold)
- Dust of Apperance (75 Gold)
- Periapt of Vitality (350 Gold)
- Potion of Invisibility (100 Gold)
- Potion of Lesser Invulnerability (150 Gold)
- Scroll of Healing (250 Gold)
- Scroll of Protection (150 Gold)
- Scroll of Town Portal (350 Gold)
- Staff of Teleportation (100 Gold)
- Tome of Retraining (300 Gold)

GOBLIN LABORATORY

The Goblin Laboratory is the place to purchase all things Goblin, such as the Goblin Shredder (which can harvest huge amounts of lumber quickly), the Goblin Zeppelin (an aerial transport), the Goblin Sapper (a demolition unit), and Reveal (which shows everything on a portion anywhere on the map for six seconds).

- Goblin Sapper (215 Gold, 100 Lumber, 2 Food)
- Goblin Zeppelin (240 Gold, 60 Lumber, 0 Food)
- Goblin Shredder (375 Gold, 100 Lumber, 4 Food)
- Reveal (50 Gold)

GOBLIN SHIPYARD

This is a key structure in many single-player missions. The Goblin Shipyard produces the Transport Ship, which can haul your units across great expanses of water.

- Transport (170 Gold, 50 Lumber, 0 Food)

TAVERN

The Tavern is one of the new structures to Warcraft III: The Frozen Throne. It allows you to purchase one of five Neutral Heroes, including the Naga Sea Witch (which you play in the single-player game), and the Pandaren Brewmaster (available in the Orc Campaign). Here's a list of the Heroes available in the Tavern.

NAGA SEA WITCH

Cost: 425 🪙 100 🪵 5	Primary Attribute: Intelligence
Attack Type: Hero	Strength Bonus per Level: 2
Range: 600	Agility Bonus per Level: 1
Defense Type: Hero	Intelligence Bonus per Level: 3
Move Speed: Fast	Production Hotkey: G

LEVEL	ATTACK (GROUND/AIR)	ARMOR	STRENGTH	AGILITY	INTELLIGENCE	HIT POINTS	MANA
1	24-34 [29 avg]	3	15	16	22	475	330
2	27-37 [32 avg]	3	17	17	25	525	375
3	30-40 [35 avg]	3	19	18	28	575	420
4	33-43 [38 avg]	4	21	19	31	625	465
5	36-46 [41 avg]	4	23	20	34	675	510
6	39-49 [44 avg]	4	25	21	37	725	555
7	42-52 [47 avg]	5	27	22	40	775	600
8	45-55 [50 avg]	5	29	23	43	825	645
9	48-58 [53 avg]	5	31	24	46	875	690
10	51-61 [56 avg]	6	33	25	49	925	735

FORKED LIGHTNING

Mana Cost: 110

Cooldown: 11 seconds

Range: 600

AOE: 125

Brings up a scorching bolt of lighting that hits a maximum of three enemy units.

Level 1 – 100 Damage per enemy unit.

Level 2 – 175 Damage per enemy unit.

Level 3 – 250 Damage per enemy unit.

FROST ARROWS

Mana Cost: 7

Range: 700

Duration: 5 seconds (1.5 for Heroes)

Adds a cold attack to the Naga Sea Witch's attacks, which both adds damage and slows the enemy that the attack hits.

Level 1 – 30% attack Rate, 30% movement rate.

Level 2 – 50% attack Rate, 50% movement rate.

Level 3 – 70% attack Rate, 70% movement rate.

MANA SHIELD

Mana Cost: 25

Cooldown: 10 seconds

Applies the Mana in the Sea Witch's cache to absorb damage from enemy attacks. In a tough melee battle, this skill can significantly extend this Hero's life.

Level 1: 1 damage per point of Mana.

Level 2: 1.5 damage per point of Mana.

Level 3: 2 damage per point of Mana.

TORNADO (ULTIMATE)

Mana Cost: 250

Cooldown: 120 Seconds

Range: 700

Duration: 40 seconds

Summons a controllable Tornado that tosses enemy ground unti into the air, damages buildings, and slows nearby units. Tornado does 50 damage per second to buildings directly under it, and 7 damage per second to nearby buildings. It's a great spell to use when trying to wipe out an entire enemy base.

DARK RANGER

Cost: 425 🔘 100 🌲 5 🍖		Primary Attribute: Agility	
Attack Type: Hero		Strength Bonus per Level: 1.9	
Range: 600		Agility Bonus per Level: 1.5	
Defense Type: Hero		Intelligence Bonus per Level: 2.6	
Move Speed: Fast		Production Hotkey: R	

LEVEL	ATTACK (GROUND/AIR)	ARMOR	STRENGTH	AGILITY	INTELLIGENCE	HIT POINTS	MANA
1	21-31 [26 avg]	4	18	19	15	550	225
2	22-32 [27 avg]	4	19	20	17	575	255
3	24-34 [29 avg]	5	21	22	20	625	300
4	25-35 [30 avg]	5	23	23	22	675	330
5	27-37 [32 avg]	6	25	25	25	725	375
6	28-38 [33 avg]	6	27	26	28	775	420
7	30-40 [35 avg]	6	29	28	30	825	450
8	31-41 [36 avg]	7	31	29	33	875	495
9	33-43 [38 avg]	7	33	31	35	925	525
10	34-44 [39 avg]	8	35	32	38	975	570

SILENCE

Mana Cost: 75

Cooldown: 15 seconds

Range: 900

Unit Duration: 16/20/24 sec (8/10/12 for Heroes)

Prevents all enemies in a targeted area from casting spells.

| Level 1 – Prevents spell casting AOE: 200 |
| Level 2 – Prevents spell casting AOE: 275 |
| Level 3 – Prevents spell casting AOE: 350 |

BLACK ARROW

Mana Cost: 6

Cooldown: 2/0/0 seconds

Range: 600/700/700

Duration: 2 seconds

Adds extra damage to attacks. Units killed while under the effect of a Dark Arrow turn into Dark Minions.

| Level 1: 2 bonus damage, 200 hit point Lesser Dark Minion. |
| Level 2: 10 bonus damage, 260 hit point Dark Minion. |
| Level 3: 20 bonus damage, 320 hit point Greater Dark Minion. |

LIFE DRAIN

Mana Cost: 75

Cooldown: 8 seconds

Range: 500

Duration: 8 seconds

Sucks the life essence out of a targeted enemy by stealing points from it every second and returning them to the Dark Ranger! Obviously, this skill can make the Dark Ranger not only lethal, but also very resilient to damage!

| Level 1: 20 hit points drained per second. |
| Level 2: 35 hit points drained per second. |
| Level 3: 50 hit points drained per second. |

CHARM

Mana Cost: 150

Cooldown: 45 seconds

Range: 700

Takes control of a targeted enemy unit. While very powerful, it cannot be use on Heroes or Creeps above level 5. Still, it allows you to control units that you would not otherwise have access to, like shamans, certain Creeps, or your enemy's troops.

PANDAREN BREWMASTER

Cost: 425 🪙 100 🌿 5 🍺	Primary Attribute: Strength
Attack Type: Hero	Strength Bonus per Level: 3
Range: Melee	Agility Bonus per Level: 1.5
Defense Type: Hero	Intelligence Bonus per Level: 1.5
Move Speed: Average	Production Hotkey: N

LEVEL	ATTACK (GROUND/AIR)	ARMOR	STRENGTH	AGILITY	INTELLIGENCE	HIT POINTS	MANA
1	24-34 [29 avg]	3	22	14	15	650	225
2	27-37 [32 avg]	4	25	15	16	725	240
3	30-40 [35 avg]	4	28	17	18	800	270
4	33-43 [38 avg]	4	31	18	19	875	285
5	36-46 [41 avg]	5	34	20	21	950	315
6	39-49 [44 avg]	5	37	21	22	1025	330
7	42-52 [47 avg]	6	40	23	24	1100	360
8	45-55 [50 avg]	6	43	24	25	1175	375
9	48-58 [53 avg]	7	46	26	27	1250	405
10	51-61 [56 avg]	7	49	27	28	1325	420

BREATH OF FIRE

Mana Cost: 75

Cooldown: 10 seconds

Range: 500/700/700

AOE: 150

Duration: 5 seconds

Sends a blast of fire at enemy units that deals extensive damage. Units under the influence of Drunken Haze also ignite and take fire damage over time! Always use Drunken Haze first, then hit them with Breath of Fire.

| Level 1: 50 initial damage, 7 damage/sec. |
| Level 2: 100 initial damage, 14 damage/sec. |
| Level 3: 150 initial damage, 21 damage/sec. |

DRUNKEN HAZE

Mana Cost: 75

Cooldown: 12 seconds

Range: 550

AOE: 200

Unit Duration: 12 seconds (5 seconds for Heroes)

Covers an enemy unit in alcohol, reducing its movement speed and giving the enemy unit a chance to miss on their attacks. When a unit with Drunken Haze is hit with Breath of Fire, they burn and incur damage over time.

Level 1: 50% movement speed loss, 45% chance to miss.
Level 2: 50% movement speed loss, 65% chance to miss.
Level 3: 50% movement speed loss, 80% chance to miss.

DRUNKEN BRAWLER (PASSIVE)

Gives an increased likelihood of avoiding attacks and a 10% chance to deal additional damage. Much like the Demon Hunter's Evasion ability, this skill helps the Brewmaster to avoid getting hit, but it also allows him to occasionally inflict massive damage on his enemies.

Level 1: 7% evasion, 2 times normal damage.
Level 2: 14% evasion, 3 times normal damage.
Level 3: 21% evasion, 4 times normal damage.

STORM, EARTH, AND FIRE (ULTIMATE)

Mana Cost: 150

Cooldown: 180 seconds

Duration: 60 seconds

Breaks the Pandaren Brewmaster into three elements, forming a trio of unique fighters. If any of the elements survive until the end of their summoned life, they return to being the Pandaren Brewmaster.

Storm: Has 1000 hit points and can use Dispel Magic, Cyclone, Wind Walk, and Resistant Skin.

Earth: Has 1500 Hit Points and can use Pulverize, Taunt, Spell Immunity, and Resistant Skin.

Fire: Has 900 Hit Points and can use Permanent Immolation and Resistant Skin.

BEASTMASTER

Cost: 425 🪙 100 🪵 5 🎈	Primary Attribute: Strength
Attack Type: Hero	Strength Bonus per Level: 2.9
Range: Melee	Agility Bonus per Level: 1.3
Defense Type: Hero	Intelligence Bonus per Level: 1.8
Move Speed: Fast	Production Hotkey: S

LEVEL	ATTACK (GROUND)	ARMOR	STRENGTH	AGILITY	INTELLIGENCE	HIT POINTS	MANA
1	27-37 [32 avg]	3	25	14	15	725	225
2	29-39 [34 avg]	4	27	15	16	775	240
3	32-42 [37 avg]	4	30	16	18	850	270
4	35-45 [40 avg]	4	33	17	20	925	300
5	38-48 [43 avg]	5	36	19	22	1000	330
6	41-51 [46 avg]	5	39	20	24	1075	360
7	44-54 [49 avg]	5	42	21	25	1150	375
8	47-57 [52 avg]	6	45	23	27	1225	405
9	50-60 [55 avg]	6	48	24	29	1300	435
10	53-63 [58 avg]	7	51	25	31	1375	465

SUMMON BEAR

Mana Cost: 125

Cooldown: 40 seconds

Duration: 70 seconds

Summons a powerful bear that attacks on the Beastmaster's behalf. This creature has Blink and Bash (Passive) abilities.

| Level 1: Summons Bear with 600 hit points. |
| Level 2: Summons Raging Bear with 900 hit points. |
| Level 3: Summons Spirit Bear with 1200 hit points. |

SUMMON QUILBEAST

Mana Cost: 75

Cooldown: 20 seconds

Duration: 70 seconds

Summons a powerful quilbeast that attacks on the Beastmaster's behalf. This creature has the Frenzy (autocast) ability and also receives area of effect damage.

| Level 1: Summons Quilbeast with 425 hit points. |
| Level 2: Summons Dire Quilbeast with 515 hit points. |
| Level 3: Summons Raging Quilbeast with 600 hit points. |

SUMMON HAWK

Mana Cost: 35

Cooldown: 70 seconds

Duration: 70 seconds

Summons a powerful hawk that attacks on the Beastmaster's behalf. This creature has the True Sight ability and also receives Invisibility similar to the Far Seer's Feral Spirit skill.

| Level 1: Summons Hawk with 300 hit points. |
| Level 2: Summons Thunder Hawk with 625 hit points. |
| Level 3: Summons Spirit Hawk with 875 hit points. |

STAMPEDE (ULTIMATE)

Mana Cost: 150

Cooldown: 180 seconds

Range: 300

AOE: 1000

Duration: 30 seconds

Calls down a herd of rampaging thunder lizards that trample the Beastmaster's enemies. Every lizard does 80 damage to each victim. Stampede is an awesome spell to use on large groups of enemies, especially on enemy bases, because it deals huge amounts of damage to enemy buildings.

PIT LORD

Cost: 425 ⚪ 100 ⛏ 5 🍖

Attack Type: Hero	Primary Attribute: Strength
Range: Melee	Strength Bonus per Level: 3.2
Defense Type: Hero	Agility Bonus per Level: 1.3
Move Speed: Fast	Intelligence Bonus per Level: 1.5
	Production Hotkey: I

LEVEL	ATTACK (GROUND)	ARMOR	STRENGTH	AGILITY	INTELLIGENCE	HIT POINTS	MANA
1	26-36 [31 avg]	2	24	14	14	700	210
2	29-39 [34 avg]	3	27	15	15	775	225
3	32-42 [37 avg]	3	30	16	17	850	255
4	35-45 [40 avg]	3	33	17	18	925	270
5	38-48 [43 avg]	4	36	19	20	1000	300
6	42-52 [47 avg]	4	40	20	21	1100	315
7	45-55 [50 avg]	4	43	21	23	1175	345
8	48-58 [53 avg]	5	46	23	24	1250	360
9	51-61 [56 avg]	5	49	24	26	1325	390
10	54-64 [59 avg]	6	52	25	27	1400	405

RAIN OF FIRE

Mana Cost: 85

Cooldown: 8 Seconds

Range: 800

AOE: 200

Duration: 3 seconds

Invokes multiple waves of fire that scorch units over an area. Each wave does damage, then continues to burn its victims for three seconds.

Level 1: 25 damage per wave, 6 waves, 5 damage per second after wave.

Level 2: 30 damage per wave, 8 waves, 10 damage per second after wave.

Level 3: 35 damage per wave, 10 waves, 15 damage per second after wave.

HOWL OF TERROR

Mana Cost: 75

Cooldown: 12 Seconds

AOE: 500

Duration: 15 seconds

A terrifying sound that causes nearby enemy units to shiver in fear, reducing their attack damage.

Level 1: 25% attack damage reduction.

Level 2: 35% attack damage reduction.

Level 3: 45% attack damage reduction.

CLEAVING ATTACK (PASSIVE)

Gives the Pit Lord an attack that damages multiple enemies instead of one.

Level 1: 25% splash damage.

Level 2: 45% splash damage.

Level 3: 65% splash damage.

DOOM (ULTIMATE)

Mana Cost: 150

Cooldown: 120 seconds

Range: 650

Marks a targeted unit for the manifestation of a Demon. The afflicted unit will take 40 damage per second until it dies. Upon its death, a great Demon called a Doom Guard spawns from its corpse! This can create some odd situations where healers are trying to keep a Doomed unit alive to prevent the arrival of the Demon! Each Doom Guard has 1350 hit points and can use Dispel Magic, War Stomp, Cripple, and Rain of Fire.

MERCENARY CAMP

The Mercenary Camp is usually a welcome sight because there are so many great Creeps that can be purchased there. Note that each camp usually only carries three Creeps. Here's a list of what's available at Mercenary Camps (descriptions of each Creep are covered in our single-player campaign strategy as you encounter the various Mercenary Camps along the way).

Forest Troll Shadow Priest		Satyr Shadowdancer		Centaur Outrunner		Makrura Snapper
Forest Troll Berserker		Furbolg Shaman		Harpy Rogue		Mur'gul Snarecaster
Mud Golem		Thunder Lizard		Harpy Windwitch		Makrura Deepseer
Ogre Mauler		Gnoll Brute		Razormane Medicine Man		Barbed Arachnathid
Assassin		Gnoll Warden		Nerubian Warrior		Blue Dragonspawn Meddler
Kobold		Ogre Magi		Nerubian Webspinner		Polar Furbolg Shaman
Kobold Geomancer		Ice Troll Trapper		Frost Revenant		Magnataur Warrior
Murloc Huntsman		Ice Troll Berserker		Burning Archer		Fel Beast
Murloc Flesheater		Gnoll Overseer		Wildkin		Draenei Disciple
Sludge Flinger		Rogue		Kobold Geomancer		Draenei Darkslayer
Satyr Soulstealer		Forest Troll High Priest		Giant Sea Turtle		Voidwalker

DRAGON ROOSTS

This is the place to buy various Dragons for your own use. They usually have Dragon Whelps, Drakes, and one of the six varieties of Dragons (Red, Black, Blue, Bronze, Green, or Nether) available for purchase.

MARKETPLACE

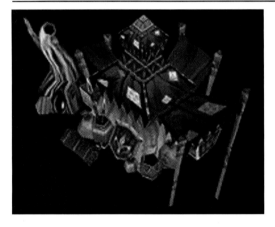

The Marketplace is a shop with a special stock of items. A new item is added to the stock every 30 seconds, so you can never be sure what you'll find there. Once an item is purchased, it's gone! Marketplaces do not stock items until two minutes into the game (multiplayer only).

FOUNTAINS OF HEALTH/MANA/POWER

These oases provide you with either Health or Mana in remote areas of the maps—and in the case of the Fountain of Power, both Mana *and* Health. They are usually well guarded by Creeps, and often become areas of contention in multiplayer games.

MULTIPLAYER TACTICS

The Warcraft III multiplayer experience has spawned vast ranks of expert gamers who have complex and highly refined strategies for playing the game on Battle.net®. The Frozen Throne will certainly not cool off their enthusiasm for this competitive environment, and you can expect these aficionados to be challenging for the top ladder positions from day one. This section will not make those gamers any better; instead, it's intended for novice Warcraft gamers who are just getting into the world of multiplayer Warcraft III. Many of these tips were culled from the Blizzard staff, and the names of those involved are noted with each tip.

ZACH ALLEN

❖ When attacking Creeps with ground troops, push them toward your troops with a small group of air units.

ANDREW BROWNELL

❖ Make your first Hero a tough melee-type, like the Paladin, the Tauren Chieftain, the Crypt Lord, or the Demon Hunter.

SUZANNE BROWNELL

❖ If you don't know the map, pay attention to the Creep camp size designated on the mini-map when engaging these foes.

❖ The Crypt Lord with Carrion Beetles and Spiked Carapace makes a good tank for an army of Crypt Fiends. Adding a Dreadlord for Vampiric Aura increases the effectiveness.

❖ Take advantage of allies' player-built shops in team games. Healing Salves, Healing Scrolls, Wands of Necromancy, and Clarity Potions are unique to some shops and are worth a trip to friendly bases.

❖ The Warden and Priestess of the Moon make for a scary combo. Shadow Strike an enemy Hero with the Warden and have the Priestess force fire on it.

❖ Use the Naga Sea Witch with other Heroes who have area damage dealing spells; such as the Far Seer, Tauren Chieftain, Lich, Dreadlord, and Warden. Three Heroes with high damage area of effect spells can wipe out entire armies by themselves.

❖ The Blood Mage's Banish skill can be used in conjunction with a Mountain King. Send the Mountain King in Banished, and have him Thunder Clap in the middle of your opponent's army, nearly invulnerable. Then run him away and Flame Strike the slowed units. Make certain your opponent does not have a lot of spellcasters when using this tactic.

MICHELLE ELBERT

❖ Remember that you can kill Critters that you see wandering the countryside. When these creatures die, they leave a corpse that can be used to raise skeletons. You can also use these corpses to have your Ghouls Cannibalize in order to restore their health!

MANUEL GONZALES

❖ When you start a game, train a Blood Mage and learn Banish. Take a Peasant with this Hero, then move to the enemy base. When your troops are near this destination, Banish your Peasant and walk around the enemy base. You can spy on them, and they can't touch you!

❖ If you like a good fight and enjoy playing the Orcs, train a Shadow Hunter and learn the Healing Wave skill. Build an army of Orc Grunts and kill the Creeps in your area. Healing Wave can save your Grunts for more combat. As you level up, learn the Serpent Ward. Now you have a formidable force early in the game with your Grunts, Healing Wave skill, and the Serpent Wards.

❖ At the beginning of a game, create a Voodoo Lounge and train a Blademaster. Buy as many Healing Salves as you can afford. Attack your enemy by killing his Peasants, Peons, Acolytes, or Wisps. Use the Healing Salves to stay alive, then run away when you are near death or out of Healing Salves.

ALEX TSANG

❖ Spell Breakers are the perfect complement to a Blizzard or Flame Strike attack. Their Spell Immunity allows them to wade through these spells without having to worry about spell damage.

JOHN YOO

❖ Upgrades are extremely important. If you and your opponent's armies are equal in strength, then upgrades will determine the outcome of the battle. Upgrade when the opportunity arises, especially when it comes to armor.

GENERAL TIPS

❖ An Archmage with Summon Water Elemental and Brilliance Aura, together with a Beastmaster who has Summon Bear and Summon Quilbeast, make for an instant army that grows throughout a battle.

❖ Using a Brewmaster and Demon Hunter in conjunction is great for a ranged army, where your Heroes take the majority of hits.

❖ Use Shades. If you really want to track the movement of your opponents, have a Shade get near your opponent's Hero, then right-click on the Hero to have the Shade follow the Hero wherever he/she goes. This gives you access to your enemy's every move!

PRIMARY RACES

The four primary races from Warcraft III have made it into The Frozen Throne. However, the Human race is slightly different in the single-player missions with the inclusion of several unique units, including Elven Archers. Indeed, all of the races feature new units and abilities that stretch the strategic possibilities of the Warcraft III universe even farther. Not only all this, but each race also contains one new Hero to lead the troops in battle.

NEW HUMAN STRUCTURES

ARCANE VAULT

Cost: 130 ● 30 ▲	
Hit Points: 485	
Fortified Defense: 5	

The Arcane Vault is basically a portable shop for any unit with an Inventory, making many key items available to your Heroes at all times (for a price). Select Build Arcane Vault for a Peasant to create this shop that sells items. The available merchandise depends on the upgrade level of your Town Hall, as well as which buildings you have to support the Arcane Vault. Once you've fully upgraded your base, the Arcane Vault reaches its zenith in terms of the variety of items it offers.

Items like Ivory Towers (cheap, portable Scout Towers) can aid greatly when establishing a low-cost, defensive perimeter around your base. Other items, like the Mechanical Critter, can be used for scouting enemy locations. In short, having an Arcane Vault is essential for victory in multiplayer games because it puts so many powerful items at the tips of the Heroes' fingers.

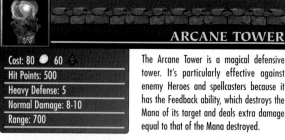

ARCANE TOWER

Cost: 80 ● 60 ▲	
Hit Points: 500	
Heavy Defense: 5	
Normal Damage: 8-10	
Range: 700	

The Arcane Tower is a magical defensive tower. It's particularly effective against enemy Heroes and spellcasters because it has the Feedback ability, which destroys the Mana of its target and deals extra damage equal to that of the Mana destroyed.

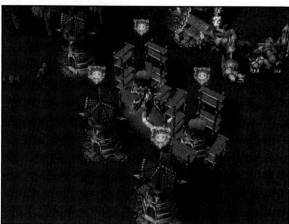

Magic Sentry

Cost: 50 ○ 50 ▲

Researched in Arcane Sanctum. Allows Human Towers (of all kinds) to see invisible enemy units. It's critical in multiplayer games because your enemies often use invisibility to get behind your front lines.

Reveal

Once you have researched Magic Sentry, Reveal allows you to view a small area anywhere on the map for 15 seconds. This ability has a cooldown of 180 seconds, but there is no specific cost associated with it.

Feedback

Feedback is an ability of the Arcane Tower that destroys 24 Mana per hit on the enemy. The Mana that's destroyed combusts, dealing damage to the unit that is being hit by Feedback! By draining away Mana and using it against the enemy, this ability makes Arcane Towers effective against any enemy that has a large pool of Mana.

NOTE

You can upgrade to a Guard Tower, a Cannon Tower, or an Arcane Tower from the Scout Tower, but once you've converted a Scout Tower into one of these other structures, that's it. You cannot upgrade a Guard Tower to a Cannon Tower or vice versa. Once the choice is made, you've committed for good. Since Cannon Towers can attack only ground units, and Arcane Towers are more effective against Heroes and spellcasters, it's a good idea to always have a variety of defensive towers in your base.

NEW HUMAN ABILITIES & UPGRADES

There are plenty of new upgrades tucked away inside the Human tech tree. This section shows you exactly what's new or changed.

Backpack

Cost: 50 ○ 25 ▲

Researched At: Town Hall/Castle/Keep   Benefits: All non-flying units

Enables Riflemen, Footmen, Knights, Priests, Sorceresses, and Spell Breakers to each carry up to two items.

Fragmentation Shards (Passive)

Cost: 50 ○ 100 ▲

Researched At: Workshop   Benefits: Mortar Teams

Upgrades the mortar shells on Mortar Teams, thus increasing the damage they inflict on unarmored and medium-armored enemy units.

Flak Cannons (Passive)

Cost: 100 ○ 150 ▲

Researched At: Workshop   Benefits: Flying Machines

Upgrades the weapons on Flying Machines, giving them an area of effect damage against air units. This is critical during large air battles against Hippogryphs or Faerie Dragons.

Barrage

Cost: 50 ○ 150 ▲

Benefits: Siege Engines

Upgrades the Siege Engine, giving it the ability to damage nearby air units. This is another excellent ability to have when the enemy swarms in with a pack of Chimaeras!

NEW HUMAN UNITS

SPELL BREAKER

Cost: 215 ● 30 ⏣ 3	
Normal Damage: 13-15	
Range: 250 (land only)	
Heavy Defense: 3	
Move Speed: Fast	
Hit Points: 650	
Mana: 250	

The Spell Breaker is an Elven warrior who's trained to destroy spellcasters. This unit starts out with Spell Steal, which manipulates magical buffs to the Spell Breaker's advantage. Spell Immunity and Feedback are also available to the Spell Breaker, as well as Control Magic, which allows him to take control of enemy summoned units.

Spell Steal

Mana Cost: 60

Steals a positive buff from an enemy unit and applies it to a nearby friendly unit, or takes a negative buff from a friendly unit and applies it to a nearby enemy unit. This valuable skill is best set to Autocast. This is the most important of the Spell Breaker's abilities because it takes a positive magical buff from an enemy and applies it to a friendly unit. It's especially important when fighting savvy enemies that use a lot of magic.

Feedback

Destroys Mana with every hit on the enemy. The bonus is that the Mana that's destroyed combusts, dealing damage to the unit that is being hit by Feedback!

Control Magic

Cost: 75 ○ 75 ▲

Mana: 30% of the targeted unit's base hit points.

Researched in Arcane Sanctum. Gives the Spell Breaker the ability to take control of enemy summoned units for Alliance use. This ability can single-handedly turn the tide of the battle by instantly changing the attacker/defender ratio.

Spell Immunity

Mana Cost: Passive

Provides a permanent immunity to magic.

 Provides a permanent immunity to magic.

DRAGONHAWK RIDER

Cost: 235 ● 40 ⏣ 3	
Piercing Damage: 19-21	
Range: 300	
Light Defense: 1	
Move Speed: Fast	
Hit Points: 575	
Mana: 300	

This swift flying unit is mounted by an Elven warrior. It has the Aerial Shackles ability, which allows it to temporarily immobilize and disarm enemy air units. The Dragonhawk Rider can also learn Animal War Training (hit point upgrade), as well as Cloud, which interferes with the ability of enemy ranged buildings to attack. As mentioned above, Cloud can also be used to take out enemy defensive structures from the air. Simply apply Cloud to all the defensive structures, then attack the buildings one at a time from the air with a group of Flying Machines or Dragonhawk Riders. You may need to occasionally reapply Cloud. Since it effectively makes the building's range zero, the defensive building will not attack air or ground units.

Cloud

Cost: 50 ○ 100 ▲

Mana Cost: 100

Provides the Dragonhawk Riders with the ability to impair an enemy ranged-attack building (like a Guard Tower or an upgraded Ziggurat). Cloud lasts 30 seconds, and is very important when it comes to protecting your aerial units during an enemy base assault. The Cloud ability allows you to completely disable all structure-based enemy defenses! By putting Cloud on a Ziggurat (for example), your Dragonhawk Riders can pummel the Ziggurat from the air without fear of counterattack.

Aerial Shackles

Mana Cost: 75

Magically blinds a target enemy air unit so that it cannot move or attack. The targeted unit takes 20 damage per second, and the Shackles last 40 seconds. This is ideal for stopping enemies that like to use large numbers of aerial units to attack your base. Use Aerial Shackles on a fleet of (rather expensive) Chimaeras to raise the ire of your attacker.

HUMANS: THE ALLIANCE   UNITS AND STRUCTURES

NEW HUMAN HERO

BLOOD MAGE

Cost: 425 ⬤ 100 ⬍ 5 ↗

| Attack Type: Hero |
| Range: 600 |
| Defense Type: Hero |
| Move Speed: Fast |
| Primary Attribute: Intelligence |
| Strength Bonus per Level: 2 |
| Agility Bonus per Level: 1 |
| Intelligence Bonus per Level: 3 |
| Production Hot Key: B |

This mystical Hero is skilled at controlling magic and ranged assaults. The Blood Mage can learn Flame Strike, Banish, Siphon Mana, and Phoenix, and can attack both land and air units with this primary attack.

LEVEL	ATTACK (GROUND/AIR)	ARMOR	STR.	AGILITY	INT.	HP	MANA
1	21-27 [24 avg]	2	18	14	19	550	285
2	24-30 [27 avg]	3	20	15	22	600	330
3	27-33 [30 avg]	3	22	16	25	650	375
4	30-36 [33 avg]	3	24	17	28	700	420
5	33-39 [36 avg]	3	26	18	31	750	465
6	36-42 [39 avg]	4	28	19	34	800	510
7	39-45 [42 avg]	4	30	20	37	850	555
8	42-48 [45 avg]	4	32	21	40	900	600
9	45-51 [48 avg]	5	34	22	43	950	645
10	48-54 [51 avg]	5	36	23	46	1000	690

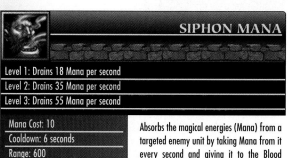

SIPHON MANA

| Level 1: Drains 18 Mana per second |
| Level 2: Drains 35 Mana per second |
| Level 3: Drains 55 Mana per second |

| Mana Cost: 10 |
| Cooldown: 6 seconds |
| Range: 600 |
| Duration: 6 seconds |

Absorbs the magical energies (Mana) from a targeted enemy unit by taking Mana from it every second and giving it to the Blood Mage. At higher levels, Siphon Mana can quickly replenish a great deal of the Blood Mage's Mana (up to 330 Mana). Although this ability has a range of 600, the targeted unit continues channeling Mana to the Blood Mage as long as they are within 850 units.

BANISH

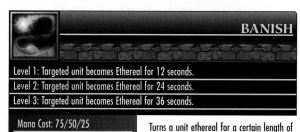

| Level 1: Targeted unit becomes Ethereal for 12 seconds. |
| Level 2: Targeted unit becomes Ethereal for 24 seconds. |
| Level 3: Targeted unit becomes Ethereal for 36 seconds. |

| Mana Cost: 75/50/25 |
| Cooldown: 10 seconds |
| Range: 800 |

Turns a unit ethereal for a certain length of time, depending on the level, and slows that unit by 50% for 36 seconds. It is effective only against non-mechanical units. Units that have been turned ethereal cannot attack, but *can* still cast spells; certain spells can also be cast upon them. In the case of spells that deal damage, casting a spell on an ethereal unit magnifies the effect of the spell by 66%.

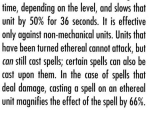

Banish is a very effective tool for removing the most powerful enemy your attack force is facing. Cast Banish on the enemy Hero, or a very powerful Creep, while your attack force deals with the other units. Likewise, if you are worried that your Hero is taking too much of a beating, you can Banish him/her to prevent damage from conventional attacks.

FLAME STRIKE

Level 1: 45 damage per second for 3 seconds, minor damage for 6 seconds.

Level 2: 80 damage per second for 3 seconds, light damage for 6 seconds.

Level 3: 110 damage per second for 3 seconds, moderate damage for 6 seconds.

Mana Cost: 135	
Cooldown: 10 seconds	
Range: 800	
AOE: 200	
Duration: 9 seconds	

Calls up a large area of fire that damages ground units inside the targeted area over time. At level 3, Flame Strike can destroy some units in a single blow, and can be used effectively to heavily damage tightly-grouped enemy structures, as well. After the initial three-second damage blast, units in the targeted area continue to take minor damage for an additional six seconds.

PHOENIX (ULTIMATE)

Cost: N/A	
Magic Damage: 61-75 (splash)	
Range: 600	
Light Defense: 1	
Move Speed: Fast	
Hit Points: 1250	
Mana: N/A	

Summons a powerful Phoenix that burns with such intensity that it damages itself, as well as nearby enemies. The Phoenix has Spell Immunity and Resistant Skin. When it dies, it creates an egg that hatches into a new Phoenix if it is not destroyed within 10 seconds.

Phoenix Egg

Cost: N/A

Heavy Defense: 0

Hit Points: 200

Mana: N/A

The Phoenix is a powerful creature that, once summoned, damages itself at a rate of 25 hit points per second and can fire flaming streams. Even when it "dies", it merely becomes a Phoenix Egg that is reborn as another Phoenix in 10 seconds if it is not otherwise destroyed. Also note that you can heal a Phoenix with items and with the Priest's Heal ability.

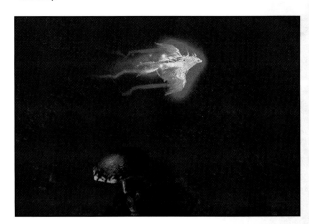

NEW ORC STRUCTURES

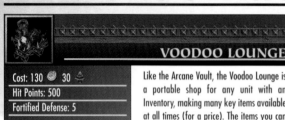

VOODOO LOUNGE

Cost: 130  30

Hit Points: 500

Fortified Defense: 5

Like the Arcane Vault, the Voodoo Lounge is a portable shop for any unit with an Inventory, making many key items available at all times (for a price). The items you can access depends on your Great Hall's level of upgrade, as well as the buildings you have already constructed. Once you've fully upgraded your base, the Voodoo Lounge is able to supply your Heroes with a wide variety of goods.

NEW ORC ABILITIES

Backpack

Cost: 50 25

Researched At: Great Hall/Stronghold/Fortress

Benefits: Grunts, Troll Headhunters, Troll Berserkers, Spirit Walkers, Shamans, Raiders, Kodo Beasts, Troll Witchdoctors, Tauren

Gives Kodo Beast the ability to hold four items. All other units can carry two.

Reinforced Defenses

Cost: 50 200

Researched At: War Mill

Benefits: Burrows, Watch Towers

Upgrades the armor in Burrows and Watch Towers. You must have upgraded fully to Fortress level before you can add this ability to your arsenal.

Berserker Upgrade

Cost: 75 175

Researched At: Barracks

Benefits: Troll Headhunters

Transforms Troll Headhunters into Troll Berserkers, giving them increased hit points and the Berserk ability.

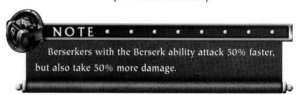

NOTE

Berserkers with the Berserk ability attack 50% faster, but also take 50% more damage.

Burning Oil (Passive)

Cost: 50 150

Researched At: Barracks

Benefits: Demolishers

Upgrades your Demolishers to fire rocks smothered in a fiery mesh of burning oil. This causes area of effect damage because the ground around it will catch fire.

NEW ORC UNITS

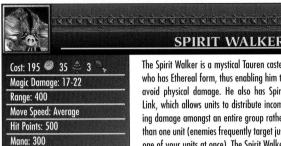

SPIRIT WALKER

Cost: 195 🔵 35 ⛏ 3 ⚔	
Magic Damage: 17-22	
Range: 400	
Move Speed: Average	
Hit Points: 500	
Mana: 300	

The Spirit Walker is a mystical Tauren caster who has Ethereal form, thus enabling him to avoid physical damage. He also has Spirit Link, which allows units to distribute incoming damage amongst an entire group rather than one unit (enemies frequently target just one of your units at once). The Spirit Walker can learn Disenchant and Ancestral Spirit.

Ancestral Spirit

Cost: 100 🔵 50 🌲
Mana Cost: 250

Raises any Tauren from the dead, including Spirit Walker. The Tauren is revived with 100% of its hit points restored. Of course, there must be a Tauren nearby that is recently deceased, but if you have a pack of Spirit Walkers traveling with Taurens, you're in business!

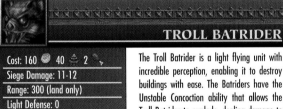

TROLL BATRIDER

Cost: 160 🔵 40 ⛏ 2 ⚔	
Siege Damage: 11-12	
Range: 300 (land only)	
Light Defense: 0	
Move Speed: Fast	
Hit Points: 500	
Mana: N/A	

The Troll Batrider is a light flying unit with incredible perception, enabling it to destroy buildings with ease. The Batriders have the Unstable Concoction ability that allows the Troll Batrider to explode, dealing damage to nearby enemy air units! The Batrider can learn Liquid Fire and is affected by Troll Regeneration (learned in the Spirit Lodge). The Batrider is a unit that is best used in groups for attacking enemy buildings because the Liquid Fire ability aids so greatly in taking down enemy structures.

 ### Spirit Link

Mana Cost: 100

Links four units together in a chain. These units will survive longer because they distribute 50% of the damage they take across the other Spirit-Linked units. This valuable skill can thwart an enemy's attempts to pick on individual units during a battle.

 ### Disenchant

Cost: 100 🔵 50 🌲
Mana Cost: 125

Removes all magical buffs from units within the targeted area, while also dealing 250 damage to summoned enemy units. Disenchant is important for removing Faerie Fire, Curse, and other damaging magical buffs that reduce your units' effectiveness.

 ### Ethereal Form

Switches the Spirit Walker between ethereal and corporal forms.

 ### Unstable Concoction

Causes a powerful explosion that deals 900 damage to a targeted air unit, and 100 damage to all nearby enemy air units! An excellent way to thwart an enemy attack by air (Wind Riders, Chimaeras, Gryphon Riders). Note that this also destroys the Batrider.

 ### Liquid Fire

Cost: 75 🔵 125 🌲

Flings a volatile liquid that causes buildings to take damage over time. Structures that are currently taking damage from Liquid Fire cannot be repaired, and have their attack rate reduced by 80%. Therefore, a team of Batriders is *the* choice to disable an enemy's defense before a large ground force moves in for attack.

NEW ORC HERO

SHADOW HUNTER

Cost: 425 ⬤ 100 ⬥ 5 ⚒

Attack Type: Hero	
Range: 600	
Defense Type: Hero	
Move Speed: Fast	
Primary Attribute: Agility	
Strength Bonus per Level: 2	
Agility Bonus per Level: 1.5	
Intelligence Bonus per Level: 2.5	
Production Hot Key: H	

This cunning Hero is skilled at healing magic and Voodoo curses. The Shadow Hunter can learn Healing Wave, Hex, Serpent Ward, and Big Bad Voodoo.

EVEL	ATTACK (GROUND/AIR)	ARMOR	STR.	AGILITY	INT.	HP	MANA
1	22-28 [25 avg]	4	15	20	17	475	255
2	23-29 [26 avg]	4	17	21	19	525	285
3	25-31 [28 avg]	5	19	23	22	575	330
4	26-32 [29 avg]	5	21	24	24	625	360
5	28-34 [31 avg]	6	23	26	27	675	405
6	29-35 [32 avg]	6	25	27	29	725	435
7	31-37 [34 avg]	7	27	29	32	775	480
8	32-38 [35 avg]	7	29	30	34	825	510
9	34-40 [37 avg]	8	31	32	37	875	555
10	35-41 [38 avg]	8	33	33	39	925	585

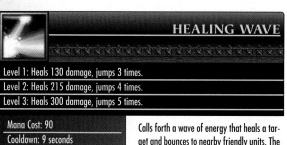

HEALING WAVE

Level 1: Heals 130 damage, jumps 3 times.	
Level 2: Heals 215 damage, jumps 4 times.	
Level 3: Heals 300 damage, jumps 5 times.	

Mana Cost: 90	
Cooldown: 9 seconds	
Range: 700	

Calls forth a wave of energy that heals a target and bounces to nearby friendly units. The wave heals less with each successive bounce, but in small groups it can be a very effective healing device.

SERPENT WARD

Level 1: 75 hit points, 11-13 damage.	
Level 2: 135 hit points, 23-26 damage.	
Level 3: 135 hit points, 41-45 damage.	

Mana Cost: 30	
Cooldown: 6.5 seconds	
Range: 500	
Duration: 40 seconds	

The Serpent Ward is an immobile serpentine being that attacks any nearby enemies. It is immune to magic, and more than one at a time can be summoned to add to your numbers in a battle!

HEX

Level 1: Lasts 15 seconds.	
Level 2: Lasts 30 seconds.	
Level 3: Lasts 45 seconds.	

Mana Cost: 70	
Cooldown: 7 seconds	
Range: 800	

Transforms an enemy unit (including Heroes) into a random critter, disabling that unit's special abilities.

BIG BAD VOODOO

Mana Cost: 200	
Cooldown: 180 seconds	
AOE: 800	
Duration: 30 seconds	

Turns all friendly units invulnerable in an area around the Shadow Hunter. The Shadow Hunter, however, does *not* become invulnerable. Having a group of god-like units for 30 seconds can allow you to rip through an enemies main line of defenses with ease.

TIP

When Big Bad Voodoo is used, the enemy goes straight after your Shadow Hunter in an attempt to end the spell early so that your invulnerable units lose this magical protection. Therefore, it's wise to ensure that the Shadow Hunter has some Health Potions ready to quaff when he goes into a battle with Big Bad Voodoo protecting his comrades.

ORCS: THE HORDE   UNITS AND STRUCTURES

NEW NIGHT ELF STRUCTURE

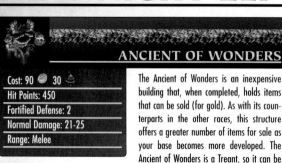

ANCIENT OF WONDERS

Cost: 90 ⬤ 30 🌲	
Hit Points: 450	
Fortified Defense: 2	
Normal Damage: 21-25	
Range: Melee	

The Ancient of Wonders is an inexpensive building that, when completed, holds items that can be sold (for gold). As with its counterparts in the other races, this structure offers a greater number of items for sale as your base becomes more developed. The Ancient of Wonders is a Treant, so it can be uprooted, moved, or used in combat. As a result, your Wisp will be lost when this building is constructed.

NEW NIGHT ELF ABILITIES & UPGRADES

Backpack
Cost: 50 ⬤ 25 🌲
Researched At: Tree of Life/Tree of Ages/Tree of Eternity
Benefits: All non-flying units, except Wisps and Siege units

Gives the ability to carry a pair of items around the map for your Heroes.

Well Spring
Cost: 75 ⬤ 150 🌲
Researched At: Hunter's Hall
Benefits: Moon Wells

Increases the amount of Mana that can be stored in Moon Wells by 200! It also upgrades the Moon Well's Mana regeneration rate by 83%! Obviously, this upgrade is extremely important for healing/replenishing damaged unit groups. It also makes a huge difference for base defense because units defending your camp have more energy (Mana and Health) to draw from the Moon Wells as the enemy hits them.

Mark of the Claw
Cost: 25 ⬤ 100 🌲
Researched At: Ancient of Lore
Benefits: Druids of the Claw (Bear)

Gives Druids the ability to cast Roar while in Bear form. The previous inability to cast this spell as a Bear required Druids to switch between forms to perform this task. With Mark of the Claw, however, Roar (which gives nearby units a 25% bonus to attack damage) can be cast when the Druid of the Claw is in any form.

Hardened Skin
Cost: 100 ⬤ 250 🌲
Researched At: Ancient of Lore
Benefits: Mountain Giants

A costly upgrade in terms of Lumber, Hardened Skin is nonetheless essential for the very expensive Mountain Giants. It provides increased resistance against attack damage.

TIP

Ben Brode at Blizzard QA says that Hardened Skin is essential to have before he will use Mountain Giants. He believes that the Mountain Giants are sitting ducks for enemy Heroes without it.

Resistant Skin
Cost: 50 ⬤ 100 🌲
Researched At: Ancient of Lore
Benefits: Mountain Giants

Gives the Mountain Giants Hero-like resistance to Spell damage. While cheaper than Hardened Skin, it *is* an important upgrade if your opponent(s) favor magic. Resistant Skin is particularly critical to avoid having your Mountain Giants turned to an Undead enemy by Banshees. Make sure that Resistant Skin has been upgraded before the enemy begins Possessing your forces away!

Mark of the Talon
Cost: 25 ⬤ 100 🌲
Researched At: Ancient of Wind
Benefits: Druids of the Talon (Storm Crow)

Allows your Druids of the Talon to cast Faerie Fire while in Storm Crow form. This ability can change matters quickly because a group of Storm Crows can move by air from battle to battle (if there is more than one in a multiplayer game) and reduce the enemy's armor considerably with Faerie Fire.

NEW NIGHT ELF UNITS

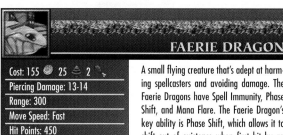

FAERIE DRAGON

Cost: 155 ⬤ 25 ⬧ 2	
Piercing Damage: 13-14	
Range: 300	
Move Speed: Fast	
Hit Points: 450	
Mana: 200	

A small flying creature that's adept at harming spellcasters and avoiding damage. The Faerie Dragons have Spell Immunity, Phase Shift, and Mana Flare. The Faerie Dragon's key ability is Phase Shift, which allows it to shift out of existence when first hit by an enemy. This makes Faerie Dragons an excellent choice for safely scouting enemy locations.

Spell Immunity (Passive)

This quite simply means that Faerie Dragons are immune to all spells. Spell Immunity is a passive skill, so it's always active.

Phase Shift

Mana Cost: 20

Causes the Faerie Dragon to phase out of existence whenever it takes damage. This lasts about one second, and enables the Faerie Dragon to avoid taking any subsequent damage from the attack that induced the Phase Shift. When in Phase Shift, all inbound missiles miss the Faerie Dragon, and all enemies attacking this unit acquire a different target. Phase Shift is set by default to Autocasting, and we recommend that this is not altered.

Mana Flare

Mana Cost: 50

Allows the Faerie Dragon to channel negative magical energies that damage nearby enemies when they cast spells. It also gives the Faerie Dragon +12 armor.

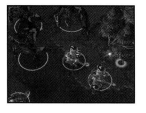

MOUNTAIN GIANT

Cost: 425 ⬤ 100 ⬧ 7	
Normal Damage: 28-40	
Range: Melee	
Move Speed: Average	
Hit Points: 1400	
Mana: N/A	

Mountain Giants are huge lumbering beasts that can disrupt enemy attackers and withstand large amounts of damage. This unit has the Taunt and War Club abilities, and can learn Hardened Skin and Resistant Skin (both of which we recommend you upgrade). Despite what you might think, a large group of Mountain Giants is *not* desirable because they have a relatively slow attack speed. They are, however, very effective as support units, and can have a great impact on your overall attack force. One tactic is to use your Mountain Giants as a sort of 'human shield', and hide Archers behind them as you advance on an enemy position.

Taunt

Cooldown: 15 Seconds

Calls all nearby enemy units and forces to attack the Mountain Giant. When you're trying to take out physically entrenched enemy defenses (Guard Towers for example), having a Mountain Giant Taunt while the rest of your troops go after the enemy structures can be very effective. Taunt is also effective as a way of drawing enemy units away from their structural defenses.

War Club

Requires a nearby tree for each Mountain Giant that uses it. When invoked, the Mountain Giant grabs a tree (and destroys it) fashioning a large club that gives him increased attack damage and greater attack range (it switches this unit's attack to Siege damage). Each War Club lasts for 15 hits.

NEW NIGHT ELF HERO

WARDEN

Cost: 425 🪙 100 🌳 5	
Attack Type: Hero	
Defense Type: Hero	
Range: Melee	
Primary Attribute: Agility	
Strength Bonus per Level: 2.4	
Agility Bonus per Level: 1.6	
Intelligence Bonus per Level: 2	
Production Hot Key: W	

This cunning Hero is adept at entering and escaping combat. The Warden can learn Blink, Fan of Knives, Shadow Strike, and Vengeance. In the single-player game, the Warden's Blink ability enables you to gain access to a plethora of otherwise inaccessible items. Likewise in multiplayer games, she is able to Blink into areas without having to use a Goblin Zeppelin to get past an obstacle.

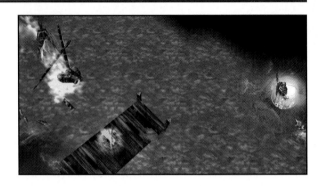

LEVEL	ATTACK (GROUND)	ARMOR	STR.	AGILITY	INT.	HP	MANA
1	22-42 [32 avg]	4	18	20	15	550	225
2	23-43 [33 avg]	4	20	21	17	600	255
3	25-45 [35 avg]	5	22	23	19	650	285
4	26-46 [36 avg]	5	25	24	21	725	315
5	28-48 [38 avg]	6	27	26	23	775	345
6	30-50 [40 avg]	6	30	28	25	850	375
7	31-51 [41 avg]	7	32	29	27	900	405
8	33-53 [43 avg]	7	34	31	29	950	435
9	34-54 [44 avg]	8	37	32	31	1025	465
10	35-56 [45 avg]	8	39	34	33	1075	495

FAN OF KNIVES

Level 1: 90 damage per target, max 350 damage (all targets).
Level 2: 135 damage per target, max 675 damage (all targets).
Level 3: 180 damage per target, max 950 damage (all targets).

Mana Cost: 100
Cooldown: 9 seconds
AOE: 400/450/475

A powerful spell that sends a wave of knives outward from the Warden, damaging all nearby enemies. Fan of Knives is effective against both land an air units, and is an important spell in missions like Night Elf Chapter 7 in the single-player game where only magic can destroy the Summoners. Fan of Knives is not aimed—it targets nearby enemies automatically, and at level 3 can destroy weaker enemies in groups.

BLINK

Level 1: Mana Cost 50, cooldown 10 seconds, Range 1000.
Level 2: Mana Cost 10, cooldown 10 seconds, Range 1075.
Level 3: Mana Cost 10, cooldown 1 second, Range 1150.

Allows the Warden to teleport short distances at will. She can move in and out of battle to confuse the enemy or save herself, and to gain access to areas that other units cannot reach. Several such areas are identified in our walkthrough for the Night Elf Campaign.

SHADOW STRIKE

Level 1: 75 Strike damage, 15 damage over 3 seconds, movement and attack rate slowed by 50%.

Level 2: 150 Strike damage, 30 damage over 3 seconds, movement and attack rate slowed by 50%.

Level 3: 225 Strike damage, 45 damage over 3 seconds, movement and attack rate slowed by 50%.

Mana Cost:	65
Cooldown:	8 seconds
Range:	300
Duration:	15.1 seconds

Hurls a poisoned dagger at a targeted enemy that inflicts large amounts of initial damage, and then deals additional damage over time. The poisoned unit also has its attack and movement rate slowed for a short duration. For mid to low-level enemies, Shadow Strike is a 'fire and forget' spell because the targeted enemy ultimately perishes from either the initial attack or from the subsequent effects of the poison.

Shadow Strike - [Level 1]
65
Hurls a poisoned dagger at a target enemy unit, dealing 75 initial damage, and 15 damage every 3 seconds for 15 seconds. The poison slows the attack rate and movement speed of the targeted unit for a short duration.

VENGEANCE (ULTIMATE)

Mana Cost:	150
Cooldown:	180 seconds
Duration:	180 seconds

Summons a powerful Avatar that can, in turn, summon invulnerable spirits from corpses. These summoned units attack the enemy with (what else) a vengeance! When the Avatar dies, the spirits vanish with her!

Maiev
Level 7

Avatar of Vengeance

Created when Vengeance is invoked. This is a powerful unit that lasts for 180 seconds.

Normal Damage:	25-36
Range:	450
Heavy Defense:	2
Move Speed:	Fast
Hit Points:	1200
Mana:	400

Spirit of Vengeance

Once created, the Avatar of Vengeance can raise up Spirits of Vengeance from nearby corpses. These units are invulnerable and last 50 seconds or until the Avatar dies (whichever comes first).

Piercing Damage:	14-18
Range:	450
Heavy Defense:	Invulnerable
Move Speed:	Average
Hit Points:	500
Mana:	N/A

UNITS AND STRUCTURES

NIGHT ELVES: THE SENTINELS

NEW UNDEAD STRUCTURES

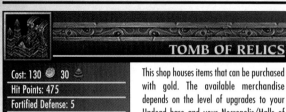

TOMB OF RELICS

Cost: 130 ⚫ 30 ♦	
Hit Points: 475	
Fortified Defense: 5	

This shop houses items that can be purchased with gold. The available merchandise depends on the level of upgrades to your Undead base and your Necropolis/Halls of the Dead/Black Citadel. A must-have if you want to be a part of any multiplayer game, the Tomb of Relics carries key items like the Sacrificial Skull (which allows you to create an area of blight anywhere, thus enabling you to build Ziggurats anywhere) and the Orb of Corruption (which greatly improves the Hero's attacks).

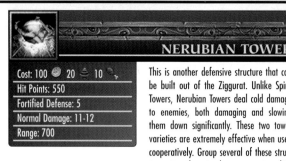

NERUBIAN TOWER

Cost: 100 ⚫ 20 ⚑ 10 ⚒	
Hit Points: 550	
Fortified Defense: 5	
Normal Damage: 11-12	
Range: 700	

This is another defensive structure that can be built out of the Ziggurat. Unlike Spirit Towers, Nerubian Towers deal cold damage to enemies, both damaging and slowing them down significantly. These two tower varieties are extremely effective when used cooperatively. Group several of these structures together to doom any straggling enemy air or ground units.

NEW UNDEAD ABILITIES & UPGRADES

There are many upgrades hidden inside the Undead tech tree. This section unveils exactly what's new or changed.

Backpack

Cost: 50 ⚫ 25 ♣
Researched At: Necropolis/Halls of the Dead/Black Citadel
Benefits: Ghouls, Crypt Fiends, Abominations, Banshees, Necromancers

Gives certain units the ability to carry a pair of items around the map for your Heroes.

Burrow

Cost: 75 ⚫ 75 ♣
Researched At: Crypt
Benefits: Crypt Fiends

Allows Crypt Fiends to burrow into the ground where they are invisible to the enemy (like StarCraft® Zerglings). Burrowed Crypt Fiends have an increased hit point regeneration, so an excellent way to both protect and quickly heal a group of Fiends is to Burrow them into the ground. Note that Crypt Fiends *cannot* attack when burrowed.

Skeletal Mastery

Cost: 125 ⚫ 150 ♣
Researched At: Temple of the Damned
Benefits: Necromancers

Skeletal Mastery causes one of the two Skeletons created by a Necromancer to be a Skeletal Mage. Skeletal Mages add another dimension to skeletal attack groups because they can attack from afar with a ranged attack, making it possible to get more hits on one enemy unit or structures than you would with just melee skeletons (due to overcrowding of space around the target).

Exhume Corpses

Cost: 125 ⚫ 100 ♣
Researched At: Slaughterhouse
Benefits: Meat Wagons

Exhume Corpses gives Meat Wagons the ability to generate corpses on the fly. The magnitude of this ability cannot be overstated. A group of Necromancers with Raise Skeleton coupled with several Meat Wagons with Exhume Corpses is a recipe for a huge army of Skeleton Warriors! Add in Skeletal Mastery (for Skeletal Mages to be added to the mix) and an Obsidian Statue refilling the Necromancer's Mana, and you have a portable army-generator!

Destroyer Form

Cost: 75 ⚫ 150 ♣
Researched At: Slaughterhouse
Benefits: Obsidian Statues

This skill allows the Obsidian Statue to transform into a Destroyer, which is a large flying unit that must devour magic to sustain its Mana. The Destroyer has Spell Immunity, Devour Magic, Absorb Mana, and Orb of Annihilation.

NEW UNDEAD UNITS

SKELETAL MAGE

Piercing Damage: 11-12	
Range: 500	
Medium Defense: 0	
Move Speed: Average	
Hit Points: 230	
Mana: N/A	

Skeletal Mages are ranged-attack skeletal warriors that are summoned by the Necromancer's Raise Dead spell once you have researched Skeletal Mastery.

OBSIDIAN STATUE

Cost: 200 ⬤ 35 🝆 3 ⚒	
Magic Damage: 7-8	
Range: 575	
Heavy Defense: 4	
Move Speed: Average	
Hit Points: 700	
Mana: 600	

This a fortified statue that can help replenish the Health and Mana of your army. Obsidian Statues can cast Spirit Touch, Essence of Blight, and can learn Destroyer Form. While primarily a backup unit, the Obsidian Statues can also attack both land and air units.

 NOTE

The Obsidian Statue is a deal-maker/breaker for the Undead. No attack group should be without a pair of them—one set to autocast Essence of Blight and the other to autocast Spirit Touch. Do this so that you have a constant source of both Health and Mana for your troops!

 ### Essence of Blight

Mana Cost: 10

When set to Autocast (we recommend this), it automatically restores 12 hit points to nearby friendly units. With a reservoir of 600 Mana, and an Obsidian Statue set to Autocast Essence of Blight, your attack group will have a significant advantage over the enemy.

 ### Spirit Touch

Mana Cost: 10

The counterpart of Essence of Blight, Spirit Touch restores five Mana to nearby friendly units! Coupled with Necromancers and Meat Wagons, one Obsidian Statue can help to raise an entire army of Skeleton Warriors.

 ### Morph into Destroyer

Cost: 100 ⬤ 50 🝆 2 ⚒

Creates a Destroyer (see next column).

DESTROYER

Cost: 100 ⬤ 50 🝆 2 ⚒ (must already have Obsidian Statue and Destroyer Upgrade)	
Magic Damage: 21-24	
Range: 450	
Light Defense: 4	
Move Speed: Fast	
Hit Points: 900	
Mana: 400	

A large flying unit that must consume magic to sustain its Mana. The Destroyer is excellent at destroying enemy casters and clusters of ground units. This unit initially has Spell Immunity, Devour Magic, Absorb Mana, and Orb of Annihilation!

 ### Devour Magic

Devour Magic consumes all magical buffs from units inside of a set area. Each unit that is devoured of magic gives the Destroyer 25 hit points and 50 Mana!

 ### Orb of Annihilation

Mana Cost: 25

Orb of Annihilation adds 20 bonus damage to the Destroyer's attack and causes his attacks to do area of effect damage. The default Autocast setting for Orb of Annihilation is 'on'.

 ### Spell Immunity (Passive)

Makes the Destroyer completely immune to all magic!

 ### Absorb Mana

Takes all of the Mana from one of your friendly units and gives it directly to the Destroyer! This is an important skill because the Destroyer does not generate his own Mana.

NEW UNDEAD HERO

CRYPT LORD

Cost: 425 🪙 100 ⬦ 5 👤

Attack Type: Hero	
Range: Melee	
Defense Type: Hero	
Move Speed: Average	
Primary Attribute: Strength	
Strength Bonus per Level: 3.2	
Agility Bonus per Level: 1.2	
Intelligence Bonus per Level: 1.6	
Production Hot Key: C	

The Crypt Lord is an ancient behemoth that was once a mighty king of the subterranean spider kingdom of Azjol-Nerub. An incredibly powerful beast, this Hero is the king of melee combat with his Carrion companions aiding in his quest.

LEVEL	ATTACK (GROUND/AIR)	ARMOR	STR.	AGILITY	INT.	HP	MANA
1	28-34 [31 avg]	2	26	14	14	675	210
2	31-37 [34 avg]	3	29	15	15	750	225
3	34-40 [37 avg]	3	32	16	17	825	255
4	37-43 [40 avg]	3	35	17	18	900	270
5	40-46 [43 avg]	3	38	18	20	975	300
6	44-50 [47 avg]	4	42	20	22	1075	330
7	47-53 [50 avg]	4	45	21	23	1150	345
8	50-56 [53 avg]	5	48	22	25	1225	375
9	53-59 [56 avg]	5	51	23	26	1300	390
10	56-62 [59 avg]	5	54	24	28	1375	420

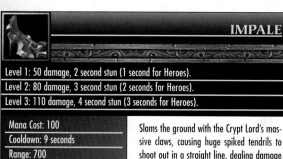

IMPALE

Level 1: 50 damage, 2 second stun (1 second for Heroes).
Level 2: 80 damage, 3 second stun (2 seconds for Heroes).
Level 3: 110 damage, 4 second stun (3 seconds for Heroes).

Mana Cost: 100	
Cooldown: 9 seconds	
Range: 700	
AOE: 300	

Slams the ground with the Crypt Lord's massive claws, causing huge spiked tendrils to shoot out in a straight line, dealing damage and hurling ground units into the air in its wake. This is a great way to stun a large group of tough units long enough for your Obsidian Statues to heal some of your nearby units, or for some of your troops to turn and run!

SPIKED CARAPACE (PASSIVE)

Level 1: 15% damage returned, 3 bonus armor.
Level 2: 25% damage returned, 5 bonus armor.
Level 3: 35% damage returned, 7 bonus armor.

Gives the Crypt Lord barbed layers of chitinous armor that increases his defense and even returns damage to enemy melee attacks, much like a weakened version of Thorns.

CARRION BEETLES

Level 1: 140 hit points, 8-9 damage.
Level 2: 275 hit points, 15-18 damage.
Level 3: 410 hit points, 22-27 damage.

Mana Cost: 30
Cooldown: 6 seconds
Range: 900

Allows the Crypt Lord to create one Carrion Beetle from a nearby targeted corpse. This Carrion Beetle then becomes a *permanent* unit in the game! While Beetles are permanent, there can be only five in the game at a time. Still, with Autocast enabled, you can always have a group of five pesky Carrion Beetles fighting on your side.

LOCUST SWARM (ULTIMATE)

Mana Cost: 150
Cooldown: 180 seconds
AOE: 80
Duration: 30 seconds

Mana Cost: N/A
Range: N/A
Duration: N/A
Cooldown: N/A

This is the Crypt Lord's big-daddy spell, and it does a whole lot of damage. It creates a swarm of angry locusts that bite and tear at nearby enemy units. As they chew through the enemy flesh, they convert it into a substance that restores hit points to the Crypt Lord when they return! In any close battle (or any battle at all), Locust Swarm makes a huge difference in your efforts. If you're losing, kick Locust Swarm into gear and watch the fun begin!

Carrion Beetle

Normal Damage: 8-9/15-18/22-27
Range: Melee
Heavy Defense: 2
Move Speed: Average
Hit Points: 140/275/410
Mana: N/A

There are three versions of the Carrion Beetle, with the major distinction between them being their hit points. The level 2 and 3 Beetle, however, can use Burrow in a similar fashion to the Crypt Fiend.

Belt of Giant Strength +6

NEW RACES

While the four primary races in Warcraft III: The Frozen Throne have all been updated and have new units and abilities, there are actually two more races (not including the Alliance's Blood Elves) that you interact with and even control in the single-player missions. In the Night Elf Campaign you fight against the Naga, and then later you actually gain control of this race and build their tech tree and units! In Human Chapters 5 and 6, you have the opportunity to use Draenei units, although you do not build Draenei structures at any time. This section of the guide describes both new races, beginning with the Draenei.

DRAENEI

The Draenei are a proud race that have been fighting the Orcs for generations. Although they have begun to lose this war in recent years, they remain vicious and capable warriors. The Draenei's underlying skill is the ability to remain invisible at all times (except when they are attacking). This skill allows them to move throughout any map without any enemies being alerted to their presence.

DRAENEI STRUCTURES

Since the Draenei structures are not something that you can build, we won't delve too deeply into this matter. One structure, however, is worth some special attention: the Boulder Tower. While you can't build Boulder Towers in any regular mission, you *can* build them in the Secret Human mission!

BOULDER TOWER

Hit Points: 1300	
Fortified Defense: 5	
Siege Damage: 90-111	
Range: 800 (land only)	

The Boulder Tower and Advanced Boulder Tower are defensive towers that hurl large boulders at enemies. These structures work much like Spirit Towers, Watch Towers, and Nerubian Towers, only they deal a different sort of damage. Boulder Towers can hit both land and air units.

DRAENEI UNITS

As mentioned previously, there are two missions in the Alliance Campaign (Chapters 5 and 6) where you have the opportunity to use Draenei units. While a host of units exist for this race, only some of them can be controlled by the gamer. This section examines in detail only those select few Draenei units.

DRAENEI VINDICATOR

Normal Damage: 29-33	
Range: Melee	
Heavy Defense: 4	
Move Speed: Average	
Hit Points: 900	
Mana: N/A	

The Vindicator is the equivalent of a Human Footman. He packs a significant attack, but has no Mana and no magical weapons. With a robust number of hit points, his fierce attack, and clever ability to cloak, the Vindicator is an outstanding 'base' attack unit.

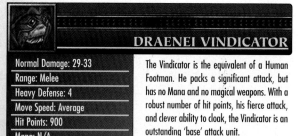

DRAENEI SEER

Piercing Damage: 36-42	
Range: Melee	
Heavy Defense: 0	
Move Speed: Average	
Hit Points: 775	
Mana: 500	

The Seer is a magical unit that has a ranged attack of lightning bolts that inflict significant damage. The Seers have Slow, Healing Wave, and Brilliance Aura at their disposal.

 Slow
Mana Cost: 40

Slows a target's attack rate by 25% and limits its movement rate by 60% when invoked. Slow can be set to Autocast.

 Brilliance Aura (Passive)

Gives additional Mana regeneration to nearby friendly units of 1 Mana per second.

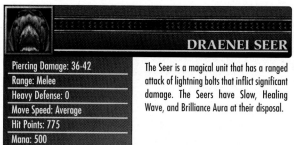 **Healing Wave**
Mana Cost: 90

Calls forth a wave of healing energy that bounces off of friendly units (up to four times), healing each unit along the way. Initially, Healing Wave heals 215 points on the primary target, then less on each subsequent target. Through the 'bounces', the Seer can actually heal himself by using Healing Wave in small groups.

DRAENEI SABOTEUR

Siege Damage: 81-90	
Range: 600	
Heavy Defense: 0	
Move Speed: Average	
Hit Points: 600	
Mana: 250	

The Saboteur is a unit that you control in Alliance Chapter 6. He has both Healing Wave and Liquid Fire, which makes him quite adept at destroying buildings (like Power Generators).

Healing Wave

Mana Cost: 90

Summons a wave of healing energy that bounces off of friendly units (up to four times), healing each unit along the way.

Liquid Fire

Flings a volatile liquid that causes buildings to take damage over time. Structures that are currently taking damage from Liquid Fire cannot be repaired, and have their attack rate reduced by 80%.

DRAENEI ELITE ASSASSIN

Normal Damage: 41-50	
Range: Melee	
Heavy Defense: 0	
Move Speed: Average	
Hit Points: 525	
Mana: 300	

The Elite Assassin is a Draenei killing machine with Howl of Terror and Critical Strike. In Alliance Chapter 6, these Assassins are the key to your victory over the Mistress of Torment and other enemies.

Howl of Terror

Mana Cost: 100

Emits a terrifying howl that reduces nearby enemy units' attack damage by 25% for 10 seconds.

Critical Strike

Provides a 20% chance of doing double damage on any given attack.

DRAENEI STALKER

Attack Type: Normal	
Damage: 32-42	
Attack Speed: Fast	
Range: Melee	
Armor Type: Heavy	
Armor: 1	
Move Speed: Average	
Hit Points: 465	
Mana: N/A	
Skills: Ensnare (lasts 10 seconds) and Evasion (15%)	

You can use the Draenei Stalker in Alliance Chapter 5. Purchase this unit in the Mercenary Camp located in the northwest corner of the map.

Other Draenei Units

Below is a list of the other Draenei units that exist, but cannot be controlled by the player.

Draenei Laborer (basic worker unit)

Draenei Harbinger (magic-using unit)

Salamander (heavy ranged unit)

Draenei Demolisher (heavy attack/siege unit)

DRAENEI HERO

ELDER SAGE (AKAMA)

Attack Type: Hero
Range: Melee
Defense Type: Hero
Move Speed: Fast
Primary Attribute: Intelligence
Strength Bonus per Level: 2
Agility Bonus per Level: 1.2
Intelligence Bonus per Level: 2.8
Production Hotkey: K

This cunning Hero has a fantastic range of abilities. Chain Lightning is a powerful attack that jumps from enemy to enemy, allowing the Elder Sage to attack groups, then become invisible and blend back into the background. Feral Spirit gives the Sage a mobile attack force of wolves, and Shadow Strike can be used as a hit-and-run attack that sucks the life out of enemies over time. The Sage's Reincarnation ability ensures that even when he's overwhelmed, he'll come back to fight again!

CHAIN LIGHTNING

Level 1 – 100 damage that hits up to 4 targets.
Level 2 – 140 damage that his up to 6 targets.
Level 3 – 180 damage that hits up to 8 targets.

Mana Cost: 110
Cooldown: 9 seconds
Range: 700

Hurls a bolt of damaging lightning that jumps from target to target, doing massive damage to several nearby enemies. Chain Lightning is also a lot of fun to watch, especially when multiple foes are getting shocked at once.

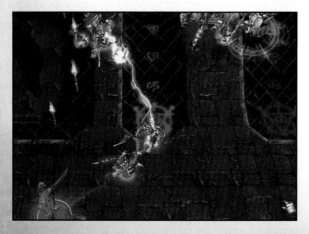

FERAL SPIRIT

Level 1 – Two, 200 hit point wolves.
Level 2 – Two, 300 hit point wolves with Critical Strike.
Level 3 – Two, 400 hit point wolves with Critical Strike and Invisibility.

Mana Cost: 100
Cooldown: 15 Seconds
Duration: 60 seconds

Summons Spirit Wolves to fight along side the Elder Sage. The only downside to Feral Spirit is that the Spirit Wolves last for just a short period of time; still, they are powerful and also gain abilities like Critical Strike and Invisibility as points are poured into this spell!

SHADOW STRIKE

Level 1: 75 Strike damage, 15 attack over short duration, movement and attack rate slowed by 50%.

Level 2: 150 Strike damage, 30 attack over short duration, movement and attack rate slowed by 50%.

Level 3: 225 Strike damage, 45 attack over short duration, movement and attack rate slowed by 50%.

| Mana Cost: 65 |
| Cooldown: 8 seconds |
| Range: 300 |
| Duration: 15.1 seconds |

Hurls a poisoned dagger at a targeted enemy. This dagger deals large amounts of initial damage and then deals damage over time. The poisoned unit also has its attack and movement rate slowed for a short duration. For mid- to low-level enemies, Shadow Strike is a 'fire and forget' spell because the targeted enemy perishes either from the initial attack or from the constant effects of the poison from the dagger.

REINCARNATION (ULTIMATE)

| Cooldown: 240 Seconds |

When killed, the Elder Sage comes back to life, effectively granting this unit a second life! The ability to pop back to life with full health can mean the difference between victory and defeat in a close battle, especially in Alliance Chapter 6 when Akama might get caught behind enemy lines and die!

The Naga spend much of the early game as your enemy, but as the story progresses you eventually find Lady Vashj and her Naga underlings make valuable additions to you arsenal.

NAGA STRUCTURES

In Alliance Chapter 5 (as well as others), you can actually build the Naga tech tree, so we felt it was important to let you know what buildings were available and what upgrades they contain.

TEMPLE OF TIDES

| Cost: 385 🔵 150 ⬆ |
| Hit Points: 1500 |
| Fortified Defense: 5 |
| Food: 15 |
| Creates: Mur'gul Slaves, Mur'gul Reavers |

The Temple of Tides is the Great Hall/Town Hall/Tree of Life for the Naga. This is where the worker units are created (Mur'gul Slaves). This structure is a prerequisite for harvesting resources! The following is a complete list of its upgrades.

 Coral Scales
Cost: 125 🔵 75 🌲
Research At: Temple of Tides
Benefits: Mur'gul Reaver, Naga Myrmidon, Snap Dragon, Dragon Turtle, Couatl

Increases the armor of Naga attack units.

 Coral Blades
Cost: 150 🔵 75 🌲
Research At: Temple of Tides
Benefits: Mur'gul Reaver, Naga Myrmidon, Snap Dragon, Dragon Turtle, Couatl

Increases the attack damage of Naga attack units.

 Chitinous Scales
Cost: 225 🔵 225 🌲
Research At: Temple of Tides
Benefits: Mur'gul Reaver, Naga Myrmidon, Snap Dragon, Dragon Turtle, Couatl

Further increases the armor of Naga attack units.

 Chitinous Blades
Cost: 225 🔵 225 🌲
Research At: Temple of Tides
Benefits: Mur'gul Reaver, Naga Myrmidon, Snap Dragon, Dragon Turtle, Couatl

Further increases the attack damage of Naga attack units.

 Razorspine Scales
Cost: 325 🔵 375 🌲
Research At: Temple of Tides
Benefits: Mur'gul Reaver, Naga Myrmidon, Snap Dragon, Dragon Turtle, Couatl

The maximum armor upgrade for Naga attack units.

 Razorspine Blades
Cost: 300 🔵 375 🌲
Research At: Temple of Tides
Benefits: Mur'gul Reaver, Naga Myrmidon, Snap Dragon, Dragon Turtle, Couatl

Further increases the attack damage of Naga attack units.

NAGA

SPAWNING GROUNDS

Cost: 250 ⬤ 60 ⬢	
Hit Points: 1500	
Fortified Defense: 5	
Creates: Naga Myrmidon, Snap Dragon, Dragon Turtle	

The Spawning Grounds is a very important structure for building the higher-end Naga units, including the Dragon Turtle—the Naga's heavy siege unit.

Research Ensnare

Cost: 50 ⬤ 75 ⬢

Research At: Spawning Grounds
Benefits: Naga Myrmidon

Enables the Naga Myrmidons to use the Ensnare ability, which is an excellent way to bring enemy air units down to earth for a little one-on-one time with your Naga melee units.

TIDAL GUARDIAN

Cost: 130 ⬤ 80 ⬢	
Hit Points: 500	
Fortified Defense: 5	
Piercing Damage: 33-45	
Range: 700	

The Tidal Guardian is the standard defensive structure of the Naga, and can attack both land and air units.

ALTAR OF THE DEPTHS

Cost: 255 ⬤ 100 ⬢	
Hit Points: 900	
Fortified Defense: 5	
Creates: Heroes	

This is where slain Heroes (in this case, Lady Vashj) are revived.

SHRINE OF AZSHARA

Cost: 180 ⬤ 70 ⬢	
Hit Points: 1050	
Fortified Defense: 5	
Creates: Naga Sirens, Couatl	

Trains Naga Sirens and Couatl. The following is a complete list of skills you can research at this structure.

 ### Naga Siren Adept Training

Cost: 100 ⬤ 50 ⬢

Research At: Shrine of Azshara
Benefits: Naga Siren

Increases Naga Siren's Mana capacity, Mana regeneration rate, hit points, and also gives them the ability to cast Frost Armor.

 ### Abolish Magic

Cost: 50 ⬤ 50 ⬢

Research At: Shrine of Azshara
Benefits: Couatl

Gives the Couatl the ability to dispel positive buffs from enemy units and negative buffs from friendly units. This also damages summoned units!

 ### Naga Siren Master Training

Cost: 100 ⬤ 150 ⬢

Research At: Shrine of Azshara
Benefits: Naga Siren

Increases Naga Siren's Mana capacity, Mana regeneration rate, hit points, and also gives them the ability to cast Cyclone.

CORAL BED

Cost: 115 ⬤ 40 ⬢	
Hit Points: 500	
Fortified Defense: 5	
Food: 15	

This the main food-producing structure of the Naga. Each Coral Bed adds 15 Food to the Naga's limit.

NAGA UNITS

There are a number of missions in Warcraft III: The Frozen Throne where you have control over the Naga, so you need to know some of the finer points of each of the Naga units under your command. The most important aspect of the Naga is, of course, that they can travel sublimely through water without so much as a pair of water wings. This capability comes in very handy when your opponent must rely on cumbersome Transports! Here's a closer look at each Naga unit.

MUR'GUL SLAVE

Cost: 75 ● 1 ⚒	
Normal Damage: 7-8	
Range: Melee	
Unarmored Defense: 0	
Move Speed: Slow	
Hit Points: 250	
Mana: N/A	

The Mur'gul Slave is the worker unit for the Naga. This little toiler can mine gold, harvest lumber, build all Naga structures, and even chip in during a fight if necessary. The Mur'gul Slave is also the unit of choice for repairing damaged structures.

MUR'GUL REAVER

Cost: 120 ● 2 ⚒	
Normal Damage: 18-21	
Range: Melee	
Heavy Defense: 0	
Move Speed: Average	
Hit Points: 400	
Mana: N/A	

The Mur'gul Reaver is the base-level fighting unit for the Naga. Cheap, effective, and vicious, the Reaver is the backbone of a solid base defense (along with some Tidal Guardians).

NAGA SIREN

Cost: 140 ● 25 ▲ 2 ⚒	
Magic Damage: 9-12	
Range: 600	
Unarmored Defense: 0	
Move Speed: Average	
Hit Points: 350	
Mana: 200	

The Naga Siren is a powerful spellcaster that can initially cast Parasite, which damages units over time and ultimately turns their corpses into Watery Minions for you to command!

Parasite

Mana Cost: 50

Afflicts a targeted enemy unit with a deadly parasite that deals 5 damage per second for 30 seconds. While this isn't often enough to destroy an enemy, it helps the cause greatly during a battle. When an infected unit dies, a Watery Minion springs up in its place to fight for your side! This spell is set to Autocast by default.

Frost Armor

Cost: 100 ● 50 ▲
Mana: 40

Creates a shield of frost around a targeted friendly unit. The shield adds 3 armor and slows melee enemy units that attack it. The slowing effect lasts for five seconds after they strike the targeted unit. Frost Armor itself lasts for 45 seconds. This spell can also be set to Autocast, which is very handy when going into battle with previously damage units.

Cyclone

Cost: 100 ● 150 ▲
Mana: 150

Throws a targeted non-mechanical unit into the air, rendering it unable to move, attack, or cast spells. This spell lasts for 20 seconds and is a great way to temporarily remove several high-powered enemies from a battle equation. Cyclone can also stop a spell that's being cast, so use it freely!

 NOTE • • • • • • •

Between Frost Armor and Parasite, it's one or the other for Autocasting—but not both. You can have only one work automatically, so we suggest a group with four Naga Sirens where two are set to Autocast Parasite and the other two are set to Autocast Frost Armor.

Watery Minion

Normal Damage: 10-11	
Range: Melee	
Heavy Defense: 2	
Move Speed: Average	
Hit Points: 240	
Mana: N/A	

This is the summoned unit that is produced once a Parasite-infected enemy dies. The Watery Minions last only about 45 seconds, but they can be very helpful in a role similar to that of the Undead's Skeleton Warriors.

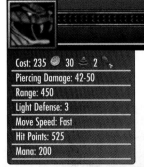

COUATL

Cost: 235 ● 30 ▲ 2 ⚒	
Piercing Damage: 42-50	
Range: 450	
Light Defense: 3	
Move Speed: Fast	
Hit Points: 525	
Mana: 200	

The Couatl is a light flying unit that can learn Abolish Magic. The beauty of the Couatl is that it can attack both land and air units, making it a valuable addition to a Naga attack force.

Abolish Magic

Cost: 50 🔵 50 🔺

Dispels positive buffs from enemy units, and negative buffs from friendly units. Against summoned enemy units, Abolish Magic deals a whopping 300 damage! It can be set to Autocast, meaning that a pack of Couatls can fly with your attack group and protect them from negative enemy magic. This is a critical combination of units against certain enemies.

NAGA MYRMIDON

Cost: 225 🔵 55 🔺 4 🗡	
Normal Damage: 33-39	
Range: Melee	
Heavy Defense: 2	
Move Speed: Average	
Hit Points: 1080	
Mana: N/A	

This powerful melee unit has the Submerge ability (much like Burrow), which allows it to hide in water. The Myrmidon can also learn the Ensnare ability.

Ensnare

Cost: 50 🔵 75 🔺

Binds a targeted enemy unit to the ground, rendering it immobile for 12 seconds. Ensnared air units can be attacked as though they were land units!

SNAP DRAGON

Cost: 200 🔵 25 🔺 3 🗡	
Piercing Damage: 25-29	
Range: 550	
Medium Defense: 0	
Move Speed: Fast	
Hit Points: 500	
Mana: N/A	

This ranged unit has a poison attack that both slows and damages the targeted enemy. Snap Dragons have the ability to Submerge, so they can hide in water like Myrmidons. They can also attack both land and air units.

Slow Poison

This poison attack deals 4 damage per second and slows the targeted enemy by 50%. It also slows the enemy's attack by 25% for five seconds.

DRAGON TURTLE

Cost: 320 🔵 65 🔺 5 🗡	
Piercing Damage: 23-26	
Range: 480 (land only)	
Siege Damage: 63-80	
Range: 450 (land only)	
Heavy Defense: 1	
Move Speed: Average	
Hit Points: 750	
Mana: N/A	

The Dragon Turtle is the Naga's siege unit, and can best be described as a powerful turtle that can devour enemy units and destroy buildings very quickly. This unit has Hardened Skin, which reduces damage taken, as well as Spiked Shell, which acts like a Thorns aura by returning damage to enemy melee units that strike it. The Dragon Turtle can attack only land units (or Ensnared air units).

Devour

The Dragon Turtle consumes an enemy unit, slowly digesting it and dealing 5 damage per second until the victim perishes. If the Dragon Turtle is destroyed with an enemy still inside, the enemy pops back out alive! Devour is an excellent way to get some higher-level units off the battlefield!

Spiked Shell

Razor-sharp spikes on the Turtle's shell deal 30% of an enemy unit's melee attack damage back to it.

Hardened Skin

Reduces all attacks on the Dragon Turtle by 12 damage, although attacks cannot be reduced below a base-damage of 3.

NAGA HERO

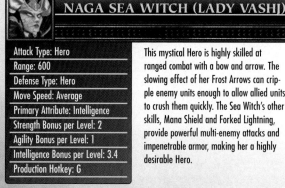

NAGA SEA WITCH (LADY VASHJ)

Attack Type: Hero	
Range: 600	
Defense Type: Hero	
Move Speed: Average	
Primary Attribute: Intelligence	
Strength Bonus per Level: 2	
Agility Bonus per Level: 1	
Intelligence Bonus per Level: 3.4	
Production Hotkey: G	

This mystical Hero is highly skilled at ranged combat with a bow and arrow. The slowing effect of her Frost Arrows can cripple enemy units enough to allow allied units to crush them quickly. The Sea Witch's other skills, Mana Shield and Forked Lightning, provide powerful multi-enemy attacks and impenetrable armor, making her a highly desirable Hero.

FORKED LIGHTNING

Level 1 – 100 damage per enemy unit.
Level 2 – 175 damage per enemy unit.
Level 3 – 250 damage per enemy unit.

Mana Cost: 110	
Cooldown: 11 seconds	
Range: 600	
AOE: 125	

Brings up a scorching bolt of lighting that hits a maximum of three enemy units.

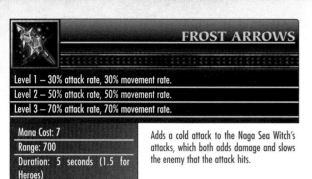

FROST ARROWS

| Level 1 – 30% attack rate, 30% movement rate. |
| Level 2 – 50% attack rate, 50% movement rate. |
| Level 3 – 70% attack rate, 70% movement rate. |

| Mana Cost: 7 |
| Range: 700 |
| Duration: 5 seconds (1.5 for Heroes) |

Adds a cold attack to the Naga Sea Witch's attacks, which both adds damage and slows the enemy that the attack hits.

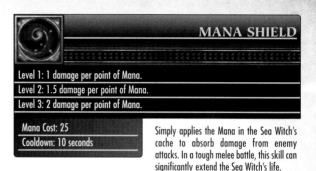

MANA SHIELD

| Level 1: 1 damage per point of Mana. |
| Level 2: 1.5 damage per point of Mana. |
| Level 3: 2 damage per point of Mana. |

| Mana Cost: 25 |
| Cooldown: 10 seconds |

Simply applies the Mana in the Sea Witch's cache to absorb damage from enemy attacks. In a tough melee battle, this skill can significantly extend the Sea Witch's life.

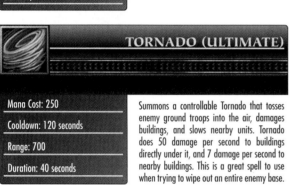

TORNADO (ULTIMATE)

| Mana Cost: 250 |
| Cooldown: 120 seconds |
| Range: 700 |
| Duration: 40 seconds |

Summons a controllable Tornado that tosses enemy ground troops into the air, damages buildings, and slows nearby units. Tornado does 50 damage per second to buildings directly under it, and 7 damage per second to nearby buildings. This is a great spell to use when trying to wipe out an entire enemy base.

ALLIANCE FORCES

While the Alliance forces are the same as Human forces in principle, there are a few unit variations that we thought were worth mentioning. Specifically, the Worker, the Swordsman, and the Archer differ between the Human multiplayer units and the Alliance Campaign in the single-player game.

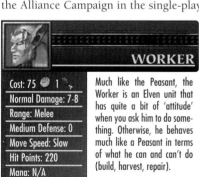

WORKER

| Cost: 75   1 |
| Normal Damage: 7-8 |
| Range: Melee |
| Medium Defense: 0 |
| Move Speed: Slow |
| Hit Points: 220 |
| Mana: N/A |

Much like the Peasant, the Worker is an Elven unit that has quite a bit of 'attitude' when you ask him to do something. Otherwise, he behaves much like a Peasant in terms of what he can and can't do (build, harvest, repair).

SWORDSMAN

| Cost: 135   2 |
| Normal Damage: 12-13 |
| Range: Melee |
| Heavy Defense: 2 |
| Move Speed: Average |
| Hit Points: 420 |
| Mana: N/A |

The Swordsman is a versatile foot soldier that can learn the Defend ability. Basically, he's a Footman in another outfit!

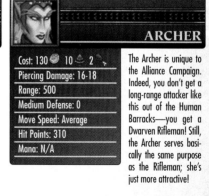

ARCHER

| Cost: 130   10   2 |
| Piercing Damage: 16-18 |
| Range: 500 |
| Medium Defense: 0 |
| Move Speed: Average |
| Hit Points: 310 |
| Mana: N/A |

The Archer is unique to the Alliance Campaign. Indeed, you don't get a long-range attacker like this out of the Human Barracks—you get a Dwarven Rifleman! Still, the Archer serves basically the same purpose as the Rifleman; she's just more attractive!

SENTINEL CAMPAIGN:
TERROR OF THE TIDES

Fresh from a victory in the original Warcraft III game, you will now be tested with new units, new weapons, and most of all, new enemies. The Naga are a race that the Night Elves will soon learn about.

CHAPTER ONE

RISE OF THE NAGA

Somewhere along the eastern coast of Ashenvale Forest, the Warden Maiev Shadowsong hunts for signs of Illidan's passing. Maiev Shadowsong finds tracks that split up, and she realizes that Illidan must be getting help. The party splits up in a quest to track Illidan down.

MAP SECRETS LEGEND

This map is rife with secret areas and power-ups, largely because of the Warden's Blink ability, which enables her to reach locations that would otherwise be inaccessible. The secrets available in this level include:

	Claws of Attack +3
	Healing Wards
	Jade Ring
	Potion of Healing
	Ring of Protection +1
GH	Rune of Greater Healing
LH	Rune of Lesser Healing
M	Rune of Mana
	Spider Ring
A	Tome of Agility
I	Tome of Intelligence +2
S	Tome of Strength

REQUIRED QUESTS

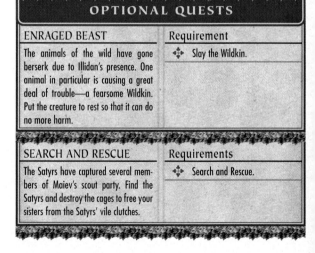

THE DEMON'S TAIL	Requirements
Illidan has sewn a path of destruction along the coastline. Hunt the Demon down and recapture him before he harms any more innocent civilians.	⚜ Follow Illidan's trail. ⚜ Maiev must survive.

BURNING SHIPS	Requirements
Illidan has taken to the sea, and you must follow. His Naga minions have begun to set fire to the few boats that are left. You must save at least two ships, or you will not have a sufficient force to give chase.	⚜ Save at least two ships. ⚜ Maiev must survive.

OPTIONAL QUESTS

ENRAGED BEAST	Requirement
The animals of the wild have gone berserk due to Illidan's presence. One animal in particular is causing a great deal of trouble—a fearsome Wildkin. Put the creature to rest so that it can do no more harm.	⚜ Slay the Wildkin.

SEARCH AND RESCUE	Requirements
The Satyrs have captured several members of Maiev's scout party. Find the Satyrs and destroy the cages to free your sisters from the Satyrs' vile clutches.	⚜ Search and Rescue.

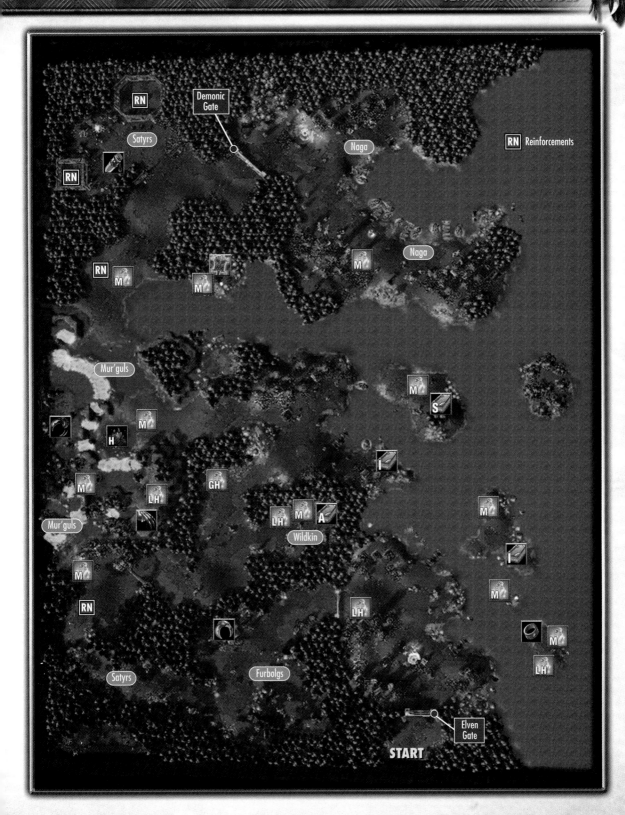

RN

Demonic
Gate

Satyrs

Naga

RN Reinforcements

RN

Naga

RN M

M

M

Mur'guls

M

H

S

I

M

GH

M

LH

LH M A

Mur'guls

Wildkin

I

M

M

RN

LH

M

LH

Satyrs

Furbolgs

START

Elven
Gate

THE PATH TO VICTORY

This first mission will help to acquaint you with the new Night Elf Hero, the Warden. Her name is Maiev Shadowsong, and she's accompanied by a five Archers and the Huntress Naisha. You must wind your way through the map, chasing Illidan. There are four quests along the way (two of them optional), and plenty of enemies—from Illidan's minions to crazed Furbolgs. You're probably anxious for your first taste of *Warcraft® III: The Frozen Throne™*, but be careful that Maiev doesn't perish, or the mission will be over.

> **TIP** • • • • • • •
>
> Use Maiev's Blink ability to reach the small islands in the southeast corner of the map to get the items hidden there.

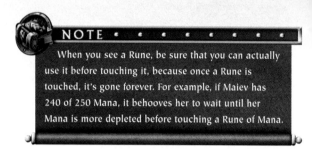

THROUGH THE ELVEN GATE

As the mission begins, your group is pinned behind an Elven Gate. Attack the gate to move past it, then cautiously patrol the area beyond. Amidst the burning buildings you'll find several Lesser Mur'guls, a **Rune of Lesser Healing**, and a secret area that's accessible only with Maiev's Blink spell!

> **NOTE** • • • • • • • •
>
> When you see a Rune, be sure that you can actually use it before touching it, because once a Rune is touched, it's gone forever. For example, if Maiev has 240 of 250 Mana, it behooves her to wait until her Mana is more depleted before touching a Rune of Mana.

The Mur'guls do not pose a serious threat to your group, especially if Maiev uses her Fan of Knives skill to quickly cut them all down. If some of your troops receive damage, have Maiev touch the Rune of Lesser Healing to replenish your Archers. After the area is clear, move Maiev to the edge of the northernmost dock and turn your attention to the land across the water. Use Blink to reach this area and find three crates, two of which contain goodies. Get the **Rune of Mana** and the **Tome of Intelligence**, then return to the group of Archers by using Blink once again.

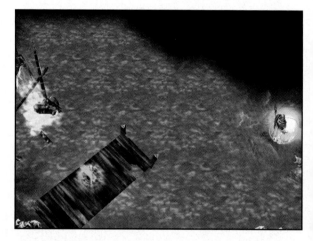

THE CRAZED FURBOLGS

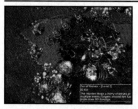 Pass through the open Elven Gate to meet your next set of foes, the crazed Furbolgs. These creatures, normally allies of the Night Elves, have been corrupted by Illidan and now want nothing more than to destroy you. Concentrate your group's fire on the Furbolgs one at a time, and they fall quickly. Maiev's Fan of Knives is also a powerful tool for reducing their hit points.

After destroying the Furbolgs, you can attack their already-burning buildings. If you look closely behind the statue of the Keeper of the Grove, you'll notice a crate that contains a **Jade Ring**, which increases Maiev's Agility by +1 when worn.

ILLIDAN'S SERVITORS

When the opposition and their structures have been decimated, you can rest your troops if necessary (remember that Night Elves recover hit points during the night). When you're ready, proceed along the path until you reach a group of Illidan's Servitors—nasty creatures that truly challenge your fighting abilities. Use your group as a whole, targeting the Servitors one at a time, to take them down without losing a single Archer.

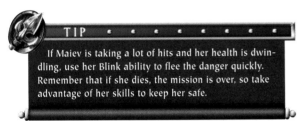

TIP

If Maiev is taking a lot of hits and her health is dwindling, use her Blink ability to flee the danger quickly. Remember that if she dies, the mission is over, so take advantage of her skills to keep her safe.

SLAY THE WILDKIN (OPTIONAL QUEST)

As you approach a group of reinforcements (the remaining units from one of the initial groups that split up at the beginning of the mission), you learn of a crazed beast known as a Wildkin that has caused great damage in the area. Your job is to destroy the beast. Your reinforcements include an Archer, a Huntress, and a Dryad. Add them to your group and move forward.

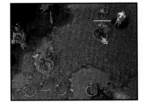

There's a crate containing a **Rune of Mana** near the waterfalls. Prepare to also meet up with a group of Wild Mur'guls. Take them out, then touch the Rune of Mana and pass below the archway that leads north. This is where you find the Wildkin. It runs away when you arrive, so pursue it with your troops.

Move in for the kill, targeting the two smaller Ferocious Beasts with *all* of your units first. They fall quickly when the power of the entire group is imposed upon them. Once the two underlings have been destroyed, bring the might of your group down on the Wildkin, all the while keeping an eye on Maiev's health. When you defeat the Wildkin, it leaves behind a **Tome of Agility**.

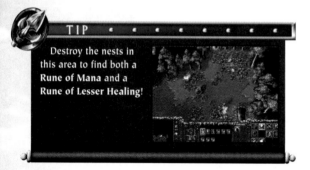

TIP

Destroy the nests in this area to find both a **Rune of Mana** and a **Rune of Lesser Healing!**

ILLIDAN'S NAGA

Move up the path to find a **Rune of Greater Healing**, which you may not need at this time. A short distance away, prepare to meet a group of Illidan's Naga—this is the first time you've seen this race. You must work as a group, using your units in unison to target the larger of the Naga before

breaking up to finish off the lesser units. Destroy the crates near the burning ships to unveil a **Tome of Intelligence +2**, then proceed north along the path.

THE WATERFALL AND THE FOUNTAIN OF HEALTH

A Rune of Mana and a Fountain of Health beside a set of Waterfalls lie ahead a short distance along the path. Look closely to see a group of Spitting Spiders at the top of the waterfall, seemingly inaccessible. Use Maiev to Blink up to the top of the Waterfall, then use Fan of Knives to destroy the Spiders and obtain the **Spider Ring**. A second set of Spiders across the way are hiding **Claws of Attack +3**! There's also a **Rune of Mana** nearby that will replenish your lost energy and allow you to Blink back to the Fountain of Health.

Spider Ring

SECRET ISLAND

Approach the coast near the burning boats and note the patch of land across the water. Use Maiev's Blink ability to actually teleport over to this island and engage one of Illidan's Naga. Destroy the foe (Fan of Knives makes this task easier) to earn a **Tome of Strength** and a **Rune of Mana**!

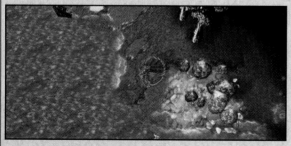

A large group of Mur'guls await your arrival just past the Fountain of Health. Although this pack of enemies seems overwhelming, a pair of blasts from Fan of Knives makes short work of them. Return to the Fountain of Health if necessary before proceeding.

SEARCH AND RESCUE (OPTIONAL QUEST)

Continue on the path to find both reinforcements and a new optional quest. After dispatching the Satyrs that are fighting your reinforcements, you learn that more of your troops have been imprisoned. Follow the path up to the camp where your troops are being held, destroy the Satyrs guarding the cages, then free your comrades. The Satyrs patrolling the far cage yield a **Potion of Healing** when vanquished.

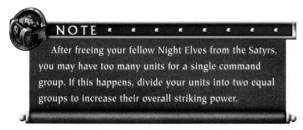

NOTE

After freeing your fellow Night Elves from the Satyrs, you may have too many units for a single command group. If this happens, divide your units into two equal groups to increase their overall striking power.

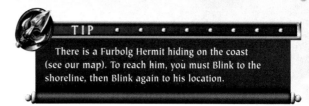

TIP

There is a Furbolg Hermit hiding on the coast (see our map). To reach him, you must Blink to the shoreline, then Blink again to his location.

THE DEMONIC GATE AND ILLIDAN

Eventually, you come to the Demonic Gate, which you must destroy in order to proceed. Simply target the gate to attack it. Once it falls, you see Illidan getting into a boat and escaping. He instructs the Naga to burn the other boats to prevent your pursuit. You must save two of the boats to claim victory in this mission, so quickly attack the Naga vigorously. If you have two attack groups, all the better!

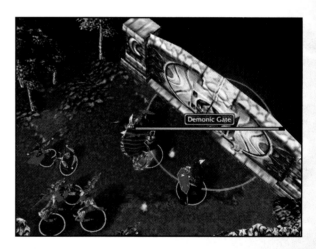

Demonic Gate

At first this task will seem insurmountable, but if you target the enemies in groups in a systematic way, you can achieve victory with at least three ships remaining. After completing the mission, you move on to Chapter 2. Don't worry about losing most of your units in the final battle with the Naga—just make sure Maiev survives.

RISE OF THE NAGA   I   SENTINEL CAMPAIGN

57

CHAPTER TWO

THE BROKEN ISLES

The next day, on the shores of a mysterious island chain, Maiev and her Watchers inspect some ancient, yet strangely familiar ruins. Maiev finds that the ruins are possibly those of an ancient city that was sunk beneath the waves. There is speculation that perhaps a magical power raised these ruins, but just what could be powerful enough to do this isn't clear.

THE PATH TO VICTORY

This mission will require the use of Transport Ships, Frigates, as well as present the likely necessity to acquire another Gold Mine in an area away from your starting point. The reward for completing the optional quest is a Robe of the Magi +6, and there are plenty of extra goodies to be had if you're willing to explore the *entire* map. After building up your base and attack force, you can move out into the unknown reaches of the map to strike fear into the hearts of your enemies.

REQUIRED QUESTS

LOCATE ILLIDAN	Requirement
Illidan and his forces are based somewhere on this chain of islands. Hunt him down and put and end to this chase.	✥ Locate Illidan.

NAGA GUARDIANS	Requirement
The Betrayer has escaped into the Tomb of Sargeras, and you must follow. To gain entrance, you must eliminate Illidan's Naga minions from the Tomb's entrance.	✥ Kill the Naga guarding the Tomb of Sargeras.

OPTIONAL QUEST

SILENCE THE GHOSTS	Requirements
Drak'thul is haunted by the ghosts of his betrayed comrades. You must find and destroy the pits from which the ghosts spawn. Within one of them lies the artifact that first raised the Orc remains. Bring the artifact to Drak'thul to show him that the curse has ended.	✥ Destroy all three Summoning Pits.
	✥ Return the Skeletal Artifact to Drak'thul.

MAP SECRETS LEGEND

While power-ups are not quite as abundant here as in the last mission, there are still numerous extras to be had on this map.

◻	Gold Coins	◻	Robe of the Magi +6
◻	Healing Wards	◻	Rune of Mana (2)
◻	Lesser Scroll of Replenishment	◻	Scroll of Healing
◻	Mana Stone	◻	Scroll of Protection
◻	Maul of Strength	◻	Skeletal Artifact
◻	Pendant of Energy	◻	Tome of Intelligence (3)
◻	Periapt of Vitality		

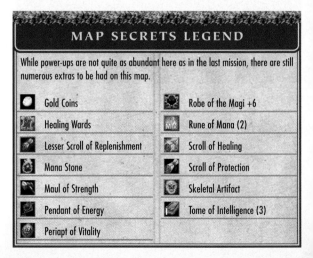

	Fountain of Health
	Goblin Merchant
	Goblin Shipyard
	Gold Mine
	Mercenary Camp

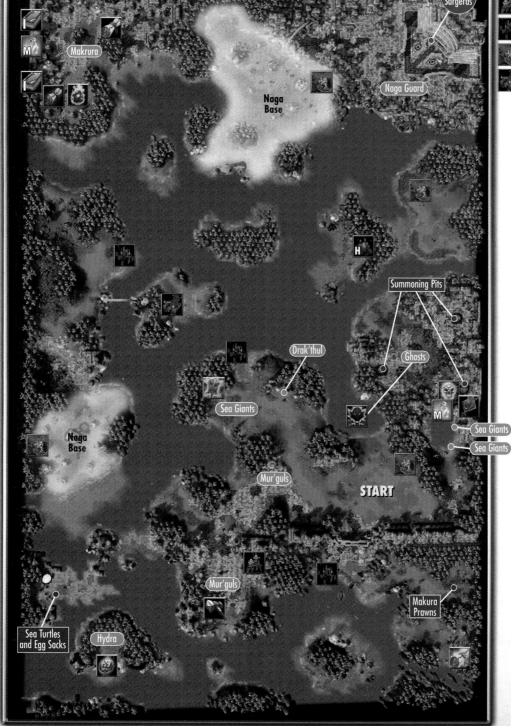

Tomb of
Sargeras

Naga
Base

Naga Guard

Makrura

Summoning Pits

Drak'thul

Ghosts

Sea Giants

Naga
Base

Sea Giants

Sea Giants

Mur'guls

START

Mur'guls

Makura
Prawns

Sea Turtles
and Egg Sacks

Hydra

FORTIFY BASE

When this mission begins, your troops are already supported by a fully functional and intact base. You need only add Moon Wells and an Ancient of Lore to complete your expansion. Of course, you also need to upgrade your units, or the enemy will cut them to ribbons. The opposition launches several attack waves on the left side of your base, so construct at least one pair of Ancient Protectors there,

and be sure to never leave the base completely unoccupied. Expect additional attacks from enemy air units, so have some Archers on hand at all times.

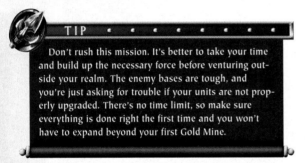

> **TIP**
>
> Don't rush this mission. It's better to take your time and build up the necessary force before venturing outside your realm. The enemy bases are tough, and you're just asking for trouble if your units are not properly upgraded. There's no time limit, so make sure everything is done right the first time and you won't have to expand beyond your first Gold Mine.

CREEP

The process of moving around any given map and killing the various non-enemy 'creeps' that guard objects, gold mines, or their own small encampments, is called creeping.

In this mission we suggest that you take Maiev and a small group of units to the southern and eastern portion of the map to clear out the various creeps that inhabit the area.

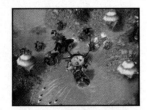

Start off by moving directly east (to the right) to meet a group of Sea Giants. There are two in front of you, but beware also of the small fins poking out of the water—these are actually dangerous

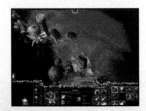

Sea Giants, too. Use Fan of Knives and your entire group to take the enemies down one at a time. After disposing them, a **Pendant of Energy** and a **Rune of Mana** become visible on the far ledge. These items are accessible only by using Blink, so have Maiev transport over and capture them.

As you move down the southeastern portion of the map, you come across Makrura Prawns. Fighting these creatures

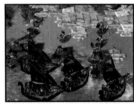

is useful for building your experience, but a victory will not net any power-ups. Further south lies a Mur'gul camp where you can get a **Scroll of Healing** if you destroy them. Maiev can even Blink over to the other islands in the south-central portion of the map, but it's just as easy to load up onto Transports and take the whole crew there.

The last two areas to 'creep' are on isolated islands in the southern portion of the map, and include a Hydra and a set of Sea Turtles. Destroy these units to yield a **Periapt of Vitality** (increasing Maiev's hit points by 150), and in the case of the Sea Turtles, the Sea Eggs yield 500 Gold (in the form of two +250 Gold Coins). Finish off these creeps and then get ready to move on the Ghosts in the east.

SILENCE THE GHOSTS (OPTIONAL QUEST)

After you've creeped the southern portion of the map, move back to the island that's home to your base, then head north to meet Drak'thul (his position is noted on our map).

Talk to Drak'thul to receive a quest to silence the Ghosts that haunt him on a nearby island. By destroying the three Summoning Pits on the island you can complete the quest and receive the **Robe of the Magi +6**.

You must load up your troops into a Transport (you start with two of them, but you can buy more at any Goblin Shipyard), and then cruise toward the shoreline near the Summoning Pits. If you need

more units, stop by the Mercenary Camp and hire a few helpers. When you reach the Summoning Pit area, *completely ignore* the Ghosts and simply target all of your units on one of the Summoning Pits. Once you destroy it, move to the second Summoning Pit, then the third. The **Skeletal Artifact** appears when you destroy the third pit, allowing Maiev to pick it up and take it back to Drak'thul for her reward.

DESTROY WESTERN NAGA BASE (OPTIONAL QUEST)

Although not required, you may still want to move your units over to the Naga base on the western edge of the map and destroy it. If you choose to pursue this option, we recommend taking two full groups of units, and a couple of Frigates for support from the sea. The Naga in this area put up a good fight, but eliminating this base prevents any further attacks on your own base from the west. If you begin to lose the battle, fall back into the Transport Ships and retreat to your base to regroup. Once the battle starts to turn against you, victory becomes impossible.

GATHER POWER-UPS IN NORTHWEST (OPTIONAL QUEST)

After the western Naga base has been destroyed, move your troops up to the northwest corner of the map, where there is no shortage of power-ups. A treasure trove of

three **Tomes of Intelligence**, a **Mana Stone**, a **Scroll of Lesser Rejuvenation**, and a pair of **Mana Runes** awaits you!

The only significant resistance in this area comes from Makrura (lobster-like Creeps), which should be a breeze to defeat compared to the Naga you've battled thus far.

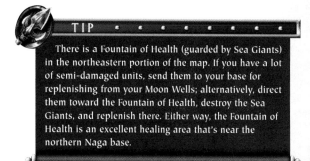

> **TIP**
>
> There is a Fountain of Health (guarded by Sea Giants) in the northeastern portion of the map. If you have a lot of semi-damaged units, send them to your base for replenishing from your Moon Wells; alternatively, direct them toward the Fountain of Health; destroy the Sea Giants, and replenish there. Either way, the Fountain of Health is an excellent healing area that's near the northern Naga base.

DESTROY NORTHERN NAGA BASE

This task is a 'must' to complete the mission. The northern Naga base lies in a large, shallow-water area. Move your Transport Ships up toward the base and drop at least two groups. One of these teams should include at least four Glaive

Throwers. Use the group with Maiev to deal with the enemy units (Fan of Knives works well in this regard) while the second group moves from one structure to next, destroying them one at a time.

When the last structure of the northern base has been destroyed, a cut-scene reveals that Illidan has escaped into the Tomb of Sargeras. Unfortunately, there are several tough Naga guarding the entrance to the tomb, which you must destroy before moving on to the next mission. Attack the guards with two groups of units to decimate them quickly. When the last guard falls, the mission ends.

SENTINEL CAMPAIGN   2   THE BROKEN ISLES

CHAPTER THREE

THE TOMB OF SARGERAS

Moments later, just inside the entrance of the shadowed tomb, Maiev and her Watchers brace themselves for an ambush. Maiev and her troops learn of Gul'dan, the Orc who came before them in search of the power of Sargeras. Gul'dan left runes on the walls that tell of his quest—and his failure….

MAP SECRETS LEGEND

The key to this mission is finding all 10 shards of the Shadow Orb. These are very cleverly hidden, with many of them requiring Maiev to use her Blink ability several times in succession. Several of the areas that hide the pieces of the Orb can be accessed only once a line of sight has been established for Maiev to 'Blink' there. Of course, there are also plenty of other items to obtain, including some important new Runes.

	Gauntlets of Ogre Strength +3
	Mantle of Intelligence
	Manual of Health
	Potion of Greater Mana
	Ring of Protection
GH	Rune of Greater Healing
LH	Rune of Lesser Healing (5)
LR	Rune of Lesser Resurrection
M	Rune of Mana (16)
Sh	Rune of Shielding
W	Rune of the Wild
◎	Shadow Orb Fragment (10)
	Stone Token
A	Tome of Agility
I	Tome of Intelligence (2)

REQUIRED QUESTS

THE SEARCH FOR ILLIDAN	Requirements
Illidan's nefarious plans have led him deep into the Tomb of Sargeras. You must find the Betrayer and discover what he's up to.	✛ Find Illidan.
	✛ Maiev must survive.

THE TOMB OF SARGERAS	Requirements
With the walls of the tomb beginning to crumble, time is running out. Maiev must use her Blink ability to reach the surface and escape before the crumbling tomb becomes her own.	✛ Bring Maiev to the tomb entrance.
	✛ Maiev must survive.

OPTIONAL QUESTS

BARRIERS	Requirement
Your Night Elf brethren have found several passageways that lead into the Tomb of Sargeras. There are only a few rock barriers remaining between you and her warriors. Destroy the rock barriers so she can rendezvous with her troops.	✛ Destroy the rock barriers.

THE SHADOW ORB	Requirement
As Gul'dan's wretched body was ripped to pieces by the tomb's Demonic guardians, his most coveted artifact was shattered. The Shadow Orb, the artifact imbued by the Shadow Council itself, was broken into 10 Fragments. Locate the missing Fragments, and reassemble the Orb. With each remnant found, the Orb's power will increase.	✛ Find the Shadow Orb Fragments.

NOTE • • • • • • •

Several Runes appear (or become available) after Illidan is uncovered, so we've presented two maps, one for each phase of the mission.

Demonic Gate

Sh

Massive Ruined Gate

Illidan

Rock Barrier

▲ Tree   + Switch

THE PATH TO VICTORY

This mission is very unique in that it can be completed without the player ever obtaining *any* of the Shadow Orb fragments. Finding these fragments, however, is something that helps Maiev a great deal, ultimately producing an item that adds +10 to her attack damage.

We not only cover the highlights of the map, but also show you exactly what must be done to uncover all 10 Shadow Orb fragments. The ultimate goal, however, is to find Illidan, so if you're not interested in solving the two optional quests, then you can simply work your way through the map toward Illidan's hiding spot.

NORTH DEMONIC GATE

Start off by moving north. Destroy the Demonic Gate, then prepare to fight four Skeletal Orcs. There are some crates and barrels behind the Orc's barricade. Open them to reveal a **Rune of Shielding**. This Rune gives your units a shield that blocks enemy spells. Once you have this important

item in your possession, move across the room to the Stormreaver Necrolyte and his pair of Skeletal Archers. Crush them to receive a **Rune of Lesser Healing** and a **Potion of Greater Mana**.

TOMB GUARDIANS

Once you've cleared out the area through the north Demonic Gate, advance to the east until you see the **Tomb of Intelligence +2** and **Rune of Mana** nearby. These items are not accessible to your group as a whole, but Maiev can use Blink to reach them. The location of these items is an indication of the kinds of tactics you must use throughout this mission if you want to retrieve all 10 Orb fragments.

Two tomb guardians, both Overlords, await your arrival to the south. Defeat them both—the easternmost foe yields a **Mantle of Intelligence +3**. There's another Demonic Gate to the west. Destroy it and pass through, then head south to face another pair of enemies guarding the area. Past the statue is a set of staircases. As you walk up the steps on the right side, the

platform between the staircases comes into view. Use Blink to transport to this platform, then Blink across to the raised platform in the south! This is the only way to reach this area.

ORB FRAGMENT #1

Once on this upper level, collect the **Rune of Lesser Healing** and **Rune of Mana**. Defeat the Skeletal Warrior to the west (left), then move to the northern edge of his

throne area. From here, you can Blink over another **Rune of Mana**. Just beyond the Rune is an **Orb Fragment**!

Grab the Fragment, then clear out the area below to retrieve a **Manual of Health** and a **Rune of Mana**. If you want your other units to join you, they must break through the second Demonic Gate. Move back up the stairs (where the Blinking began) and continue all the way up to the switch in the floor.

ORB FRAGMENT #2

Step on the floor switch and you receive another optional quest (the Barrier quest). Ignore it for now, and go back down to the area on the map that was just unlocked by the floor switch (a green circle appears on the map briefly after the switch is activated to show you where to go). This newly revealed area boasts a **Rune of Mana**, a **Ring of Protection +2**, and another **Orb Fragment**! Although only Maiev can reach the Orb, the ranged-attack units in your group can still help with the fight from across the water.

ORB FRAGMENT #3

Return to the area near the floor switch to find a Rock Barrier. Break through it to access some reinforcements. With a little Blinking you can also find another piece of the Orb! Hack through the rocks to expose a walkway to the left. Blink Maiev over there, then follow the pathway around the outside to the **Orb Fragment** below.

ORB FRAGMENT #4

Continue north along the path (past the floor switch) to the area with waterfalls on either side. Defeat the enemies in this area and then take in the view of the walkway on the left side. Blink Maiev over to this spot to retrieve a **Rune of Mana**, and battle several more enemies. More importantly,

though, there's another **Orb Fragment** there. Once you have your fourth piece of the Shadow Orb, Blink Maiev back to her comrades and continue north.

REINFORCEMENTS

Following a cut-scene depicting the discovery of some Runes left by the Orcs, head north to fight two groups of Mur'guls and retrieve a **Tome of Intelligence**. Continue west to fight again, this time against Hydra that use Faerie Fire on each of your units. Blast through the rock wall on the far western edge of this area to release a pair of friendly Dryads—their Dispel Magic ability will save the day.

ORB FRAGMENT #5

With the Dryads in tow, find the tree in the middle of the area. If it seems like a strange place for a tree, you're on to something! Use one of your Huntresses to place a Sentinel on the tree to reveal the fifth **Orb Fragment** (or at least the platform necessary to Blink over to it). The Orb Fragment is revealed when Maiev Blinks over to one corner of this platform.

ORB FRAGMENT #6

The next Orb Fragment is on a platform in the upper north-west corner of the map. Move directly north from the tree, take out the Giant Sea Turtle (who leaves behind a **Healing Salve**), then use Blink to cross the chasm over the water. The platform holds a **Rune of Mana** and some crates and barrels. The sixth **Orb Fragment** is within one of the barrels.

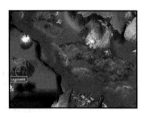

> **TIP**
>
> Maiev will likely level up at some point during this mission. Where you put this new skill point can have a significant impact on the last portion of the mission. Maiev must escape from Sargeras' Tomb while relying heavily on her Blink ability, and since the level 3 of Blink has a cooldown of only one second, it's a good idea to invest this skill point into Blink now! If you have to wait 10 seconds for Blink to become available again (while the clock ticks down), you won't be a happy Warden!

ORB FRAGMENT #7

The next Orb Fragment is in the north-central area of the map. Position a Sentinel on the nearby tree to illuminate the way for Maiev to Blink over to it. When the Sea Turtle dies, it drops the **Orb Fragment**!

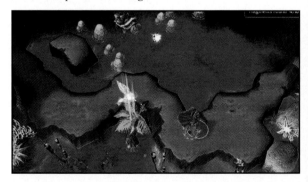

FOOT SWITCH

From the northern edge of the caverns, move back to the east. Expect an encounter with Hydra and Sea Turtles before you reach an impassible area. You can see the floor switch in the distance, so use Blink to send Maiev over to it. Activate it, and a bridge rises from the ground, allowing your comrades to follow Maiev.

NAGA DEFENDERS

Head east. After the cut-scene, keep going east until you come to a shrine located in the middle of the water—this area is defended by the Naga, who put up a significant fight. Still, with Fan of Knives and concentrated attacking (focusing on one enemy unit at a time), victory is possible. Once this area is clear, continue east, then take the first turn to the north.

ORB FRAGMENT #8

The northeast corner of the map contains an area accessible only to Maiev with her Blink ability. From the watery area you can see where she can climb up on the right side (after defeating a Hyrda). From this perch she can also see the other side and Blink over to it, retrieving a **Rune of Mana**

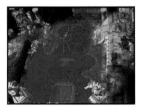

COMPLETE THE BARRIERS QUEST AND FACE THE NAGA

With another Orb Fragment in your possession, turn your attention to the nearby line of rocks. Crush these stones to receive reinforcements, as well as complete the optional Barriers quest. From this location, move directly south through the ruined gate.

You are immediately swarmed by Naga. Eliminate them one at a time, then use the **Rune of Healing** that they leave behind before moving to the west along the path. Expect two more waves of Naga, including a pack that's guarding a **Rune of Lesser Resurrection**. This valuable item resurrects any unit in your group that died nearby!

ORB FRAGMENT #9

Move along the pathway to the south, toward the Massive Ruined Gate. After the cut-scene, hack your way through the gate and turn north. From this location, Blink down to the platform on your left. Move to the edge of this platform to illuminate another **Rune of Mana** across the walkway below. Blink all the way across to this new location to find the ninth **Orb Fragment**.

ORB FRAGMENT #10

There's a **Rune of Mana** directly to the south in some water below your location. Blink down to it, then follow the water to the east (right) until you find the tenth, and final, **Orb Fragment**. Congratulations!

ILLIDAN

The game will suggest that you save at this point, and we concur because the fight that's coming is fairly tough. As you approach the second Massive Ruined Gate, you face another group of Naga bent on preventing your advance. Use every tool at your disposal, including the Stone Token if you have it. After destroying the enemy, wait until Maiev's Mana has been restored, then blast through the last Massive Ruined Gate. Following a cut-scene, the mission changes to one of escape for Maiev.

MAIEV'S ESCAPE

Once Illidan is found, you have only three minutes and thirty seconds to get Maiev out of the Tomb alive! The collapsing walls have opened several rooms that contain Runes, and there have been some other new Runes dropped (such as Runes of Speed). The path out is littered with heavy-duty battles. The enemy units involved in these frays quickly turn their attention to Maiev when she draws near. If you use Blink carefully, however, you can jump past these firefights and skip over the dangerous areas quickly and effectively. By moving fast, you should be able to reach the exit within two minutes, and once you're there, the mission is over!

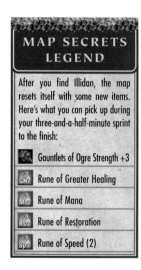

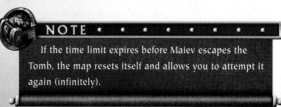

NOTE

If the time limit expires before Maiev escapes the Tomb, the map resets itself and allows you to attempt it again (infinitely).

CHAPTER FOUR

WRATH OF THE BETRAYER

Hours later, suffering from grievous wounds and exhaustion, Maiev stumbles back to the relative safety of her base camp. Upon her arrival, she decides that Shan'do Stormrage must be informed of the situation, and hopefully he will send reinforcements to help in the fight against Illidan's forces.

REQUIRED QUESTS

THE RUNNER'S TRANSPORT	Requirements
The pressure of Illidan's Naga forces bears down heavily on Maiev's base. You must reach the Night Elf Transports quickly so that you can bring the Runner through the next leg of the journey out to sea. Protect the Runner at all costs; she is your only hope.	⟡ Rescue the Night Elf Transports. ⟡ The Runner must survive.

ESCAPE TO THE SEA	Requirements
Only a few Naga defenses lie between the Runner and the open sea. Protect the Transport vessels as they pass through the dilapidated ruins, and get the Runner though the Pillars of Aszune. Once she has reached the safety of the ocean, Elune will see that she reaches Shan'do in time.	⟡ Bring the Runner in a Transport out to sea. ⟡ The Runner must survive.

OPTIONAL QUEST

NAGA EXCAVATORS	REQUIREMENTS
Your Watcher scouts have spotted several Naga excavation crews working on strange caves in the surrounding ruins. Kill the Excavators to deny Illidan the use of any powerful artifacts that they might hold.	⟡ Kill the first Naga Excavator. ⟡ Kill the second Naga Excavator. ⟡ Kill the third Naga Excavator. ⟡ Kill the fourth Naga Excavator.

MAP SECRETS LEGEND

Although there are several extras available on this map, they are not essential for the completion of the mission. Still, the Orb of Slow, the Staff of Teleportation, the Staff of Negation, and the Mana Stone are all excellent items that you can obtain from the Excavators optional quest.

🪙	Gold Coins (each holds +250 Gold)	🔮	Rune of Mana
🟦	Mana Stone		Slippers of Agility
🟫	Mantle of Intelligence		Staff of Teleportation
⚫	Orb of Slow		Staff of Negation
		🅰	Tome of Agility

THE PATH TO VICTORY

The storyline of this mission leads you to believe that there is a great rush to complete the tasks at hand (specifically to get the Runner to the exit point), but there is actually plenty of time to explore the map and complete the mission at your leisure. Although getting the Runner to the exit is the ultimate goal, there are several goodies to be had in out-of-the-way areas of the map, including some Slippers of Agility and a Mantle of Intelligence.

Legend: Goblin Shipyard — Path on Foot — Path in Ships — **F** Fortify Here — **TG** Tidal Guardian — Bridge

The goal is to build up the defenses in your base to the point where you won't have to micro-manage the periodic attacks that are sent against it. Also, your base is there for you to upgrade your units to their full potential, thus making the escape for Maiev and the Runner much easier when the time comes to run the gauntlet toward the exit.

NOTE

While there is no way to get reinforcements from the main base to the Runner's group, Maiev *can* use the Staff of Teleportation to teleport back to the base, where she can purchase items from the Ancient of Wonders. There are also several items in the southeast corner of the map that only a Blinking Maiev can reach.

FORTIFY BASE AND UPGRADE

Two main Naga bases constantly send units to attack your main base. While your home turf is initially well defended, wave after wave of enemy attacks will eventually destroy your base if nothing is done to bolster its defenses. The Naga attack from three main fronts, and simply bolstering these defenses with some extra Ancient Protectors and Moon Wells (to automatically heal defending units) make the base more or less self sufficient, requiring very little of your attention.

NOTE

If you attempt to destroy the enemy Naga bases, you will quickly find that a lack of gold prevents you from succeeding.

We have identified specific areas on the map that you must fortify. Place one extra Ancient Protector and two Moon Wells at each of these locations. Set the Moon Wells to automatically Replenish Mana and Life, then divide your troops equally between the three areas. As you are doing this, initiate the Hunter's Hall upgrade as soon as possible to help your troops defend more effectively, and also to make the Runner's quest easier.

BEGIN RUNNER'S QUEST

Once the base is fortified and the upgrades are nearly complete, you can begin the Runner's Quest by moving the Runner's group south (see our map for the optimal path). You quickly run into some Naga, including a Naga Excavator working at an archeological site. As you approach these enemies you receive the optional 'Naga Excavators' quest. Destroying the first Excavator earns you

the **Staff of Teleportation**, which enables Maiev to teleport back to the main base and use the Ancient of Wonders to purchase useful items.

FIND KEEPER OF THE STORMS SHRINE (OPTIONAL)

Once back at the main base, Maiev can use her Blink ability to move toward the area to the south of your camp. As you can see from the map, there are several useful items in this location, including a **Rune of Mana**, a **Tome of Agility**, and several **Gold Coins**. This is completely optional, but if covering every possible inch is your goal, then take Maiev out for a spin in the lower-right

corner of the map to mop things up. To reach this area, known as the Keeper of the storms shrine, Maiev must Blink up and over the waterfall on the eastern edge of the southern Naga base, then defeat a Royal Guard.

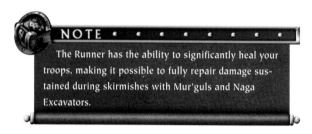

NOTE

The Runner has the ability to significantly heal your troops, making it possible to fully repair damage sustained during skirmishes with Mur'guls and Naga Excavators.

EXCAVATOR #2

Use the Staff of Teleportation to bring Maiev back to the Runner, then proceed along the designated path to the south to meet a group of Mur'guls in front of a staircase. If you want to complete the Excavator quest, then climb the stairs, eliminate the Naga guards, and destroy the second Excavator. Your efforts yield a **Staff of Negation** and two **+250 Gold Coins**, which can be put to use in defending your base.

EXCAVATOR #3

Follow the path north, and two Huntresses join your party. Continue north and cross a narrow dirt bridge. The third Excavator is just beyond this catwalk, to the right of the path. Move in and sweep the Naga away with Maiev's Fan of Knives to retrieve an **Orb of Slow**, which not only adds 6 bonus damage to Maiev's attacks, but also makes her attacks more effective against air units and has a chance to slow the enemy considerably.

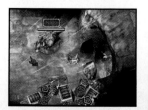

THE GOBLIN SHIPYARD

Continue along the path until you reach the Goblin Shipyard (there are two packs of Mur'guls to fight along the way). When you reach the Shipyard, you discover two Transport Ships (more than you need to complete the mission), three Hippogryphs, and two Glaive Throwers. This completes the Get the Transports quest, and also triggers the beginning of the Escape to the Sea quest.

EXCAVATOR #4

You must defeat one more Excavator at the Shipyard before making a run for the exit in the Transport Ships. To reach the fourth Excavator, you must pack your troops into the Transports and move them around the watery channel so that they can disembark up the ramp. Once face-to-face

with the enemy, use Maiev's Fan of Knives to dice up the guard and the Excavator. This completes the Excavator quest and rewards you with a **Mana Stone** for your trouble.

THE WESTERN EXTRAS (OPTIONAL)

Although not necessary to completing this mission, there are several extras that you can obtain on the western side of the map as you make your way toward the exit point. Specifically, there are **2,250 Gold Coins** and **Slippers of Agility**. The latter item is acquired by approaching Mushi Ale-Hearth, the Pandaren Brewmaster. He simply gives the Slippers up when you get close enough. You can disembark in the southern portion of the map and climb the stairs to get some extra gold—you may need it to purchase items in the main base or to build units to defend the base. There are also several groups of Gold Coins on the western edge of the map, but it is certainly not necessary to grab them unless you relish the challenge.

ESCAPE TO THE SEA

The final goal in this mission is to get the Runner to the escape point in the upper-left (northwest) corner of the map. The final stretch of water is littered with Tidal Guardians (the Naga's defensive turret unit), Naga Sirens, Sea Turtles, and Couatls (Naga flying units). You must disembark to destroy the two gates before proceeding to the exit area. If you are interested in grabbing the Gold Coins and the Slippers of Agility, then you must disembark from the Transport Ships two more times to eliminate the enemies in each area.

WARNING
If your ship goes down with units onboard, those units are lost forever!

After nabbing the Slippers, we recommend that you take the time to have the Runner heal up the troops before you move to the next gate. Each gate is guarded by several Tidal Guardians, which require your full attention. Once the second gate has been breached, ready the Runner's Transport and get it up to the exit as fast as possible. The Naga are persistent, and the Tidal Guardians have the ability to destroy your Transports in short order. You can use Maiev's Blink ability to provide a distraction for the Naga, and the Hippogryphs are also excellent as escorts for the Runner's ship.

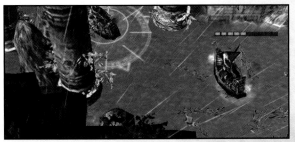

CHAPTER FIVE

BALANCING THE SCALES

Late that evening, in the secluded Moonglade, Malfurion Stormrage, and Tyrande Whisperwind discuss the aftermath of the Legion's invasion. The next day, on the shores of the Broken Isles, Maiev and her Watchers attempt to hold the line against Illidan's final assault.

REQUIRED QUESTS

MAIEV'S DISTRESS

Maiev and her Night Elf forces have been holding off Illidan and the Naga for weeks. With her defenses weakened and her gold supply exhausted, she cannot last much longer. You must bring Tyrande and Malfurion to Maiev's base and crush the imminent Naga threat.

Requirements
✥ Reach Maiev's base.
✥ Tyrande and Malfurion must survive.

ILLIDAN'S MINIONS

The Naga forces are still poised to attack. Destroy them and send Illidan's foolish minions back to the sea so that you can recapture Illidan.

Requirement
✥ Destroy Illidan's base.

OPTIONAL QUEST

NIGHT ELF FLEET

The Night Elf fleet was separated when crossing the perilous ocean. Now the three remaining ships are stranded offshore, unable to safely land. Reach all of the ships and clear a path for them to land upon the shore.

Requirements
✥ Reach the first ship.
✥ Reach the second ship.
✥ Reach the third ship.

MAP SECRETS LEGEND

There are plenty of extras in this mission, many of which can be obtained as you accomplish your quests.

	Amulet of Spell Shield		Scroll of Regeneration
	Bracer of Agility		Rune of Mana
	Circlet of Nobility		Scroll of Mana
	Gold Coins		Scroll of Replenishment
	Lesser Replenishment Potion		Tome of Agility
	Minor Replenishment Potion		Tome of Intelligence
	Moonstone		Tome of Strength
	Ring of Protection		

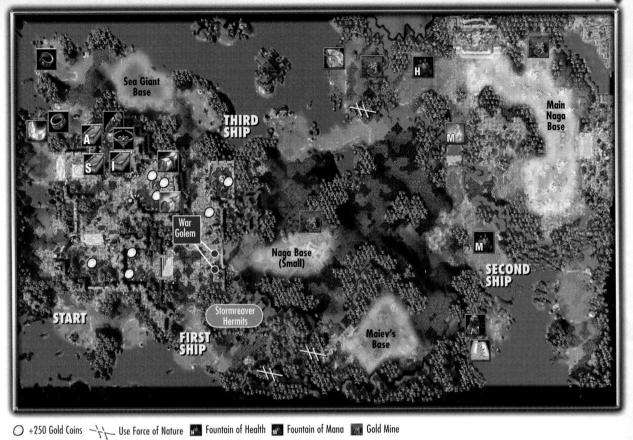

○ +250 Gold Coins   ⤬⤬ Use Force of Nature   🅷 Fountain of Health   🅼 Fountain of Mana   ▦ Gold Mine

THE PATH TO VICTORY

This is a long and complex mission that involves several different strategic elements. First, you must move Tyrande's group across the map, past treacherous enemies. While you're doing this, you need to also defend Maiev's base from constant attacks on two fronts! Once the two groups are united, you must seek out another Gold Mine so that you can build your forces up to the point where the Naga's main base can be destroyed completely.

This mission requires you to switch between Tyrande and Maiev every few minutes (if not more frequently). To streamline this action, assemble your units into two distinct groups by using hotkeys. This allows you to switch between them quickly when you hear an alert that the other party is under attack.

FORTIFY MAIEV'S BASE

You begin this mission in the southwest. Before you move Tyrande's group, however, it's important to relocate to Maiev's base, then group *all* of the units there together and hotkey them. Once this is done, set all of the Moon Wells in Maiev's base to automatically heal and replenish Mana (this act alone strengthens the base's defenses considerably).

75

Since the resources available to Maiev are extremely limited, it's important to use the gold she has wisely. All of the units in the game are base-level (meaning they have no upgrades). Consequently, start one of the upgrades in the Hunter's Hall, and use the remaining gold to enable one of the Wisps to repair the buildings in Maiev's base. Expect an attack (most likely from the east) while you're putting all of this in motion, and defend against it with *all* of Maiev's units, then resume control of Tyrande's group.

TIP

There's a secret room with a **Tome of Agility**, a **Tome of Strength**, and a **Tome of Intelligence**, as well as a **Circlet of Nobility** and a **Minor Replenishment Potion**. To access this room, Malfurion must use Force of Nature to remove the trees that block the path.

MOVE TYRANDE AND MALFURION NORTH

After Maiev's base is set, move Tyrande and her group north. There are plenty of enemies along the way, so keep your group tight and be prepared to use Tranquility to heal the entire force when necessary. Not far from the start location is a set of ruins that Tyrande and her group can explore (indeed, they must go through this area to reach Maiev). There are also

some goodies to collect, including **Gold Coins**, which provide Maiev with much-needed cash to help in the defense of her base.

Tyrande and Malfurion will encounter stiff resistance in the ruined temple area, so consider sending Treants (created with Force of Nature) into battle ahead of the rest of the group.

Advance into the temple and grab any **Gold Coins** that you find (see our map for all Coin locations), then approach the secret room and use Force of Nature to open the path that leads inside.

The adjacent area (to the east) holds a wealth of items, including three **Gold Coins**, a **Scroll of Mana**, and a **Scroll of Healing**. Enter this area, defeat the Naga, and scoop up the bonus items, then turn back to the west and keep moving.

BEGIN THE NIGHT ELF FLEET QUEST

As Tyrande and Malfurion move west and north, they arrive at the shore and receive the Night Elf Fleet quest. A new unit is hinted at (the Mountain Giant), but you won't receive its assistance until you reach the second ship. When the quest cut-scene ends, grab the **Moonstone** and the **Ring of Protection** from the crates, then heal up your troops (with Malfurion's Tranquility) if necessary. While the troops are healing up, return to Maiev's base and spend some of the newfound money toward creating an Ancient Protector or two (or building new units).

THE FIRST SHIP

The First Ship is docked in the southern area of the map, so Tyrande and Malfurion have a fair distance to travel before reaching it. First, move them to the east to contend with a Sea Giant base. Sweep through the base and then

move south, through the ruins again. Along the way, they will find more Gold Coins (guarded by Naga, of course), which can instantly be turned into money for Maiev's base.

A pair of War Golems stand guard by an archway en route to the First Ship. Leave these units alone for now—the archway leads to a small Naga base, and passing through it not only summons the wrath of the rather tough War Golems, but also invites the Naga base to attack your units, who will suffer quick deaths in their un-upgraded state. Don't worry, you'll get your chance to take down these War Golems later. For now, just keep moving toward the ship.

BALANCING THE SCALES   5   SENTINEL CAMPAIGN

When you reach the First Ship, some ghosts pop up to fight your troops, but they won't be a match for Tyrande and Malfurion. Two Huntresses and an Archer join your party at this time, as well.

TO MAIEV'S BASE!

After the First Ship is uncovered, blast through the group of Stormreaver Hermits to the east, picking up the **Rune of Mana** that is hiding in one of their tents. Once cleared, use Force of Nature to cut through the forest that lies between Malfurion and Maiev to the east. Two well-placed Force of Nature spells unite the two groups!

ACQUIRE GOLD MINE

Once Tyrande and Malfurion reunite with Maiev, it becomes clear that a source of gold is necessary if you hope to defeat the main Naga base in the east. The game hints that the mine in the central area of the map is the best choice, but there's another mine in the north-central territory (see our map) that can be accessed only by Malfurion's Force of Nature. Still, destroying the small Naga base near the central Gold Mine should be your first priority. Bring the combined might of Tyrande, Malfurion, and Maiev down upon the central Naga base, decimating it completely! When dust settles, move your Tree of Life up to the Gold Mine and begin harvesting.

THE SECOND SHIP

After securing the Gold Mine, you can build up your forces and upgrade their abilities quickly. Move an attack group to the location of the Second Ship. There is a Fountain of Mana nearby, and the entire area is defended by Mur'guls, but the Force of Nature ability allows you to defeat these enemies quickly. Rendezvous the Second Ship to add a Dryad and two Mountain Giants to your arsenal (plus the ability to make them).

BUILD ATTACK FORCE AND EXPAND

Expect a visit from Illidan himself (in the form of an attack on your base) once you find the Second Ship! Use everything you've got to defeat him, and continue to expand and upgrade your base, adding all of the buildings, including a Chimaera Roost.

There's a Gold Mine in the upper area of the map that can be reached only with Force of Nature. The extra gold you can garner from this location definitely comes in handy for the fight against Illidan's base. We strongly recommend that you do *not* attack Illidan's base until you've upgraded your units fully and have created a strike force of four or five Chimaeras to help with the attack on the base.

THE THIRD SHIP

As your base grows and the upgrades fall into place, you can move one of your attack groups north toward the Third Ship. Upon discovering the ship and defeating the Sea Elementals that surround it, you receive a Huntress and two Druids of the Claw to help in your fight. It also completes the optional quest.

This is when you should use Malfurion's Force of Nature to gain access to the extra Gold Mine if you need the money. The mine contains 12,500 Gold, and there's an **Amulet of Spell Shield** nearby that you may also claim once the Giant Sea Turtles are destroyed.

READY ATTACK FORCE AND DESTROY NAGA BASE

Build your Moon Wells to the point where your 100 Food maximum is possible, then produce a 'ground group' of Mountain Giants, Archers, Dryads, Druids of the Claw, and your Heroes, as well as an 'air group' comprised of four or five Chimaeras. Once you've assembled these two formidable forces, charge toward the main Naga base and attack, using the Chimaeras to destroy the Naga buildings while your ground force fights the Naga units. Use Malfurion's Tranquility skill to heal your ground units during the battle. The Chimaeras will quickly break the back of the Naga by leveling their structures, thereby eliminating their ability to generate resources and units!

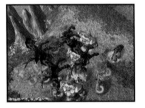 

There's a Fountain of Health along the northern route. This is an excellent fallback location for obvious reasons. However, if your troops are fully upgraded, you should have no problem defeating the Naga base.

> **TIP**
>
> Use your three Heroes' abilities when attacking Illidan's base. Malfurion's Tranquility heals, Maiev's Vengeance creates powerful Avatars, and Tryande's Starfall lays waste to large areas.

At this point, the enemy may be counterattacking your base, but as long as the main Naga base is near total destruction, you need not worry about this. When the last Naga structure collapses, victory is yours!

CHAPTER SIX

SHARDS OF THE ALLIANCE

Three days later, on the western coast of Lordaeron, the Night Elves venture cautiously into the shifting shadows of Silverpine Forest. The Night Elves find themselves in Lordaeron, an area consumed by the Undead Scourge. While Malfurion convenes with the forest, Maiev and Tyrande meet with Prince Kael'thas and agree to help his caravan weave its way through the Undead-laden country-side in return for help in finding Illidan.

REQUIRED QUEST

ESCORT KAEL'THAS AND HIS CARAVAN	Requirements
Escort Kael'thas and his supply caravan across the River Arevass.	✛ Lead the caravan across the river.
	✛ At least two Supply Wagons must survive.
	✛ Tyrande, Maiev, and Kael'thas must survive.

OPTIONAL QUEST

RETRIEVE SUPPLIES	Requirements
Kael'thas has stashed some gold and lumber nearby. Retrieve the resources to allow the purchase of mercenaries and other supplies.	✛ Recover the first gold cache.
	✛ Recover the second gold cache.
	✛ Recover the third gold cache.

MAP SECRETS LEGEND

As with the other maps you've explored thus far, there are a few bonus items that only the truly observant (or those with this guide) will find.

⬤	Gold +600	📜	Scroll of Animate Dead
🗡	Potion of Mana	📜	Scroll of Mana
🧪	Potion of Replenishment	🔮	Talisman of Evasion
💍	Ring of Protection	⚜	Wand of Mana Stealing
🔱	Rune of Lesser Healing		

MERCENARY CAMPS

There are three Mercenary Camps in this mission, and each offers a different selection of units. Here's a breakdown of the help offered at each site. (Corresponding Gold/Lumber/Food costs appear in parentheses beside each mercenary.)

MERCENARY CAMP #1

- **Forest Troll Berserker** (195/30): Axe thrower.
- **Forest Troll High Priest** (245/40)
- **Ogre Mauler** (240/0): Large, brutal warrior of the Ogre Legion.

MERCENARY CAMP #2

- **Assassin** (200/30): Medium-ranged unit that fires envenomed bolts. (No Shadowmeld)
- **Kobold Geomancer** (205/30)
- **Kobold Taskmaster** (255/50): Heavy melee unit with Command Aura. Can Bash opponents.

MERCENARY CAMP #3

- **Forest Troll Trapper** (170/20)
- **Renegade Wizard** (255/50)
- **Elder Sasquatch** (290/80): Heavy melee unit that can Bash opponents. Can cast Force of Nature.

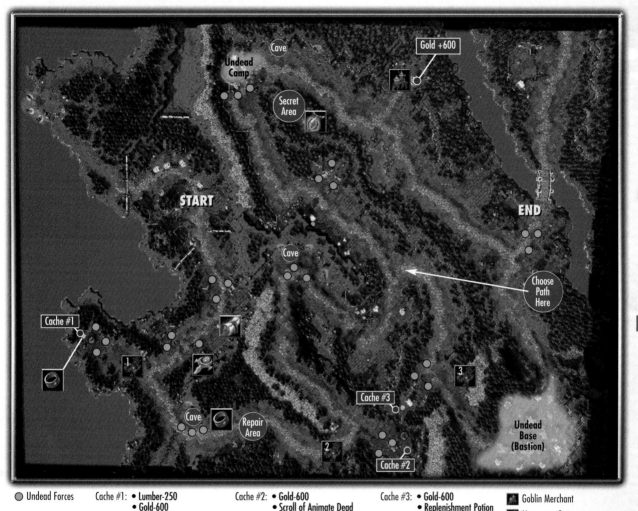

Undead Forces

Cache #1: • Lumber-250
• Gold-600
• Rune of Greater Healing

Cache #2: • Gold-600
• Scroll of Animate Dead
• Rune of Lesser Healing

Cache #3: • Gold-600
• Replenishment Potion

Goblin Merchant

Mercenary Camp

Ring of Protection

THE PATH TO VICTORY

This mission requires the careful defense of Kael'thas' caravan, so it's important not to send your troops too far away from the caravan. Although there are frequent surprise attacks on the rear of the caravan as it winds through the paths, the Blood Elf units shadowing the caravan can handle these skirmishes, allowing your forces to concentrate on the dangers that lie in front instead. In short, as long as you keep your units close to the enemy,

and use Maiev's Vengeance spell as frequently as possible, you'll be able to defeat the Undead units you face.

There are three Mercenary Camps and three gold stashes along the way. Each gold discovery allows you to purchase mercenary units, strengthening your ability to overcome the Undead. The three gold stashes are part of the optional quest, and all three must be liberated to succeed in this challenge.

MOVE SOUTH

As soon as the mission begins, assemble your units into a single group and proceed down the path to the south. The

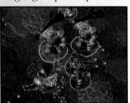

caravan automatically follows your units, so you don't have to worry about coaxing them into remaining nearby. A short distance beyond the starting point of the mission, you face a mob of Undead, including plenty of Ghouls. Maiev's Fan of Knives is very effective against large numbers of the Scourge, but it's better to use Vengeance here because the Avatar she raises converts any corpses into allies for your cause. This is very important because the Undead Necromancers will use those corpses if you don't!

TIP • • • • • • •

There's a **Scroll of Mana** near the starting location (see our map).

MERCENARY CAMP #1/GOLD CACHE #1

As you continue down the map, a Mercenary Camp comes into view to the west. Proceed past the camp to find the first **Gold Cache**, which is guarded by some Undead, including a level 1 Dreadlord. Clear them out and then pick up the **600 Gold**, **250 Lumber**, and **Rune of Lesser Healing** for the effort. With those newly acquired resources burning a hole in your pocket, head over to the Mercenary Camp and hire some help to aid you in your quest. Once you're stocked up with mercenaries, move along the path to the repair area (see our map). Another group of Undead greets you on the way, so take care of them before the caravan catches up.

NOTE • • • • • • • •

If your units are damaged heavily, remember that there's relief in the caravan! The two Priests you're escorting through danger can heal your units automatically. Simply position your wounded close enough to them so that their healing ability is within its effective range.

HINT - Pick up a tree with the Mountain Giant's War Club ability to give the Giant Siege damage, and increased attack range.

MERCENARY CAMP #2/GOLD CACHE #2

As you move into the repair area, the caravan is repaired by the Blood Elves, so any damage thus far will be patched up, giving the caravan a fresh start. The second **Gold Cache** is just beyond this area, and there's also another Mercenary Camp nearby. The stash is well defended by a Crypt, a Graveyard, and a Ziggurat (upgraded with defensive capabilities), so be sure to use Vengeance and Starfall to soften up the enemy. Once cleared, claim the **600 Gold**, a **Rune of Lesser Healing**, and a **Scroll of Animate Dead**, then pay a visit to the Mercenary Camp and hire some more help.

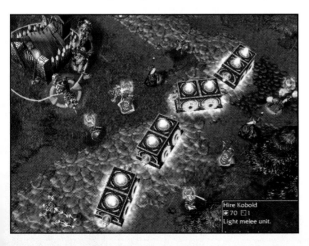

Hire Kobold
⊙ 70 ☐ 1
Light melee unit.

THE FORK IN THE ROAD

At this point, the road loops back to the north. Keep moving, stopping only to fight any Undead that get in your way or threaten the caravan. There are some caves at the northern bend in the road where various Ghouls, Crypt Fiends, and another level 1 Dreadlord attempt to impede your progress. Use Vengeance and Fan of Knives to make them wish they had stayed in their tomb. When the caravan reaches the town (just before the fork in the road), Kael'thas announces that the caravan will stop for repairs one more time before making a final rush toward the bridge.

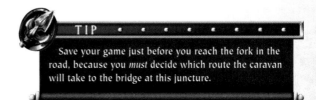

TIP

Save your game just before you reach the fork in the road, because you *must* decide which route the caravan will take to the bridge at this juncture.

SHARDS OF THE ALLIANCE 6 SENTINEL CAMPAIGN

The fork in the road offers you a choice. You must decide which path the caravan will take. You can either pass through the Undead base (which you must then destroy) along a shorter route, or take the longer but less perilous route. After making your decision, the caravan will follow *only* that path. In other words, once you've committed to one path, you can't change your mind.

MERCENARY CAMP #3/GOLD CACHE #3

Regardless of the path you follow, the third **Gold Cache** is down the right side of the fork in the road. It holds **600 Gold** and a **Replenishment Potion**. This is just enough cash to pick up some more helpers from the Mercenary Camp before moving on. Once you've captured the cache site and purchased some mercenaries, you can either continue down toward the Undead bastion (short route) or turn around and move back up the path (long route).

THE LONGER PATH (LEFT)

If you choose the path to the left, you'll have an easier time of it, but the journey is a fair bit longer, thus extending your mission. After you've made the choice, ignore the selection (for a moment) and turn to the right to collect the goodies from the third **Gold Cache** and visit the nearby Mercenary Camp. Once you've completed the Retrieve Supplies quest and purchased more mercenaries, move back up the path to the north, keeping an eye out for any Undead along the way. Expect a group of Abominations,

Crypt Fiends, and Ghouls before you reach the small Undead camp at the apex of the road. Level the base, then make the turn and resume your trek southward.

> **TIP**
>
> There's a secret area that's accessible only by using Maiev's Blink ability. After you turn south on the long path, hug the inside of the roadway and look for a single tree stump. Move Maiev into this area, then have her Blink over to the area inside the trees, which will be just barely visible, to receive a **Talisman of Evasion**!

As the caravan proceeds south, you approach a Goblin Merchant in the northeast (accessible by a short road). This lightly guarded area also contains a Gold Coin worth **600 Gold**! Pick up any necessary items like a Scroll of Protection for the final battle, then continue south.

THROUGH UNDEAD BASTION (RIGHT)

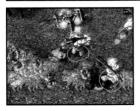

If you've chosen the more difficult path, then turn right at the fork in the road, move to the third **Gold Cache**, clean out the enemies, get the money, then hire some more mercenaries—you'll need them! The Undead bastion is tough, but still manageable if you keep your units grouped closely together. Enter the enemy base and attack their structures one at a time. Use Maiev's Vengeance right away—the resulting Avatar concentrates on enemy units while your group makes quick work of the buildings. Tyrande's Starfall is also an excellent way to damage both Undead units and their structures.

Manage this battle carefully to sweep through the bastion. Doing so leaves only a short distance to travel before reaching the final battle near the bridge.

THE FINAL BATTLE

Regardless of the path you choose to follow at the fork in the road (easy or hard, left of right), you'll still end up in the town near the bridge. When you get there, you are welcomed by a massive attack from the Scourge. At this point, you need only hold off the attack. Do this, and the mission is a success. Maiev warns that the Undead's forces are unending, but there is a finite number that you must destroy to complete the mission. Vanquish the attack waves of the Undead, and you move on to the next mission!

CHAPTER SEVEN

THE RUINS OF DALARAN

At the moment of Tyrande's success, deep within Silverpine Forest, Malfurion attempts to commune with the spirits of the wild. Later that evening, at the Night Elves' base camp, Malfurion returns to warn Maiev and Tyrande of his brother's dangerous sorcery. It becomes clear that there are four Naga Summoners around the Eye of Sargeras. You must destroy these Summoners in order to save the world.

THE PATH TO VICTORY

Your goal is to destroy the four Summoners in the northwest corner of the map. Unfortunately, these enemies are ethereal, and can only be damaged with magic. Add to this the fact that the Summoners are extremely well defended behind multiple layers of Naga units and structures, and it becomes clear that you have your work cut out for you if you want to be successful in this mission.

Scroll of Mana (NumPad 4)
Left-Click to Use
Restores 100 mana to all friendly units in an area around your Hero.

This is your ultimate destination. It's very well defended.

REQUIRED QUEST

SPELL OF DESTRUCTION	Requirement
Illidan's Naga Summoners have begun channeling a powerful spell through the Eye of Sargeras that threatens to tear the planet asunder. Time is running out as they come ever closer to finishing their chanting. You must slay all four Naga Summoners before time runs out. Unfortunately, the Summoners have turned ethereal and can only be harmed by magic. Use one of the following to damage the Naga Summoners: Faerie Dragon's Mana Flare, Chimaeras' regular attack, Druids of the Talon's regular attack, Maiev's Fan of Knives or Shadow Strike spells.	✦ Destroy the Naga Summoners.

OPTIONAL QUEST

SAVE THE PALADIN	Requirement
There is a Paladin being held behind the Naga. Break him free of his cage, and he may aid you in the destruction of Illidan's forces.	✦ Free the Paladin.

MAP SECRETS LEGEND

Although there are several extra items on this map, the time limit prevents most players from exploring every area. There is one area, however, that you can reach only with Maiev that's well worth the trip. It's near the Paladin's cage and it contains four distinct items! Here's a complete list of what this map holds:

Amulet of Spell Shield		Robe of the Magi +6
Claws of Attack +9		Rune of Mana
Helm of Valor		Scroll of Mana
Lesser Replenishment Potion		Scroll of Protection
Potion of Greater Healing		Tome of Agility
Potion of Greater Mana		Tome of Intelligence
Potion of Mana		Tome of Strength

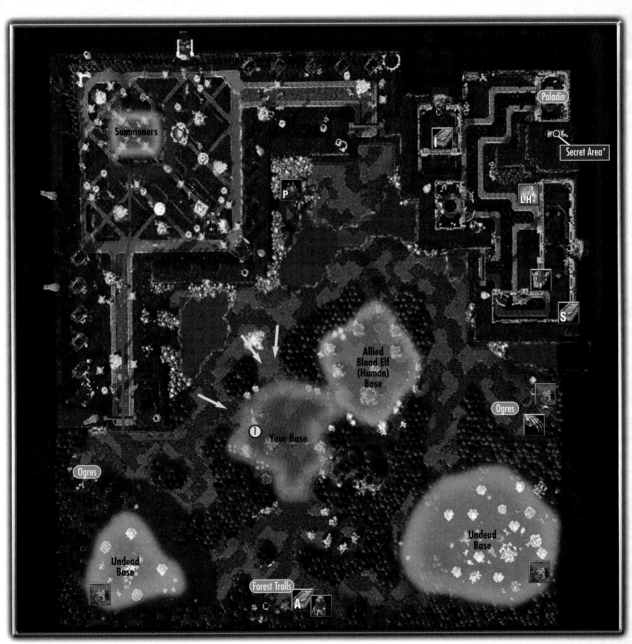

Summoners

Paladin

I

Secret Area*

L H

S

P

Allied Blood Elf (Human) Base

Ogres

① **Your Base**

Ogres

Undead Base

Undead Base

Forest Trolls

A

SENTINEL CAMPAIGN   7   THE RUINS OF DALARAN

⟵ Your path to the Summoners   ⟵ Enemy attacks will come from here

Gold Mine   P Fountain of Restoration (Power)

① Contains:
- Amulet of Spell Shield
- Scroll of Mana
- Potion of Mana
- Scroll of Protection

***Secret Area:** Use Maiev's BLINK to reach this area; it contains:
- Rune of Mana
- Robe of the Magi +6
- Potion of Greater Healing
- Potion of Greater Mana

The main goal for the first 20-25 minutes of the mission is to gather sufficient resources to upgrade your units to their maximum levels while building an attack force that consists of the following: a ground group with two or three Mountain Giants, Maiev, Malfurion, the Paladin, two Archers, two Dryads, and two Druids of the Claw. You also need an air attack group consisting of five or six Faerie Dragons and three to five Chimaeras (upgraded). When you attack, these two groups will work in unison. The secondary goal during the first 25 minutes is to move up toward the northeast corner of the map and rescue the Paladin that is imprisoned there. This is an optional quest, but having the Paladin on your side is a huge bonus when you make your run at the Summoners.

> **NOTE** • • • • • •
> There is a 30-minute time limit on this mission. This time constraint magnifies the significance of each and every decision you make, so when you need a moment to think, pause the game (F10) to stop the action while you consider your next move.

FORTIFY BASE AND UPGRADE

As mentioned above, your first task is to lightly fortify your base (don't pour too many resources into it) and begin the upgrading process immediately. You must upgrade your Tree of Ages into a Tree of Eternity, create three new Wisps, set your Moon Wells up to automatically replenish health and Mana, and build new Moon Wells and a Chimaera Roost.

Completed: Moon Well

Illidan and his Naga forces attack both the Human base and your camp repeatedly, but you won't have to worry about helping out the Humans—they are more than capable of fending off Illidan themselves. As for your base, it's not a bad idea to move your extra Ancient Protector up to the area where the Naga attacks come (see our map). It's also wise to leave a few units behind when you go after the Paladin so that your base doesn't get destroyed while you're away.

Completed: Hardened Skin

> **TIP** • • • • • • •
> The Human base next door always lends a hand when Illidan and the Naga attack you, so all you really have to do is fend the attack long enough for Kael'thas' troops to show up and save the day.

RESCUE THE PALADIN (OPTIONAL)

Shortly after the mission begins, you receive an optional quest, to free the trapped level 8 Paladin, Magroth the Defender. He resides in a cell in the northeast (upper-right) corner of the map. A small party of units (including Malfurion and Maiev) can easily deal with the Naga units that guard him. Once the upgrades in the base are underway, you can move your attack group up to free the Paladin, who returns the favor by assisting your efforts later.

The area where the Paladin is trapped is easily reached. There are also several other closed-off areas that contain both enemies and items. Refer to our map and decide if any of the items is worth spending the time to capture. Once the Paladin is free, return to your base and resume your defensive stand, then assess the status of your upgrading/attack force-building efforts.

READY ATTACK FORCE

It is plausible to create an aerial attack group with six Chimaeras and six Faerie Dragons (both of which are capable of damaging the Naga Summoners), so shoot for these numbers in your airborne group. For the ground units, you'll need some fighting units, but remember that only Maiev's spells and the Druid of the Talon's attacks will actually damage the Summoners, so you'll have to choose your units carefully. Several fully upgraded Mountain Giants will most certainly help in your efforts to clear a path up to the Eye of Sargeras.

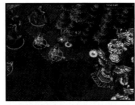

SECRETS

As mentioned earlier, there isn't a great deal of time to spend patrolling the map looking for secret items. Still, there are a few key items that are well worth your attention, especially the small area adjacent to the Paladin's cage where you can use Maiev's Blink ability to get a **Robe of the Magi**, a **Rune of Mana**, and **Potions of Greater Healing and Mana** all at once! There's also some **Claws of Attack +9** in an Ogre camp, and a **Helm of Valor** that drops from one of the Kobold Taskmasters near the Paladin.

Time Left 00:13:04

DESTROY THE SUMMONERS!

As soon as your attack force is fully built (you should be able to have this completely done with about 10 minutes left on the clock), move your two groups toward the Naga base following the path charted on our map. Before you leave, ensure that Maiev and Malfurion's Mana levels are maxed-out, and also purchase some Mana Potions from the Ancient of Wonders because it is often Maiev's Fan of Knives that ends up doing the most damage to the Summoners.

As you enter the Naga base, work hard to keep your units all grouped together, with your aerial units targeting first the Tidal Guardians, then the other structures. A group of five or six Chimaeras and an equal complement of Faerie Dragons can destroy a structure in just a few seconds when working cooperatively, so keep them all on the same page, attacking structures one at a time.

> **TIP**
>
> If your aerial units become damaged during early attacks on the Naga positions, you can quickly fly them back to your base for your Moon Wells to replenish their health and Mana. You can also use Malfurion's Tranquility to heal them if necessary.

While it may seem like a good idea to simply run a large group of aerial units up to the Summoners' position, this always ends in failure because of the vast number of Naga units and Tidal Guardians in the area. By far the most effective approach is to inch your units up the path toward the Summoners' position, reaching them with your troops relatively intact. Malfurion's Tranquility spell is absolutely essential in this assault because you can use it two or three times during the attack, with each casting fully healing the bulk of your units.

When you reach the Summoners' area, your first goal is to have your Chimaera group destroy the four Tidal Guardians, one at a time. With these structures in ruins, you can turn the Chimaera's attention toward the Summoners (their attacks effectively damage these powerful foes), while also advancing Maiev with her Fan of Knives and Shadow Strike to finish the Summoners off. The mission ends when the Summoners are history!

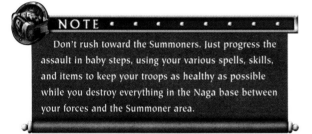

> **NOTE**
>
> Don't rush toward the Summoners. Just progress the assault in baby steps, using your various spells, skills, and items to keep your troops as healthy as possible while you destroy everything in the Naga base between your forces and the Summoner area.

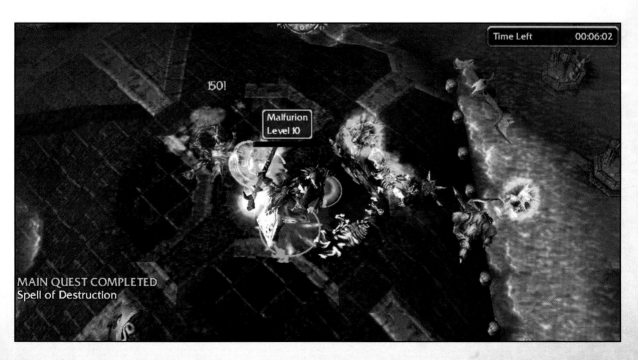

MAIN QUEST COMPLETED
Spell of Destruction

Time Left 00:06:02

150!

Malfurion
Level 10

CHAPTER EIGHT

THE BROTHERS STORMRAGE

Illidan and Malfurion join forces to find Tyrande. Maiev is bound by Malfurion's Entangling Roots, and Malfurion and his brother Illidan move forward to fight the Undead. Hours later, along the banks of the River Arevass, Malfurion and Illidan work together to pick up Tyrande's trail. Moving quickly through the woods, their skills and senses start working in unison—their twin wills bent on finding their beloved priestess before it's too late.

THE PATH TO VICTORY

This is the most difficult mission yet. There are now two distinct camps to manage, and one of them consists of the Naga, which until now have been your sworn enemy. Illidan's Naga base is in the northeastern (upper-right) corner of the map, and Malfurion's Night Elf Base is located on the western (left) edge of the map. You have control over both, but your goals with each are different. Malfurion needs only to defend his position and keep his base from being destroyed by constant Undead attacks, while Illidan must complete the optional quest (to break open the dams), and then decimate the Red Undead base completely.

REQUIRED QUEST	
TYRANDE'S RESCUE	Requirements
Illidan and Malfurion must work together to save the woman they love from the clutches of the Undead. Malfurion must hold out against the Undead forces, while Illidan must crush the massive Undead base surrounding Tyrande. Only then can she be brought to safety.	Illidan must destroy the red Undead base. Malfurion must defend his Night Elf base.

OPTIONAL QUEST	
DAM TROLLS	Requirement
The Trolls have constructed several dams that block your way to the red Undead base that attacks Tyrande's camp. You must destroy Krag'jin, the Troll Chieftain, in order to break the dams and gain access to the Undead bases.	Slay the Trolls and their Chieftain.

MAP SECRETS LEGEND

Here is the list of items you can collect from this map:

Claws of Attack +15		Pendant of Mana
Crown of Kings +5		Ring of Protection +5
Healing Wards		Rune of Greater Resurrection
Inferno Stone		Rune of Restoration
Mask of Death		Rune of Shielding

NOTE

Often when two camps are used on the same map, resources are shared between them, making it easier for you to manage your lumber and gold. In this mission, however, the resources are decidedly separate and *cannot* be shared, so you must keep a close eye on both economic situations.

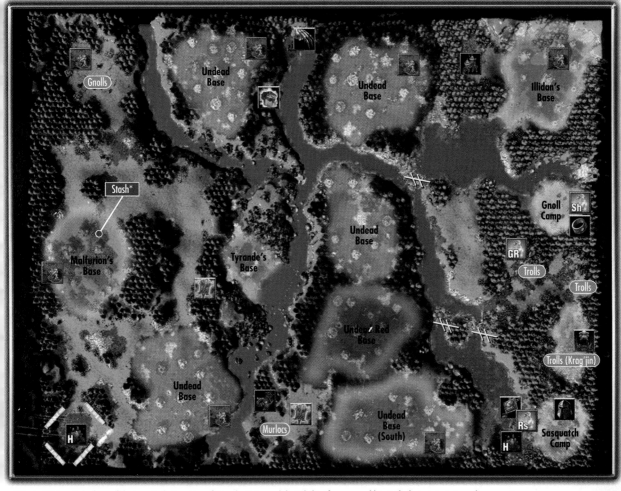

*Stash: This is a stash of ALL of the items in the inventory of Tyrande, Maiev, and the Paladin (if you rescued him in the last mission). Depending on what items you picked up in missions 1-7 with those three Heroes, they will be sitting in Malfurion's base at the beginning of this mission!

✕—✕ Dam

🔲 Fountain of Health   🔲 Goblin Merchant   🔲 Gold Mine   🔲 Mercenary Camp

While the goal is to simply keep Malfurion's base intact, you *can* attack the orange Undead base and 'bring the fight to them' instead of the other way around if you're feeling adventurous. This feat requires significant micromanagement and frequent switching between Illidan's forces and Malfurion's. For many, setting up Malfurion's base to automatically defend itself is much more desirable because it allows you to concentrate on controlling Illidan and the Naga.

FORTIFY MALFURION'S BASE

As soon as the mission begins, upgrade Malfurion's base to withstand the imminent Undead attacks from the south. First, group Malfurion together with his forces and hotkey them so that you can select and maneuver them quickly.

Secondly, begin upgrading the Night Elf units in the Hunter's Hall. Finally, build two more Ancient Protectors at both the north and the south entrances to Malfurion's base; this greatly improves the early defense of the area. Eventually, you'll also want to increase the number of Moon Wells in the base, but that can wait until later.

An attack comes quickly from the south, so move Malfurion into position before the enemy arrives.

WARNING

The Undead Meat Wagons always target Ancient Protectors first, and a pair of these horrific enemy units can destroy an Ancient Protector in a hurry. For this reason, we recommend that you position some Wisps near the Ancient Protectors (have them harvest lumber during non-combat situations), then you can quickly rush the Wisps to repair your damaged Ancients when they're under attack.

Upgrade Illidan's Forces

While you're improving Malfurion's base, set the Naga units to upgrading so that Illidan's units become more powerful. Ultimately, the attack on the Undead is made entirely by Illidan's Naga, so it's important to upgrade as quickly as possible. Since the Undead throw frequent attacks at Illidan's base, you'll also want to build several new Tidal Guardians to bolster the defenses.

The mission starts with plenty of resources for the Naga, but lumber quickly becomes scarce, so create a couple more Mur'gul Slaves to harvest it early on.

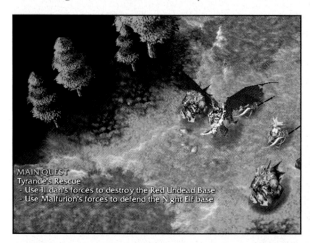

MAIN QUEST
Tyrande's Rescue
- Use Illidan's forces to destroy the Red Undead Base
- Use Malfurion's forces to defend the Night Elf base

NOTE

Don't forget to put the nearby Goblin Merchant to use for Illidan. The Scrolls of Protection and Healing, along with Invulnerability Potions all come in *very* handy throughout this mission, so stock up early and often.

Dam Trolls Quest

After a short time you are alerted to the fact that there are dams blocking Illidan's access to the Undead bases in the central portion of the map. The only way to destroy these dams is to attack the Trolls that manage them. There are three Troll groups in the eastern region of the map, including their Chieftain, Krag'jin. Once Krag'jin has been destroyed, the dams fall, allowing Illidan to confront the Undead that continue to be a thorn in Tyrande's side.

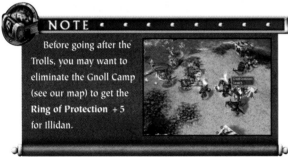

> **NOTE**
>
> Before going after the Trolls, you may want to eliminate the Gnoll Camp (see our map) to get the **Ring of Protection + 5** for Illidan.

One solid group of upgraded Naga units is all it takes to conquer the Trolls, especially if Illidan has a Scroll of Healing and a Scroll of Protection or two handy. Move to the south and into the Troll's area, attacking each group en masse (see our map). The battle with Krag'jin can present a significant challenge, so use a Scroll of Protection before venturing into battle to succeed with flying colors. Defeating Krag'jin not only demolishes the dams, but it also yields a **Mask of Death**, a very powerful vampiric item.

SASQUATCH CAMP

Once the dams have been opened, Illidan's troops can move all the way south down the waterway to the Fountain of Health and the Sasquatch Camp. Obviously, the Fountain of Health becomes an outstanding base camp and launching point for attacks on the Undead bases (which are just to the west of this location), but if you take the time to clear out the Sasquatch Camp to the east you'll also get a **Crown of Kings +5**! Either way, securing the Fountain of Health is essential, so be sure to do that before moving on the Undead.

> **WARNING**
>
> The Elder Sasquatch in the Sasquatch camp and by the Fountain of Health have the ability to resurrect after you've killed them once, so be prepared to fight each of these large beasts *twice*.

MALFURION'S FOUNTAIN OF HEALTH

If you are not content to let Malfurion sit back and relax in his base, you can always move him south to claim the Fountain of Health, then send his troops to attack the orange Undead base (the one responsible for most of the attacks on Malfurion). The choice is yours. There's no strategic advantage to doing this, but it might provide an acute level of enjoyment after taking a licking from the Undead for the last 30 minutes.

READY ILLIDAN'S FORCES AND ATTACK THE UNDEAD

Once you've secured the Fountain of Health and your Naga units are fully upgraded, build an attack force of two

groups: one with Illidan and a mix of units, and the other comprised of Mur'gul Reavers and Dragon Turtles. This second group should specifically target Undead

buildings while the first group deals with the swarms of Skeleton Warriors that the Necromancers raise.

We suggest that you destroy the green Undead base in the south-central area of the map before moving up to the red base. This is partly because there's a Gold Mine in this area that you may need, but also because there's a Mercenary Camp to the west that will aid you in your fight if you can secure it.

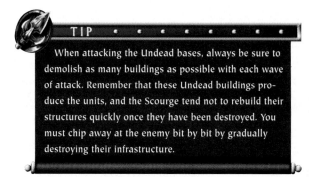

> **TIP** • • • • • • • •
>
> When attacking the Undead bases, always be sure to demolish as many buildings as possible with each wave of attack. Remember that these Undead buildings produce the units, and the Scourge tend not to rebuild their structures quickly once they have been destroyed. You must chip away at the enemy bit by bit by gradually destroying their infrastructure.

Once the southern green Undead base is yours, you can even build a Temple of Tides by the Gold Mine and harvest some gold for the purchase of Mercenaries.

DESTROY THE RED UNDEAD BASE

No doubt Illidan's forces will have taken some heavy losses in the battle for the bottom of the map, so take some time

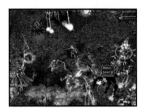

to rebuild the attack force, then move over to the Mercenary Camp to hire some help before attacking the red Undead base.

MERCENARY CAMP

Here's a list of the units available from the Mercenary Camp in this area. (Corresponding Gold/Lumber/Food costs appear in parentheses beside each mercenary.)

- **Murloc Tiderunner** (85/0/1): Light melee unit.
- **Murloc Huntsman** (120/10/2): Light melee unit that can Ensnare opponents.
- **Murloc Nightcrawler** (170/20/2): Light melee unit that poisons opponents. Can also use Shadowmeld.

The goal here is to destroy the red Undead structures. Before claiming victory, every *structure* must be demolished, not the units. For this reason, we recommend that you use Dragon Turtles again to target enemy buildings en masse and clear the area out quickly. When the last enemy structure is smoldering on the ground, victory belongs to you!

ALLIANCE CAMPAIGN:
CURSE OF THE BLOOD ELVES

These aren't just Human missions—they also involve the Blood Elves. Although part of the Human Alliance, there are several unique aspects to this race that are now available to you.

CHAPTER ONE

MISCONCEPTIONS

At Grand Marshal Garithos' base camp, near the outskirts of Dalaran, Kael'thas and his warriors arrive bearing ill news. Marshal Garithos instructs Kael'thas to repair the three Arcane Observatories, a task which does not please Kael'thas. Still, he will follow Garithos' orders to the letter.

REQUIRED QUESTS

OBSERVATORY REPAIR	Requirement
The Observatories in this area served Lordaeron well when they were operational. Repair them to reveal a large area of vision for your army, and comply with Garithos' command.	✛ Find and Repair the Observatories.

OPTIONAL QUESTS

HIDDEN CACHES	Requirement
There are four hidden caches of gold, lumber, and items hidden around this map. Find them to bolster your resources and power.	✛ Find all four hidden caches.

MAP SECRETS LEGEND

This map is loaded with hidden items—including numerous Runes!

	Claws of Attack +3		Rune of Mana (8)
	Manual of Health		Rune of Rebirth
	Maul of Strength		Scroll of the Beast
	Potion of Mana (2)		Scroll of Healing
	Rune of Greater Healing (2)		Scroll of Protection
	Rune of Greater Mana (2)		Tome of Intelligence
	Rune of Greater Resurrection		Tome of Strength
	Rune of Healing (2)		
	Rune of Lesser Healing		

THE PATH TO VICTORY

This mission has several stages. The first involves getting Kael'thas and his troops out of the town that occupies most of the right side of the map. Once this is done, you must sail across to the central island and build a base to accrue adequate resources to both uncover the other caches and repair the Arcane Observatories. It's very important to take your time in this mission, and be sure not to leave your base (once it's built) undefended, as it will fall prey to frequent Undead attacks.

Arcane
Observatory

GH

Gnolls

Gnolls

Gnolls

Gnolls

Cache #4*

Gnolls

GH

Golems

Gnolls

M H

M

Arcane
Observatory

M

Murlocs

Forest Trolls

Ivory
Tower x2

Arcane
Observatory

Cache #1*

M

GM

Undead
Base

M

GM

M

M

S

Felguards

I

M

Ogres

M

Moss Covered
Granite Golem

RN

Ogres

RN

M

Ogres

M

Ogres

Cache #3* Rb

L H GR

M

Cache #2*

M

MISCONCEPTIONS   1   ALLIANCE CAMPAIGN

 RN Reinforcements

|||||||| Trees to be destroyed with
Flame Strike

 M Fountain of Mana

Goblin Merchant

Goblin Shipyard

*Cache #1: • Tiny Castle
• Rune of Lesser Healing
• 200 ○
• 250 🌲

*Cache #3: • Scroll of Healing
• Periapt of Vitality
• Tome of Intelligence

*Cache #2: • Tiny Altar of Kings
• Tiny Barracks
• 200 ○

*Cache #4: • Ring of Protection +1
• Healing Wards
• Scroll of Healing

MURLOC SECRET AREA

As the mission begins, a single Peasant works feverishly to repair an Arcane Observatory. When it's complete, a large portion of the map is revealed. Before venturing south into the town, use Flame Strike to obliterate the row of trees blocking your path north (see our map), then move up and defeat the Murlocs to acquire a **Maul of Strength** and a **Rune of Mana**.

Select Target

HIDDEN CACHE #1

After your troops are fully healed (be sure your Priests are set to 'auto heal'), move to the south and into the town. You must immediately fight some Dalaran Mutants, followed by Felguards and a Fel Stalker—the latter yields a **Rune of Mana** when destroyed. This is when you receive the optional quest "Hidden Caches."

Two groups of Wizards protect the area with the first Cache. Both are best handled with Flame Strike, which destroys the weaker units before it burns out! After eliminating the Wizards, you can break through the Iron Gate and capture the first **Hidden Cache**.

OPTIONAL QUEST UPDATE
Hidden Caches
 - Hidden Caches Found (1 of 4 Found)

Bundle of Lumber

Fountain of Mana and the Felguards

After clearing out the Cache and repairing the rest of the first Arcane Observatory (which happens automatically), move your troops down to the Fountain of Mana and eliminate the guards. In this mission, the Fountain of Mana is essentially a Fountain of Health because it constantly replenishes your Priests' Mana, allowing them to heal all your nearby units completely.

Next up is a fight against a group of Felguards, Bloodfiends, and an Overlord. This is the toughest encounter yet, so keep your Priests in the back so that they can heal injured units during the fight, and use Kael'thas' Flame Strike to wear down the enemies as often as possible. You get a **Rune of Lesser Resurrection** and a **Tome of Intelligence** in return for outlasting these foes. The Rune brings back one of your lost units if you had a casualty during the battle.

Hidden Cache #2

Before moving out of the town, your troops can visit the southern portion of the town and battle some Renegade Wizards. Take them out, then destroy the crates and barrels to reveal a **Rune of Mana**. There are also several groups of creeps outside of town that are just itching for a fight. Accept this challenge if you want to acquire more experience, along with a **Tome of Strength**.

The second **Cache** is hidden behind some trees, so use Flame Strike to remove this natural barrier. The Cache contains a **Tiny Altar of Kings**, a **Tiny Barracks**, and **200 Gold**.

BUILD BASE

After securing the Cache, go west to meet a Naga who's willing to lend a hand. She offers you two Transports, so take one of them and move your men over to the shore directly to the north. Drop your Tiny Castle, Tiny Altar of Kings,

and Tiny Barracks here and make an instant base! There's also a nearby Goblin Merchant that sells, among other things, Scrolls of Town Portal.

TIP • • • • • • •

The Town Center supplies only 12 Food, so if you haven't lost a large number of units, you won't be able to create Peasants (if you're over your food limit). For this reason, you should probably have the Peasant come down from the first Arcane Observatory to the Transport Ship site.

Once the core structures are in place, quickly build up a force of Peasants to harvest the much needed nearby resources. Also build an Arcane Vault as soon as possible because it has Ivory Towers for sale at only 30 Gold and 20 Lumber! Ivory Towers are Scout Towers that can be upgraded to Guard, Cannon, or Arcane Towers! Use Kael'thas to buy these Ivory Towers and then place them around your base to create an inexpensive perimeter defense.

ARCANE OBSERVATORY #2

Even though the second Arcane Observatory is basically adjacent to your new base, we still recommend that you put up a defensive perimeter and upgrade your units somewhat before venturing out to secure it. When your troops are ready, move out and capture the Observatory, then set a Peasant to work repairing it. This requires a great deal of lumber, so keep your Peasants harvesting this important resource.

The next item on your agenda is to sweep through the island and destroy the various creeps that inhabit it. There are several groups of Forest Trolls that yield some useful items, so make sure you scour the map to get all that you deserve. A Goblin Shipyard also lies in your path; buy additional Transport Ships here if you need them.

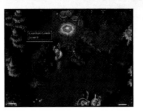

area of the Gold Mine (set up another base if necessary) before continuing to the southwest to reach the Hidden Cache.

Hack your way through several packs of pesky Gnolls, then unleash Flame Strike to obliterate the trees that stand in your way. Crush the Guardian Golem and Defender Golem on the other side and pick up the last **Hidden Cache** to finish the optional quest.

HIDDEN CACHE #3

The third **Hidden Cache** is tucked away in the far southwest corner of the map, and you must cross over two Ogre-

infested islands to get there. Fortunately, you can also pick up a few items on this trek. Just before you reach the Cache, you get a little more help as two Riflemen join your party as reinforcements. Defeat the Ogre Warchief guarding the Cache to receive a **Rune of Rebirth**, which resurrects the unit that dropped the Rune and makes him one of your minions

(permanently). This is a very powerful Rune, and the Ogre Warchief becomes an impressive and helpful addition to your forces.

THE THIRD ARCANE OBSERVATORY

Now that you've come this far, you should have a decent supply of lumber in your coffers. The only task left to complete is the restoration of the final Observatory. Using only one Peasant requires 1428 Lumber to repair it completely. If you're

at the Observatory with a single Peasant and have enough lumber, then you can just let the Undead destroy your base, because you have all you need to claim victory. Defeat Snarlmane the Bloodgorger, the Gnoll Warden that guards the Observatory, then get your Peasant(s) over there to repair it as quickly as possible. When the job's done, the mission ends.

HIDDEN CACHE #4

You're almost done! Take a strong attack force (one or two groups, depending on your level of confidence) to the northwestern island. Gnolls and Golems guard the Observatory and the fourth Hidden Cache in this area. We suggest that you first move north and claim the

CHAPTER TWO

A DARK COVENANT

The next day, at the Alliance base camp, Prince Kael'thas and his men ready themselves to move out. The Observatories noted a large Undead force that Kael'thas is responsible for taking out. Unfortunately, Garithos has ordered all foot soldiers and Knights out of the area, making Kael'thas' job considerably more difficult.

THE PATH TO VICTORY

When the mission begins, you have control of four outlying bases (labeled as Bases 1-4 on our map). Unfortunately, each of these camps immediately falls under *heavy* attack by Undead units, and is ultimately destroyed despite your best efforts. For this reason, we recommend moving each and every unit from these bases out of harm's way (see our map). When the dust settles, the Naga come to your aid, enabling you to strike out and recapture one of the recently-lost bases. From this point, you can build up an attack force capable of destroying the green Undead base.

This mission has several possible solutions, from destroying every single Undead base on the map, to simply securing one base (for the gold), and then moving to destroy the green Undead base. The path we present is just one of the many ways to do it, not the *only* way.

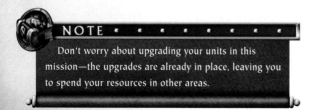

NOTE

Don't worry about upgrading your units in this mission—the upgrades are already in place, leaving you to spend your resources in other areas.

REQUIRED QUEST

CRUSH AND DESTROY	Requirements
From the shadows, Dalvengyr commands his Undead Scourge to surround your encampment. Seek out Dalvengyr, destroy him, slay his troops, and raze every last one of his buildings!	✦ Destroy the green Undead base.

MAP SECRETS LEGEND

While the goal of this map is strictly to execute a military campaign to destroy the green Undead base, there are a also few items of note:

Claws of Attack +3		Ring of Superiority
Gold Coins +200		Rune of Greater Mana
Lesser Scroll of Replenishment		Rune of Mana (2)
Mana Stone		Scroll of Healing
Pendant of Energy		Scroll of Protection
Potion of Greater Healing		Tome of Agility +2
Replenishment Potion		Tome of Intelligence
Ring of Regeneration		

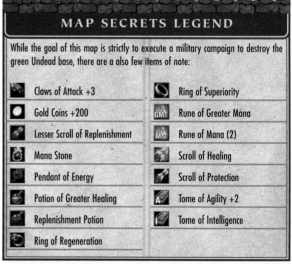

Gnolls

Orange
Undead
Base 1

Tiny Castle in crate

Base 2

Forest Trolls

Lightning Lizards
Storm Wyrm

M

Observatory

Undead Main
Green Base

Ogres

M

Observatory

Gnoll Wardens

Observatory

GM

Ogres

Main Base

Forest Trolls

Forest Trolls
(Warlord)

Forest Trolls

Ancient Hydra

A +2

Base 4

Base 3

M

Gnolls

Tiny Castle in crate

 Initially move all non-main-base units to these two locations.   → Recommended Path   Gold Mine

RESCUE THE OUTLYING UNITS

The Undead are too powerful for your forces to overcome initially. The best plan is to immediately move all of the units

from the outlying bases (1-4 on our map) to one of two rescue points (also see map).

FORTIFY THE MAIN BASE AND READY ATTACK FORCE

Move the rescued troops into your base and immediately get the workers started on harvesting the various lumber supplies on the island. Group the rest of the units together, and use the Gryphon Aviary to create at least two more Dragonhawk Riders. Although your gold supplies are certainly limited, these new units have the 'Cloud' ability, which greatly aids an attack to reclaim one of the outlying bases.

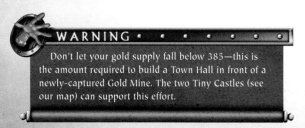

WARNING

Don't let your gold supply fall below 385—this is the amount required to build a Town Hall in front of a newly-captured Gold Mine. The two Tiny Castles (see our map) can support this effort.

It's also a good idea to create three or four Blood Elf Swordsmen to help defend the main base while your primary attack force is gone. Vashj and the Naga show up and offer their help. This group of Naga are extremely tough and can single-handedly defend your base or attack Undead bases. Whether you decide to use the Naga as your main attack force, or Kael'thas and the Blood Elves, the Dragonhawk Riders must be teamed with them.

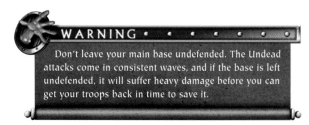

WARNING

Don't leave your main base undefended. The Undead attacks come in consistent waves, and if the base is left undefended, it will suffer heavy damage before you can get your troops back in time to save it.

RECLAIM BASE 2

Although Bases 2 and 4 are both logical choices to be reclaimed initially, Base 2 isn't actually in the path of Undead attack waves, so you can harvest its gold and lumber in relative peace once it's captured. Move your attack force and a group of four Dragonhawk Riders north toward Base 2. If you're using the Naga to attack, you won't need a Transport Ship (the Naga can swim), but if Kael'thas is your attack kingpin, you must bring a ship to aid in his movement.

Base 2 isn't well defended, and falls without too much effort on your part. The key is to move the Dragonhawk Riders in first to use Cloud on the three Spirit Towers (the Undead's defensive struc-

tures), then charge with the attack group. Continue to use Cloud on the Spirit Towers, and these Undead structures effectively have a range of zero, rendering them unable to fire on your units. Once the base is secured, ferry a few workers over to build a new Town Hall near the Gold Mine.

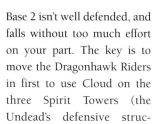

CREEP THE MAP (OPTIONAL)

Even though it's not a priority, you may still want to move around the map and destroy the various Creeps to collect items. Check out our map for the various Creep camp locations, along with what they have to offer for your efforts. Of course, if you're looking to gain experience, then you'll want to eliminate all the Creeps regardless, but if your goal is to complete the mission, then just pick and choose which group of Creeps guard the items that most interest you.

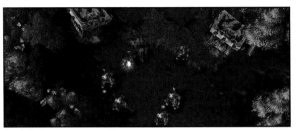

> **NOTE**
>
> Only the main Undead base actually sends units to attack you. However, if you attack and destroy one of the other Undead bases, then the adjacent Undead base will 'wake up' and send waves of attacks on you. In other words, you must only deal with attacks from the main Undead base until you attack one of the other bases. Attacking one of the other bases increases the number of units that you must fight.

RECLAIM BASE 1

At this point, you have a strategic choice to make. You can either move your attack force to the south and secure Base 3, or you can move directly to the west of Base 2 and secure Base 1 (the orange Undead base). If you move to Base 3, you must still blast through another base before reaching the green base (your target), so we suggest that you build up a significant attack force (two full attack groups, complete with a third group of Dragonhawk Riders for Cloud support) and move against Base 1 (the orange Undead base). After leveling this base, you have only a short trip to your next target, the adjacent green base.

> **NOTE**
>
> The process of destroying the Undead bases is not a quick one. Expect to have considerable downtime while you replenish your health and vanquished units between attacks. You'll also be fending off attacks on your main base throughout the entire mission.

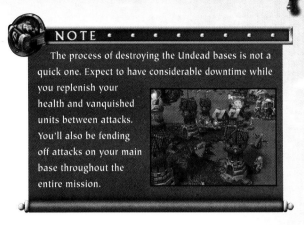

ELIMINATE GREEN UNDEAD BASE

Eventually, your conquest of the green Undead base comes into focus. It can be destroyed with a similar two-group (plus Dragonhawk Riders) attack force. Once you've secured Base 1 (or Base 4, depending on which way you're approaching the green base), heal your troops and replace any losses, then move in, concentrating all of your firepower on the buildings one at a time. Victory is yours when all the structures have been destroyed in the green Undead base—don't worry about the Scourge units. Also, once it's a forgone conclusion that your forces are going to decimate every last building, it's no longer necessary to save your main base from attack.

> **TIP**
>
> Use your Dragonhawk Riders to 'Cloud' defensive enemy structures, and target their buildings with everything you've got one at a time.

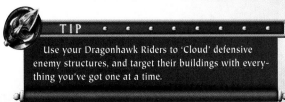

CHAPTER THREE

THE DUNGEONS OF DALARAN

Two days later, within the magically shielded dungeons of Dalaran, Kael'thas and his Blood Elf brethren languish in their cells, awaiting their inevitable executions.

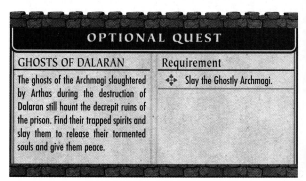

REQUIRED QUESTS

BLOOD ELF LIEUTENANTS	Requirements
Garithos has imprisoned your Blood Elf Lieutenants within special magical cages. Break them free so that they can release your brethren and prepare for the upcoming battle with Garithos.	❖ Free the Blood Elf Lieutenants. ❖ Kael and Vashj must survive.
JAILOR KASSAN	Requirements
The old Jailor of the sewer prison of Dalaran blocks the final gate to the surface. Kill him and those guarding the gate with him so that the wrongfully imprisoned Blood Elves can push the fight into the city.	❖ Slay Jailor Kassan and his guards. ❖ Kael and Vashj must survive.

OPTIONAL QUEST

GHOSTS OF DALARAN	Requirement
The ghosts of the Archmagi slaughtered by Arthas during the destruction of Dalaran still haunt the decrepit ruins of the prison. Find their trapped spirits and slay them to release their tormented souls and give them peace.	❖ Slay the Ghostly Archmagi.

MAP SECRETS LEGEND

Here's a complete rundown of the many useful items hidden throughout this map:

Boots of Speed		Rune of Restoration (2)	
Claws of Attack +3		Scroll of Mana	
Claws of Attack +6		Scroll of Regeneration	
Essence of Aszune		Shamanic Totem	
Frost Wyrm Skull Shield		Stone Token	
Medallion of Courage		Tome of Agility	
Ring of Protection +1		Tome of Intelligence	
Rune of Healing (3)		Tome of Knowledge	
Rune of Mana (2)		Tome of Strength	

THE PATH TO VICTORY

This is a very complex dungeon mission with myriad extra elements that are not crucial to victory. However, it also gives your Heroes plenty of extra items and experience points. One of the most fascinating aspects of this endeavor is the introduction of active Runes. Runes are symbols on the floor that do something when two units stand on a matching pair. This can be anything from a door opening to the appearance of a key item. Some of these Runes *must* be activated, while others are simply extras or related to optional quests.

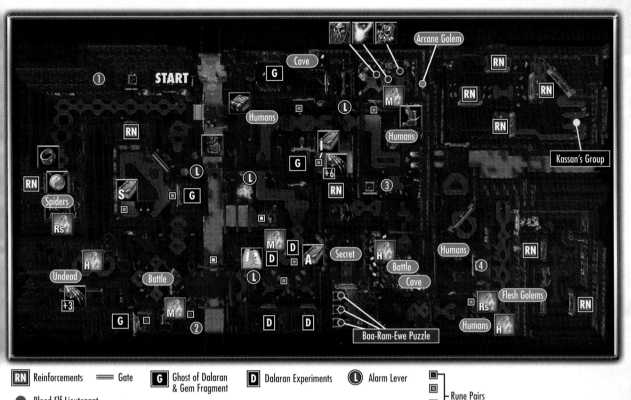

Map labels: Cave · Arcane Golem · RN · RN · RN · RN · START · ① · G · M · RN · Humans · L · Humans · Kassan's Group · RN · I · G · +6 · RN · ③ · S · L · L · G · RN · Spiders · Rs · M · D · A · Secret · H · Humans · RN · Undead · H · Battle · D · Battle · Cave · ④ · +3 · L · Flesh Golems · G · M · D · D · Rs · Humans · H · ② · Baa-Ram-Ewe Puzzle

Legend:

RN Reinforcements ═══ Gate G Ghost of Dalaran & Gem Fragment D Dalaran Experiments L Alarm Lever

Rune Pairs

● Blood Elf Lieutenant

The path through the dungeon is long and winding, but fairly linear. Therefore, we will not focus on every twist and turn, but rather the key areas that you need to be aware of. There is also a puzzle in this mission that, when solved, unlocks The Crossing (the secret level of the Alliance Campaign)!

THE FIRST BLOOD ELF LIEUTENANT

You're locked in a cell when the mission begins. Fortunately, Lady Vashj is nearby and releases you from your bondage. With Vashj by your side, blow open the nearby cells to release the first Lieutenant (which triggers the main quest) and the other Blood Elves being held captive.

SPITTING SPIDERS

The path through the dungeon leads east, but start off by heading west to first explore a corridor full of Egg Sacks and guarded by Spitting Spiders. Destroy these vile arachnids to

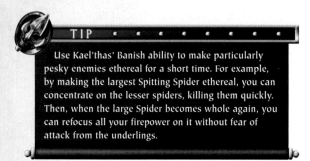

acquire another Priest, a **Medallion of Courage**, and a **Ring of Protection +1**. The Egg Sacks are full of Spider Broodlings, so open them one at a time and kill the emerging spawn. If you open too many sacks at once, you'll have a bevy of Spider Broodlings at your throat, and it's very important to avoid losing any units in the dungeon.

> **TIP**
>
> Use Kael'thas' Banish ability to make particularly pesky enemies ethereal for a short time. For example, by making the largest Spitting Spider ethereal, you can concentrate on the lesser spiders, killing them quickly. Then, when the large Spider becomes whole again, you can refocus all your firepower on it without fear of attack from the underlings.

BONUS ITEMS

Before moving to the gate, cross the green water duct to the Magic Vault. Destroy the Rock Golem that guards the vault, then open it to reveal a **Tome of Knowledge**. Use Kael'thas' Flame Strike to take down the mushrooms that block access to the Stone Token in the middle of the water. Only Lady Vashj is capable of moving through the water to get the Stone Token, so use her to grab the item, then go back up the stairs to the gate.

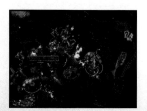

THE GHOSTS OF DALARAN (OPTIONAL QUEST)

When you approach the gate, the Human guards automatically start attacking the lever in an attempt to activate the 'alarm', which opens the gate and means more fighting for you. To stop this from happening, use Banish to make the unit ethereal (which prevents him from doing anything at all). This way, you can destroy the other guards first, then destroy the lever guard quickly when he becomes whole again.

Smash the gate and move into the room beyond. Once inside, you receive the Ghosts of Dalaran optional quest. This is your first exposure to the active Runes that have a cause-and-effect relationship with the dungeon. Notice the two green Runes in the room, then position one of your units on each one. When both of the Runes are occupied, the door opens to reveal the first Ghost of Dalaran (an Archmagi). Use your troops to destroy the Archmagi and then claim a **Gem Fragment**.

LIEUTENANT #2 AND THE SECOND GHOST

Proceed south along the passageway until you reach a battle that's raging between the Undead and the Alliance. Keep

your troops back and use Flame Strike to wipe out the tightly-grouped fighting units (they are *both* your enemy), then move in to clean up any remaining opposition.

Free the Lieutenant and the Archer in the adjacent cell, then smash a nearby crate to uncover a red Rune; its match is in the Archer's cell. Stand on the Runes to open up the pen that holds the second Ghost (Conjurus Rex), then defeat him to receive another **Gem Fragment**.

Finally, before leaving this area move to the west (left) to fight a group of Undead. Open the farthest cell to reveal **Claws of Attack +3**. Again, Flame Strike is a good spell to use against the Undead Necromancers who tend to hang back behind the frontline action.

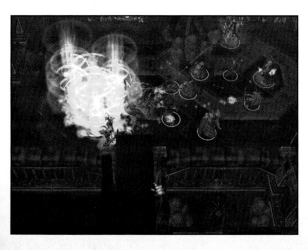

THE DALARAN EXPERIMENTS

You can now pass over the bridge and destroy the next gate. A significant force awaits just beyond this barrier, guarding the Dalaran Experiments. Before looking more closely at the Experiments, crush the Alliance guard force with

extreme prejudice. The other option is to destroy the lever on the far side of the gate, thus releasing the Dalaran Experiments, who then fight the Alliance guards, doing at least part of your job for you!

Either way, the Dalaran Experiments are *very* tough hombres, so you must keep a close eye on your troops when you're fighting them. To better preserve your units, it's best to keep your trigger finger on Banish so that you can stop the carnage long enough for your troops to either heal or run away. Once the two caged experiments are destroyed, two large Dalaran Experiments (1000 HP each) come into view on either side of a **Scroll of Mana**, which is guarded by two War Golems. Grab the Scroll of Mana to activate the Rune beneath it, then destroy the Dalaran Experiments one at a time. This is a good time to use your Stone Token to get some help for your troops! Once the area is clear, stand on the two green Runes to obtain a **Tome of Agility**.

TOME OF INTELLIGENCE

Move to the next gate and destroy the two guards before they can activate the lever (use Banish to prevent the guard from attacking it). Then, send Lady Vashj down to the Rune in the canal (she is the only unit that can reach it), and have a second unit stand on the other nearby Rune. This summons a **Tome of Intelligence**.

GHOST OF DALARAN #3

Another significant enemy force awaits just beyond the gate. Manage this one like the last, using a combination of Flame Strike, selective targeting, and Banish on the tougher units, such as the Knights. There's another Rune surrounded by some crates, and its match is down the ramp in the water. As you approach the nearby gate, Banish the guard that attempts to activate the alarm. Waste him, then move down the ramp to find the second Rune.

Reveal and defeat the next Ghost, then add another **Gem Fragment** to the Ring of the Archmagi. It's also important to look carefully at the area in the water and pick up a **Claws of Attack +6**!

LIEUTENANT #3

Past the gate is a Demon Gate (which you cannot open now), and a room full of crates guarded by some Footmen. Move through these areas and proceed through the gate to the south. Release the third Lieutenant after fighting some Human troops. As you enter the rooms past the Lieutenant's cell, an Archer and a Priest join your party, and you find a **Rune of Healing**!

THE SECRET LEVEL

After the third Lieutenant is freed, move south into the site of a huge battle. Stay out of the way and use Kael'thas' Flame Strike and Vashj's Forked Lightning to hasten the destruction of the combatants. As a rule, you can just hang back and let the enemies destroy each other.

When the battle is over, move your troops through the room and then open the gate to the west. There are three pens inside (each containing a sheep), and three switches on the floor.

If you've seen the movie 'Babe' (the one about a little pig that goes a long way), then you'll know how to solve this puzzle. If not, then read on. Hit the switches in this order: Top, Bottom, Middle. This opens the door to the north, allowing you to move one of your Heroes inside to claim the **Secret Level power-up**, which unlocks the secret mission as soon as this one ends!

SECRET LEVEL FOUND
You have unlocked a secret mission. Complete this mission to play.

THE CAVE AND THE FOURTH GHOST

After you've discovered the secret level, head for the cave (see our map) and send one of your troops inside. That unit appears in the north-central area of the map on a platform beside a red Rune. The matching Rune is nearby, so move your troops back up to the area and step on the second Rune to open the door-way to the fourth Ghost of Dalaran!

Once you've activated the Runes, enter the newly opened room and eliminate the Ghost to get the fourth **Gem Fragment**. When all is finished, move your troops back down to the area in the south near the cave entrance.

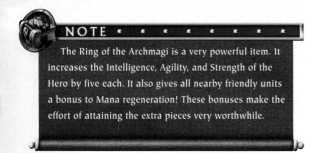

NOTE • • • • • • • • •

The Ring of the Archmagi is a very powerful item. It increases the Intelligence, Agility, and Strength of the Hero by five each. It also gives all nearby friendly units a bonus to Mana regeneration! These bonuses make the effort of attaining the extra pieces very worthwhile.

THE ARCANITE GOLEM

As you move to the east and fight with the large Human force there, you'll notice a group of mushrooms on the northern edge of the hallway. Level this stand of fungus with a blast from Flame Strike to reveal another Rune. The match is back in the north-central area by the Demon Gate. Step on both Runes to open the gate and reveal an Arcanite Golem (level 11). This is entirely optional, and we recommend that you save *before* you open this gate. The Arcanite

has 5000 (count 'em) hit points, and is *very* difficult to destroy. The plus side is that the destruction of this enemy grants you access to the crates inside the room, and all that they hold…

Essence of Aszune – Legends speak of an intelligent Orc who found the Heart of Aszune. This is the essence of her heart, precious to the Night Elves. It has the power to heal the Hero that wields it. This item is permanent.

Shamanic Totem – This powerful Orc artifact channels Shamanic powers through its user, allowing them to cast Purge.

Frost Wyrm Skull Shield – This ancient Frost Wyrm skull has been equipped with handles, turning it into a powerful shield. Increases armor by 5 when worn and reduces Magic damage dealt to the Hero by 33%.

THE FOURTH LIEUTENANT

As you round the corner and travel north into the unexplored dungeon, two Human guards release three Flesh Golems on you. They put up a tough fight, but you can damage them with Flame Strike. Use Vashj's Mana Shield to protect her, then put her on point. When the Golems fall, you get a **Rune of Healing**. Continue north, kill the guards, then explore the cells in the southeast corner of the map to acquire additional reinforcements.

Approach the Lieutenant's cell (see our map) and prepare to fight a group of Footmen and Riflemen. After decimating this force, free the Lieutenant to complete the main quest!

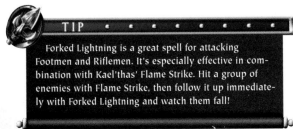

TIP

Forked Lightning is a great spell for attacking Footmen and Riflemen. It's especially effective in combination with Kael'thas' Flame Strike. Hit a group of enemies with Flame Strike, then follow it up immediately with Forked Lightning and watch them fall!

KILL THE JAILOR

Move to the north and take in the cut-scene depicting Kassan the Jailor advising you to turn back. Thumb your nose at him and continue north into the final room. Expect stiff resistance. Use Flame Strike on the groups of Knights, then follow it up with Forked Lightning. If the battle seems to be going the wrong way, target the gates to the cells to release more Blood Elves.

After defeating the Humans in the western edge of the room, release the rest of the Blood Elves and get ready for the final battle. Kassan's group is in the eastern edge of the room by the doorway to freedom. Kassan himself is immune to magic, making it impossible for you to Banish him. Keep your Heroes *behind* the front lines, and use their abilities (such as Flame Strike on Knights) aggressively to ensure victory.

THE CROSSING

Moments later, as the allied Blood Elves and Naga spill into the back alleys of Dalaran. Engineers begin to rebuild Dalaran's defenses while Lady Vashj attempts to open the Portal.

THE PATH TO VICTORY

Your goal in this mission is to protect the Portal from 30 separate waves of Garithos' units. To emerge victorious, you must place enough towers throughout the map to destroy each wave as it approaches you. Enemies that get through to the Portal will damage it, and when the Portal's health reaches zero, the mission is over and you continue on to Alliance Chapter 4. If you survive all 30 waves, the Panda-n-Cub image will flash briefly on your screen during the end cinematic before moving on to the next mission.

Since this is a bonus level, it needs to be handled differently than the other missions in *Warcraft III: The Frozen Throne*. This task is markedly more difficult than any other you've faced thus far, and you proceed to the next mission whether you win or lose in your attempts to protect the Portal. We'll discuss a general strategy for placing the Towers along the enemy's path, then list the 30 waves of attackers and their respective hit points.

REQUIRED QUEST

DEFEND THE PORTAL

Garithos is sending his men on a *suicide* mission to destroy the Portal. You must hold out long enough for all of the Blood Elves to get through to Outland. Place defensive towers in strategic locations to stop Garithos' army from reaching and destroying the Portal. Defend the Portal from Garithos' troops while the rest of the Blood Elves escape.

Requirements

- ⊹ Build Towers to stop Garithos' men.
- ⊹ The Portal must survive.

MAP SECRETS LEGEND

The secret items on this map are *very* difficult to obtain because you must concentrate on enemy waves, rather than collecting loot. If you want to get these items, you need to send one of your units out early for them.

Gloves of Haste (2)		Ring of Regeneration	
Lesser Scroll of Replenishment		Rune of Mana	
Orb of Slow		Rune of Restoration	
Potion of Greater Healing		Rune of Speed (2)	
Potion of Speed		Scroll of Animate Dead	
Ring of Protection +2			

Garithos' Elite Guard Base

M

Rs

Sp

M

Sp

THE OVERALL STRATEGY

The key to victory in this mission (and we should warn you that as a secret mission, it is plenty difficult) is to place the defensive towers in exactly the right locations to maximize their effects as the mission wears on. Check out our map to find the prime locations for Boulder Towers, Energy Towers, Flame Towers, Cold Towers, and Death Towers.

↗ Attack wave path

■ Place Flame Towers here

■ Place Cold Towers here

□ Place Death Towers here

Goblin Merchant

You must build the towers as quickly as possible and continue building them throughout the entire mission as your resources allow (gold is consistently poured into your coffers as time goes by). Put the most effective towers in the key corner locations with the greatest amount of time to target enemy units in their line of sight. Ideally, you should leave some corner positions open until later in the mission when you gain access to the Flame Tower, the Cold Tower, and finally, the Death Tower.

Use both Flame Strike and Forked Lighting to help your cause when foes slip past your defenses.

NOTE • • • • • • • •

Even though we have suggested tower placements on the map, you must ultimately cover every inch of the gauntlet with towers of all sorts.

TIP • • • • • • • •

It's important as you're playing the Human missions to make sure that Kael picks up all of the items that increase his Mana recharge and Mana level. Then, you can move Kael up to the enemy gate and destroy the two towers (with Flame Strike) that guard the gate. Once these towers are gone, you can use Flame Strike right on the enemies as they *gather* for their next run of the gauntlet! Using this technique greatly enhances your ability to manage the later waves, when the enemy has 5000 + hit points per unit.

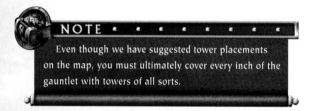

Completed Advanced Energy Tower

THE WAVES

Each wave usually consists of 12 units, plus a leader. The following page lists all 30 waves and what you can expect from each one. (HP = hit points per unit.)

NOTE • • • • • • • •

If you survive all 30 waves in Normal or Hard, you will start Alliance Chapter 4 with a Pandaren Brewmaster as a bonus! This Neutral Hero has no Inventory and does not carry-over to Alliance Chapter 5.

Experiment with the exact locations of your towers. Most of the path that the enemies follow has a narrow strip of grass where towers can be constructed. You should strive to build the towers along the *entire* length of the path so that the enemy experiences constant bombardment.

Don't worry about losing towers, because the enemy won't attack your units or towers; they only move ceaselessly toward the Portal in an effort to destroy it.

NOTE

Each named unit drops Gold Coins, which increase in value in the later waves.

WAVE #	LEAD UNIT	GROUP UNIT
1	None	Peasants – 176 HP
2	None	Militia – 176 HP
3	Captain – 480 HP	Footmen – 336 HP
4	None	Flying Machine – 140 HP
5	Buri Frostbeard (Mountain King) – 560 HP	Mortar Team – 288 HP
6	None	Riflemen – 416 HP
7	Aurrius the Pure (Paladin) – 560 HP	Knights – 640 HP
8	None	Gryphon Riders – 660 HP
9	None	Siege Engine – 680 HP
10	Peril Spellbinder (Archmage) – 420 HP	Apprentice Wizards – 560 HP
11	Bandit Lord – 880 HP	Enforcer – 800 HP
12	Forest Troll Warlord – 960 HP	Forest Troll Berserkers – 800 HP
13	None	Goblin Zeppelins – 400 HP (Note: Zeppelins are loaded with Goblin Sappers)
14	Thordin Rockbeard (Mountain King) – 740 HP	Ogre Warriors – 1200 HP
15	Ogre Lord – 1000 HP	Ogre Magi – 1280 HP
16	Gavinrad the Dire (Paladin) – 720 HP	Royal Guards – 1520 HP
17	None	Red Drakes – 1600 HP
18	Grim Thunderbrew – 860 HP	Siege Engines – 680 HP
19	Overlord Arachnathid – 2000 HP	Warrior Arachnathids – 2160 HP
20	Storm Wyrm – 4800 HP	Thunder Lizards – 5320 HP
21	Dalar Dawnweaver (Archmage) – 560 HP	Water Elementals – 1960 HP
22	None	Goblin Zeppelins – 400 HP (contain Goblin Shredders)
23	None	Rock Golems – 2040 HP
24	Deeplord Revenant – 6400 HP	Ice Revenants – 7520 HP
25	Ancient Sasquatch – 5040	Elder Sasquatch – 2400 HP
26	None	Red Dragons – 4400 HP
27	None	Siege Golems – 5800 HP
28	None	Centaur Khan – 5000 HP
29	None	Gargantuan Sea Turtle – 5960 HP
30	Tatsa Sweetbarrow (Pandaren Brewmaster)	Pandarens – 6120 HP

The final attack is led by Tatsa Sweetbarrow, a level 15 Pandaren Brewmaster with a bunch of Pandarens behind him.

THE CROSSING

ALLIANCE CAMPAIGN

CHAPTER FOUR

THE SEARCH FOR ILLIDAN

After three days of fruitless searching, Prince Kael'thas and Lady Vashj realize they are lost in the barren wilderness of the Hellfire Peninsula. Kael'thas and Vashj find Illidan locked inside a Night Elf cage, and vow to rescue him at all costs.

THE PATH TO VICTORY

The Search for Illidan can be likened to an old-fashioned game of tag. The goal is to reach Illidan's cage and destroy Maiev so that you can gain control of the cage (just getting close to it in the absence of Maiev is enough). Once the cage is under Kael'thas' control, it turns and moves slowly toward the Circle of Power in the Alliance base. Likewise, if Maiev has control of the cage, it rolls toward her Night Elf base. You must maintain control of it and get it to the Circle of Power in your base to emerge victorious.

KILL MAIEV!

When the mission begins, *immediately* send both Heroes toward the Mercenary Camp to the south. As soon as they arrive, purchase two or three Mercs, then move everybody to the east after Maiev as quickly as possible.

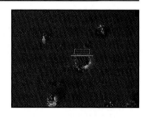

When you reach Maiev, hit her with Flame Strike, Chain Lightning, Forked Lightning, and whatever else you've got in your bag of tricks (along with the Mercenaries). Aggressively targeting Maiev specifically should be enough to destroy her. The cage then turns around and starts rolling toward your base. Once the cage is yours, the challenge is to hold it, and that can be difficult indeed.

REQUIRED QUESTS

THE DEMON WITHIN	Requirements
Lord Illidan has been captured by the cunning Warden in a cage of magical enchantments. Slay the guardians of the cage and take it from the Night Elves before they reach the safety of their base.	✥ Recapture Illidan's cage.
	✥ The cage must not reach the Night Elf base.

ESCORT ILLIDAN	Requirement
Though free from the Warden's grasp, Illidan remains weak, and the enchantments on the cage cannot be broken easily. You must escort Illidan's cage to the Blood Elf base, where the protection of Kael's army will give you time to break the magical locks.	✥ Bring Illidan's cage to the Blood Elf base.

SECRETS

This map has no secret items—only the Goblin Merchants, Fountain of Power, and Mercenary Camp can provide Kael'thas and Lady Vashj assistance.

MERCENARY UNITS

The Mercenary Camp contains some very buff units that can provide major help in this mission. Here's what's available (Gold/Lumber/Food):

Draenei Darkslayer (260/0/4): A medium melee unit with Immolation.

Fel Stalker (275/0/4): A Demonic beast that can cast Mana Burn.

Greater Voidwalker (300/0/5): Heavy ranged attack unit that can cast Chain Lightning and Frost Armor.

Eredar Diabolist (320/0/5): Heavy ranged unit that casts Firebolt and Parasite.

Circlet of Power

Alliance Base

Circlet of Power

P

Night Elf Base

● ● ● ● The corridor that Illidan's cage moves along

━━━ Drop Dead Point. If the cage is past this line and your Heroes are dead (respawning in your base), you are in real trouble and may want to restart the mission.

 Fountain of Power

 Goblin Merchant

 Mercenary Camp

HOLD THE LINE!

As the cage begins to roll back toward your base, direct your group (which should consist of Kael'thas, Vashj, and a Mercenary or two) to the Fountain of Power and heal them up for Maiev's next arrival. Like your Heroes, Maiev respawns almost immediately and quickly attempts to reclaim the cage. Groups of Blood Elf and Naga units continually stream from your base; your job is to support them as best you can, using your Heroes' special abilities to turn fortune in your favor.

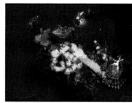

Maiev and the Night Elves hit you with an enormous number of units that sweep down the path like a blue wave of death. Even if Maiev gets to your base with her units and retakes the

cage, don't give up! Your Heroes continually respawn, and eventually you'll be able kill Maiev and recover the cage. Indeed, you may lose control of it several times during the mission, but as long as you're persistent, you'll eventually be able to move the cage to your Circle of Power. If the cage gets past a certain point (see our map) and both of your Heroes are dead, you may want to restart the mission, because it becomes very difficult to recover from such a disadvantage—still possible, just very difficult.

COAX IT IN

As the cage approaches your Circle of Power, you must give it everything you've got to prevent Maiev from wresting control back at the last second (and, trust us: it happens). When the cage finally reaches the Circle, it's over!

CHAPTER FIVE

GATES OF THE ABYSS

Hours later, at Illidan's base camp, Prince Kael'thas finally approaches the former Demon Hunter and asks for his aid. Then, two days later, upon the desolate plains of Outland, Illidan and Prince Kael'thas prepare to assault Magtheridon's dimensional gateways.

THE PATH TO VICTORY

The primary goal of this mission is to close the four Dimensional Gates that are spread out over the entire map. The first one is at your starting point, and holding off the enemy in that location closes it within a few minutes. As you explore the map, however, you learn of a way to get your hands on a new race's units, the Draenei! If you want to complete both the quest and the optional quest, this mission is enjoyably time consuming, so settle in for the long haul.

REQUIRED QUEST

DIMENSIONAL GATES	Requirements
A brutal Pit Lord named Magtheridon commands a vast army that moves through the Dimensional Gates daily. Only Illidan has the power to close each Gate by stepping onto the Dimensional Nexus. Kael'thas will need to protect Lord Illidan while he works his powerful magic for three minutes.	✛ Close each Dimensional Gate. ✛ Guide Illidan to each Dimensional Nexus. ✛ Illidan must survive three minutes per gate.

OPTIONAL QUEST

DRAENEI VILLAGE	Requirement
For centuries, the Draenei have been battling the Fel Orcs, but in the last hundred years the Draenei have been slowly losing. With the help of Illidan and Kael'thas, the Draenei would be able to turn the balance in their favor and rid themselves of the Fel Orcs once and for all.	✛ Destroy the orange Fel Orc base.

MAP SECRETS LEGEND

This mission is loaded with secrets and power-ups. Use our map to see where everything is hidden.

Belt of Giant Strength +6	Potion of Greater Healing
Claws of Attack +12	Ring of Protection +4
Greater Scroll of Replenishment	Rune of Dispel Magic
Healing Salve	Rune of Lesser Healing
Hood of Cunning	Rune of Shielding
Khadgar's Gem of Health	Runed Bracers
Pendant of Energy	Scroll of Resurrection

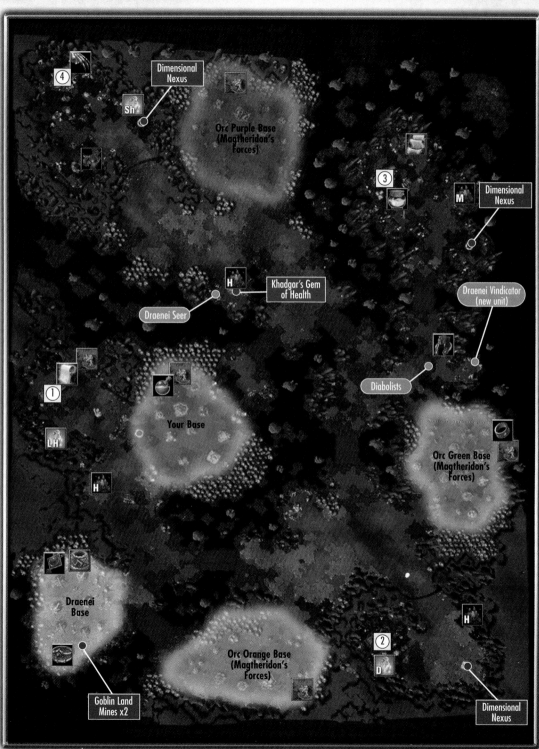

Dimensional
Nexus

Sh

④

Orc Purple Base
(Magtheridon's
Forces)

③

M

Dimensional
Nexus

H

Khadgar's Gem
of Health

Draenei Seer

Draenei Vindicator
(new unit)

Diabolists

①

Your Base

Orc Green Base
(Magtheridon's
Forces)

LH

H

Draenei
Base

Orc Orange Base
(Magtheridon's
Forces)

②

D

H

Goblin Land
Mines x2

Dimensional
Nexus

 Dimensional Gate   Fountain of Health   Fountain of Mana   Gold Mine   Mercenary Camp

UPGRADE AND BOLSTER BASE (CLOSE FIRST GATE)

The mission begins with Illidan closing the first of the four Dimensional Gates. We recommend grouping of all of your units tightly together, then setting your Barracks and Arcane

Sanctuary to build Swordsmen, Archers, and Priests as quickly as possible (set their waypoints to the area in front of Illidan so that they automatically engage in combat.

As the battle rages, the newly made Priests help to heal the damaged units. The gate closes after three minutes. Once

this happens, immediately begin upgrading both the Naga and the Blood Elf tech trees, while continuing to create new units to help defend your base.

DESTROY ORANGE ORC BASE

As soon as you move one or more of your units slightly to the south, a cut-scene introduces the optional quest for this mission. In order to get some help from the Draenei base in the southwest corner of the map, you must first destroy Magtheridon's orange Orc base in the south-central region of

the map. To do this, you need a fully upgraded attack force of 12 units, or a group of 12 units plus a small siege group, such as Dragon Turtles, to quickly bring down enemy buildings.

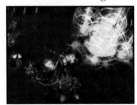

The enemy has clustered Orc Burrows and Guard Towers in tight groups of three, the perfect target for a blasting of Flame Strike! A few hits from this attack soften them up

before you move in to finish these clusters off with your main attack group. Once the base is destroyed, the Draenei begin to attack the other enemy bases in waves.

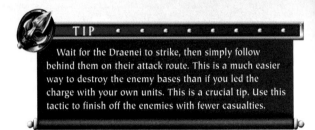

TIP

Wait for the Draenei to strike, then simply follow behind them on their attack route. This is a much easier way to destroy the enemy bases than if you led the charge with your own units. This is a crucial tip. Use this tactic to finish off the enemies with fewer casualties.

CLOSE DIMENSIONAL GATE 2

For the purposes of this walkthrough, the second Dimensional Gate is in the southeast corner of the map. Take a crack group of 12 units (including Illidan) down to the gate

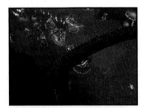

and clear away the areas both in front of the gate and around the Fountain of Health. Once this is done, buff up your units around the Fountain, then send Illidan into the Nexus.

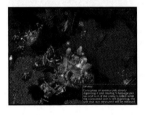

As soon as Illidan is in the Nexus, the enemies start to pour out of the gate. It's the same drill as you had when the mission started—keep the enemies away from Illidan for three minutes. If

any of your units become significantly damaged, you can send them back to the fountain for repair. Be sure to use Flame Strike and Forked Lightning to further cripple the enemies that emerge from the gate. When the gate's closed, move your troops back up to your main base.

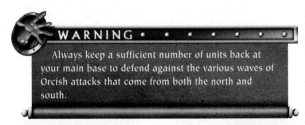

WARNING

Always keep a sufficient number of units back at your main base to defend against the various waves of Orcish attacks that come from both the north and south.

DESTROY PURPLE ORC BASE

This base is very difficult to defeat because it is defended by multiple Red Dragons. Replenish your main attack group, then wait for the Draenei to send a force up to the purple Orc base. When they go, follow along and work with them to destroy the base quickly. When nothing but ashes remain, build a Town Hall to harvest the gold from the recently liberated mine.

> **NOTE**
> If the purple base proves too strong, then consider ignoring it—the green base is an easier target.

CLOSE DIMENSIONAL GATE 3

With two of the three Orc bases destroyed, the defensive burden on your home base is considerably lessened. Move your troops up to the Gate Nexus and destroy the Doom Guards

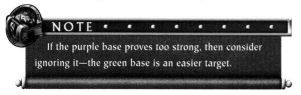

that stand in your way. This is a tough fight, and you may lose several of your units, so continue to create new units in your base to replace those lost in battle.

> **NOTE**
> If Illidan dies while trying to close a Dimensional Gate, the three-minute timer *resets* back to the *full* three minutes.

Again, move Illidan into the Nexus, and stand tall against the enemies that flow out of the gate. There's a **Rune of Shielding** in one of the nearby crates to help your cause. This is, by far, the most difficult gate to manage (and so you may want to handle it last). Instead of 12 units, bring 24, along with all the magic and items you can get your hands on! When the gate closes, you have only one more to close!

CREEP THE MAP

Because there is only one gate left to close, and doing so ends the mission, you may want to tackle the green Orc base in the east, and/or find the other hidden bonus items (see our map), such as the two Draenei units locked in cages in the east and central areas of the map. There are also some items, a **Pendant of Energy**, **Runed Braces**, and **Khadgar's Gem of Health**, that may be worth going after.

CLOSE DIMENSIONAL GATE 4

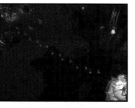

This is it! Close the fourth gate, and victory is yours at last. You don't have to destroy the remaining Orc base (in the east), but you can if you want to. The fourth gate is covered by Bloodfiends and Vile Temptresses, so don't expect a walk in the park. Send every unit on the entire map to this area, because this is now the only show in town.

After the initial enemies are cleared away, go to the Fountain of Mana and recharge. If you have Priests handy, they will soak up the Mana and convert it into health for all of your units. Battle courageously against these remaining enemies and protect Illidan for another three minutes to complete the mission!

> **TIP**
> If you're having trouble securing victory at Gates 3 or 4, then try placing Tiny Towers (or have Peasants construct some towers) around the gates.

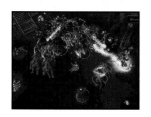
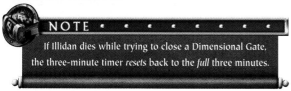
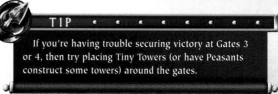

CHAPTER SIX

LORD OF OUTLAND

Hours later that same day, at the base of Magtheridon's Black Citadel, Illidan marshals his forces for their final strike.

REQUIRED QUESTS

SHADOWKEYS

The Pit Lord, Magtheridon, rules with the absolute power of the Black Citadel and its regime of Demonic minions. Slaughter Magtheridon's two dark lieutenants, the Master of Pain and the Mistress of Torment, in order to seize their Shadowkeys and gain access to his throne chamber.

Requirements

- ✧ Slay the Master of Pain.
- ✧ Defeat the Mistress of Torment.

SLAY MAGTHERIDON

The gates to Magtheridon's throne chamber have been thrown wide open, leaving the Pit Lord vulnerable to attack. Destroy Magtheridon so that Lord Illidan can claim power over Outland and take the Citadel as his fortress.

Requirement

- ✧ Slay the mighty Pit Lord, Magtheridon.

MAP SECRETS LEGEND

Here's a list of all of the useful (and unusual) items hidden around this map—including a body part that will be familiar to Diablo® II players!

	Claws of Attack +12	Sh	Rune of Shielding
	Claws of Attack +15	Sp	Rune of Speed
	Gold Coin +250 (2)		Scroll of the Beast
	Healing Salve		Scroll of Healing (2)
	Helm of Valor		Scroll of Protection
	Manual of Health		Scroll of Restoration
	Mask of Death		Shard of Summoning
	Orb of Venom		Stone Token
	Periapt of Vitality	A	Tome of Agility (2)
	Potion of Greater Healing (2)	I	Tome of Intelligence (2)
	Ring of Protection +5	S	Tome of Strength (2)
	Robe of the Magi +6	S	Tome of Strength +2 (2)
	Rune of Greater Resurrection		Wirt's Other Leg
M	Rune of Mana		

OPTIONAL QUESTS

MAGICAL GENERATORS

The seemingly impenetrable defenses of Magtheridon's Black Citadel are powered by a series of magical Generators. If someone could sneak past the guardians and destroy the Generators, each layer of defenses could be negated, allowing easy access to the rest of the stronghold. Perhaps Akama and his Draenei followers would be up to the task.

Requirement

- ✧ Destroy the Power Generators (four total).

SIEGE BASTION

Within the many halls of the Black Citadel lie old armaments of now-forgotten wars. Find and seize the old Chaos Orc Demolishers so that you can bring them to bear against Magtheridon's defenses.

Requirement

- ✧ Slay the Demolisher guards.

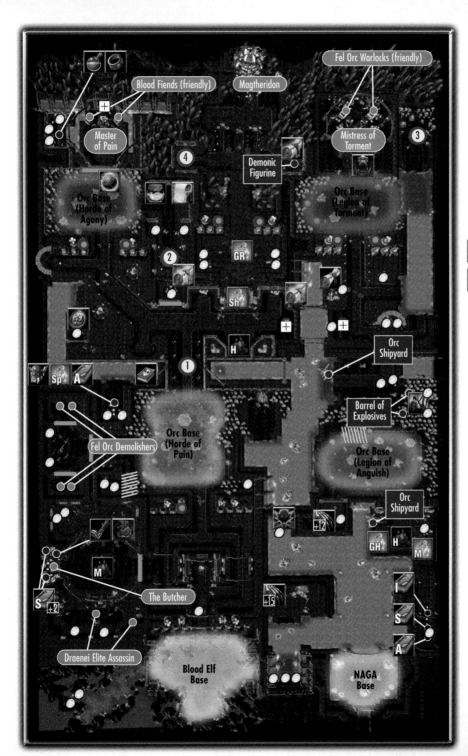

Fel Orc Warlocks (friendly)

Blood Fiends (friendly)

Magtheridon

Master
of Pain

Mistress
of Torment

4

Demonic
Figurine

3

Orc Base
(Legion of
Torment)

Orc Base
(Horde of
Agony)

2

GR

Sh

H

Orc
Shipyard

Sp A

1

Orc Base
(Horde of
Pain)

Fel Orc Demolishers

Barrel of
Explosives

Orc Base
(Legion of
Anguish)

Orc
Shipyard

+12

GH H

M

M

The Butcher

+15

I

S

A

S +2

Draenei Elite Assassin

Blood Elf
Base

NAGA
Base

M	Fountain of Health
H	Fountain of Health
+	Floor Switch
—	Gate (destroyable)
●	Juggernaut
////	Use Flame Strike Here
○	Power Generator
○	Gold Coin +250

LORD OF OUTLAND

6

ALLIANCE CAMPAIGN

129

THE PATH TO VICTORY

Since this is the last mission of the Alliance campaign, one might expect it to be a large and complex endeavor. Fortunately, it *is* a large and complex mission, involving the use of three classes of units (the Draenei, Naga, and Blood Elves) and taking you down multiple paths. There are many 'extras' on this map, most of which can be bypassed, but since the goals of this mission are so interwoven with one another, it's usually worthwhile to seek out as many as you can.

SURVEY THE DOMAIN

You have three full groups to manage right from the start: Vashj and the Naga, Akama and the Draenei, and Illidan/Kael'thas and the Blood Elves. Hotkey the three groups as you see fit, then

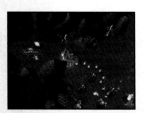

take the time to survey the two bases (Naga and Blood Elf). There's 500 Gold in the southwest corner of the map that Illidan can acquire before doing anything else.

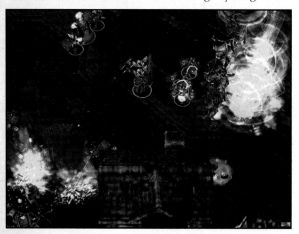

The Draenei are completely invisible, and as such are hugely important to your later efforts to destroy the Power Generators. For this reason, we suggest keeping the Draenei away from all no-win situations—protect them fiercely.

THE BUTCHER

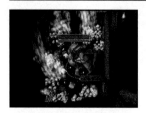

Group your Humans together, then move north to clear out the area around the Draenei. Once this area is secure, take both groups to the west and claim the Fountain of Mana. Vast gold reserves lie both to the north and south of the fountain (1000 Gold total). Two Draenei Assassins also reside in cages to the south. Free these prisoners and add them to the Draenei group.

After clearing this area out, it's time go after the Butcher (anyone who played *Diablo® II* will remember this gentleman). Throw everything you've got at the Butcher, and he falls quickly. You may still suffer some casualties, so keep the units you are least willing to part with in the rear. Use Akama's Feral Spirit to ensure that summoned units take the Butcher's wrath rather than your own precious minions. After this grisly foe is raw meat, pick up the two **Tomes of Strength**, the **Stone Token**, and **Wirt's Other Leg**.

> ### TIP
> The Butcher is tough to kill, so use Kael'thas' Banish ability to prevent him from damaging you, while still allowing you to cast deadly magic!

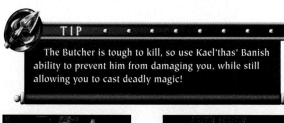

> ### NOTE
> We haven't mentioned the Naga yet. If you want to grab them and get the ball rolling, that's perfectly fine, but you don't necessarily need them at this point. Either way, you must 'take care' of the eastern edge of the map with your Naga troops.

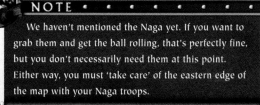
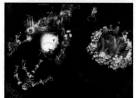

THE FIRST POWER GENERATOR

The path north is guarded by two Juggernauts. These powerful defensive creatures reduce your *entire* attack force to ashes in just a few seconds, so don't even think about trying to get past. This is where the Draenei and their invisibility to enemies comes in very handy. Move the Draenei group north, past the Juggernauts, through the Orc base, and up to the first Power Generator.

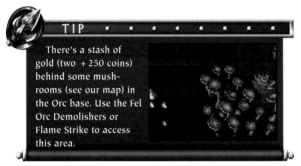

TIP

There's a stash of gold (two + 250 coins) behind some mushrooms (see our map) in the Orc base. Use the Fel Orc Demolishers or Flame Strike to access this area.

When you reach the Generator, simply attack it with all the Draenei; the Generator soon collapses, and the Juggernauts disintegrate immediately. You can now move all of your troops up into the Orc base and lay waste to it. We suggest targeting one building at a time with all of your units, while the Draenei concentrate on the Orc units. Level the base completely, then blast through the gates to the west and destroy the Overlord and his minions. This provides access to four Fel Orc Demolishers, a group of units that makes the destruction of future Orc bases much easier.

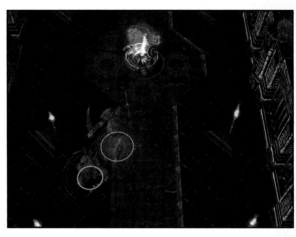

HINT - With the Generator destroyed, the gate's defenders are no longer able to fight.

ALLIANCE CAMPAIGN **6** LORD OF OUTLAND

THE NAGA

Now that you've moved the Draenei and Blood Elves up to mid-map and have destroyed an Orc base, it's time to get

the Naga rocking, too. With the group of Naga (led by Lady Vashj), clear out the nearby areas of Doom Beasts. There's some **Claws of Attack +12** and several **Gold Coins** to be had.

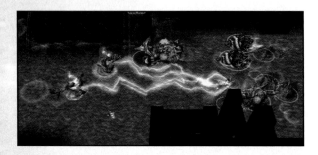

The Orcs have Frigates and Fel Orc Juggernauts in the water, all of which must be destroyed by your Naga. There's

a Fountain of Health to the north, near the Orc Shipyard. Heal your units, destroy the Shipyard, then eliminate any stray Frigates that may be patrolling the waters.

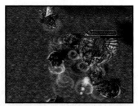

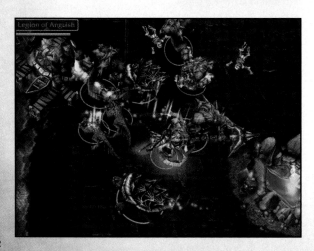

THE GOODY BAG

There's an area directly to the south of the Fountain of Health that contains two each of these items: **Tome of Strength**, **Tome of Agility**, **Tome of Intelligence**, and **Gold +250**. Best of all, this area is undefended! The catch is that

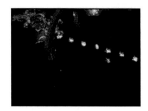

the entrance to this area is easy to miss if you're not looking for it. Take Lady Vashj down and have her grab these great power-ups before moving on.

THE LEGION OF ANGUISH

Before joining forces with the Humans/Draenei, you need to defeat the Legion of Anguish on the eastern edge of the map. If your Naga troops have been thinned, spend some of your money to create new units, then mob the base and decimate it quickly. Vashj's Forked Lightning effectively thrashes the Orc troops. Have your Dragon Turtles concentrate their attacks on the Orc buildings one at a time. Once the base is destroyed, you can join up with the other groups.

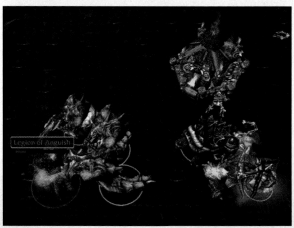

JOINING FORCES

Once the Legion of Anguish Orc base is secure and the Orc Shipyard is dust in the wind, you have a chance to join the Naga, Draenei, and Blood Elf groups into a single powerful strike force. If you choose to join them together, use Flame Strike or the Fel Orc Demolishers to destroy the mushrooms (beside the Fountain of Mana) that block the path between the two groups. If you don't want the two groups to meet up yet, you can wait until the bridge is activated by the two floor switches a little later.

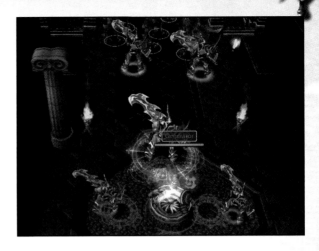

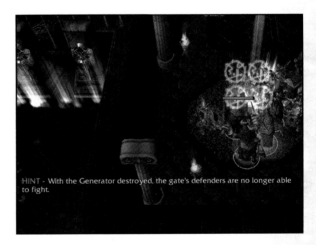

HINT - With the Generator destroyed, the gate's defenders are no longer able to fight.

THE SECOND GENERATOR

The second Generator is located to the north and, once again, it is behind a pair of Infernal Juggernauts. Move your Draenei force up through the Horde of Agony's base, then to the east and down to the next Power Generator. This Generator is defended by one Overlord and some Fel Guards and Blood Fiends. Fortunately, the enemies from the Orc base are not alerted when your Draenei attack the Power Generator and its guards. This is not a tough fight, and if you concentrate your attack on one enemy at a time, you'll defeat them very quickly. Knock out the Power Generator so that your other troops can move north.

TIP

There's a **Periapt of Vitality** and a **Manual of Health** along the western edge of the map that you can pick up en route to the Horde of Agony.

THE HORDE OF AGONY AND THE MASTER OF PAIN

The Horde of Agony is the Orc base that guards the doors to the Master of Pain's chamber. Bolster your Blood Elf attack

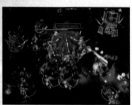

force, then move up (with the Fel Orc Demolishers in tow) to destroy the Horde of Agony's base.

Once the base is secure, heal your units and enter the Master of Pain's chamber. We recommend that you keep

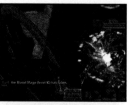

the Draenei back, because you'll need their stealth abilities later in the mission, and they are irreplaceable. When the Master of Pain has been vanquished, you receive an **Orb of Venom** and two Blood Fiends to bolster your numbers. There's a floor switch just behind the Master of Pain's throne—step on it to gain access to the **Ring of Protection +5** to the west.

JOINING FORCES

The time has come to join forces with the Naga (if you haven't already). Move your troops to the central area of the map (there's a Fountain of Health there). Just to the west is a floor switch that raises half of a bridge to the other side

of the map. Have a Naga unit hit the switch on the Naga side to join your forces together before going after the Legion of Torment and its Mistress.

THE THIRD GENERATOR

The next Power Generator lies in the northeast corner of the map, behind both the Legion of Torment and another pair of Infernal Juggernauts. Again, take your Draenei

secretly up to the location of the Power Generator and destroy it quickly, then simply hide your Draenei to avoid involving them in a futile fight.

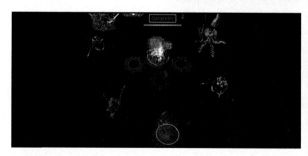

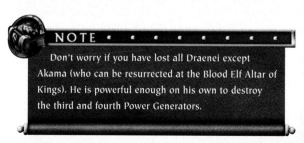

NOTE • • • • • • •

Don't worry if you have lost all Draenei except Akama (who can be resurrected at the Blood Elf Altar of Kings). He is powerful enough on his own to destroy the third and fourth Power Generators.

THE LEGION (AND MISTRESS) OF TORMENT

Use some of your gold to replenish lost units before moving against the Legion of Torment's base. You may also want to spend some time exploring the map to recover a few more hidden items, like the **Shard of Summoning** (it's buried behind some mushrooms that can be destroyed with Exploding Barrels).

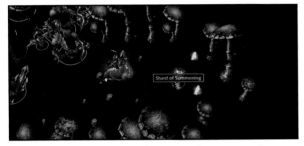

Once your troops are ready, move them up and sweep through the Legion of Torment's base. The level of resistance you face is similar to what you encountered in the other Orc bases, so use the same tactics to achieve victory here. When the base is leveled, take the time to move back to the Fountain of Health (or Mana) to replenish/heal your troops before going after the Mistress of Torment. She's tough, but manageable when all three groups of units are summoned against her. When she's dead, the doors to Magtheridon's lair open wide!

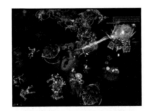

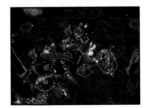

THE FOURTH GENERATOR

Another pair of Infernal Juggernauts prevents all but the Draenei from entering this area. Move up to the Power Generator and destroy it (thankfully, this does not alert any nearby units).

MAGTHERIDON

Once the Generator is destroyed, you may be tempted to rush in and attack the first chamber of enemies guarding Magtheridon. This, however, is usually a recipe for disaster. Remember, you have only a limited amount of gold, and so you really have only one solid chance to defeat Magtheridon. We suggest moving Akama into the antechambers. Once in place, have him use his Chain Lightning, followed by Hide. The result is that Akama, by himself, can destroy most of the enemies guarding Magtheridon by using Chain Lightning and Shadow Strike followed by Hide. The use of these spells gets the attention of the enemies, but once Akama Hides, the enemies simply turn back and stand their ground! It takes some time, but we recommend this tactic because it saves your core units for the fight with Magtheridon, who has no fewer than 4600 hit points!

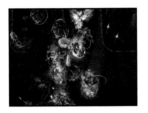

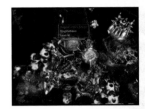

Once Akama has thinned the enemies to just Magtheridon and one or two more, move *all* of your troops into his chamber and attack Magtheridon exclusively! With 4600 hit points, this guy is extremely tough to destroy, so

unleash *all* of your Heroes' abilities in concert to bring him down. If you throw 25 units against Magtheridon, it's not unusual to leave with just five or six when the battle finally ends!

SCOURGE CAMPAIGN:
LEGACY OF THE DAMNED

Although a Bonus Campaign featuring the Orcs still remains, the Undead missions represent the final third of the Frozen Throne story. Each challenge is tough, requiring patience, cunning, and a little luck to achieve victory. Expect a lot of fun getting there!

CHAPTER ONE

KING ARTHAS

The Alliance is attempting to save themselves (and all of humanity) by escaping into the mountain canyons, where they can hide from the Scourge. Arthas gives the order to have them all slaughtered before they can escape.

THE PATH TO VICTORY

This mission presents another unique situation. You have control over three bases: one in the southeast, another in the southwest, and a third in the northeast corner of the map. Each one has a Hero (Arthas, Sylvanas, and Kel'Thuzad), and the ability to produce Ghouls and one other unit. Arthas can produce Abominations, Sylvanas can create Banshees, and Kel'Thuzad can generate Necromancers.

REQUIRED QUESTS

SLAUGHTER HUMAN REFUGEES	Requirements
There are several bands of Human refugees attempting to escape to the recently captured city of Dalaran. Rout them and burn down their pathetic villages and encampments to show them the folly of trying to escape Arthas' wrath.	⊕ Destroy the refugee towns (9 total).
	⊕ Do not allow more than 20 refugees to escape.

SLAY THE PALADINS	Requirements
The Paladin order has emerged again from the rubble of the Lordaeron Empire. Destroy the Altars of the three Paladins that have set up camps here.	⊕ Destroy the three Altars.

MAP SECRETS LEGEND

The secrets in this mission aren't essential, but it's always fun to acquire some of these goodies before the mission comes to an end:

Bracer of Agility		Rune of Mana	
Claws of Attack +3		Rune of Restoration (3)	
Gauntlets of Ogre Strength +3		Scroll of Healing	
Mantle of Intelligence +3		Slippers of Agility +3	
Manual of Health		Tome of Intelligence	
Ring of Protection +1		Tome of Strength	
Rune of Healing (3)		Voodoo Doll	
Rune of Lesser Healing (2)			

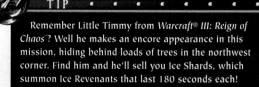

TIP

Remember Little Timmy from *Warcraft® III: Reign of Chaos*? Well he makes an encore appearance in this mission, hiding behind loads of trees in the northwest corner. Find him and he'll sell you Ice Shards, which summon Ice Revenants that last 180 seconds each!

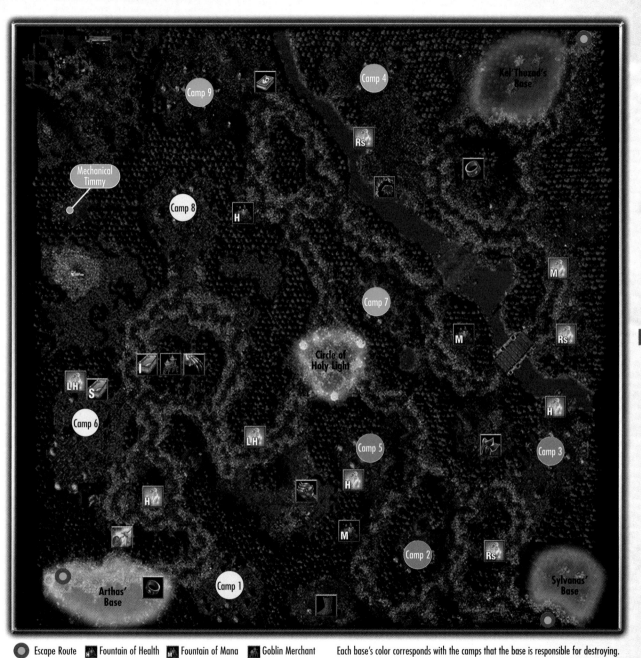

Kel'Thuzad's Base

Camp 9

Camp 4

Rs

Mechanical Timmy

Camp 8

H

M

Camp 7

M

Rs

Circle of Holy Light

I

LH S

H

Camp 6

LH

Camp 5

Camp 3

H

H

M

Camp 2

Rs

H

Arthas' Base

Camp 1

Sylvanas' Base

⭕ Escape Route　🅗 Fountain of Health　🅜 Fountain of Mana　🖼 Goblin Merchant　　Each base's color corresponds with the camps that the base is responsible for destroying.

The main goal is to destroy the nine Human camps that dot the map. These vary greatly in composition, with some consisting of just a few tents and Farms, while others are well-defended bases with Guard and Cannon Towers. Although you can destroy all of the nine camps by using units from one of your three bases, we recommend that each of your three bases destroy one of the three Human camps. We've color-coded the corresponding camps and bases (see our map) to make this match-up tactic easy to follow. Simply attack the green Human camps with an attack force from the corresponding green base (Sylvanas' in this case). Note that this is just a suggestion for completing this mission (one that works). You can also combine elements of all three bases into one cohesive attack force if that's the route you'd rather take.

The secondary (but equally important) goal is to prevent the Humans from escaping to the canyon passes. There's an Escape Route circle behind each of your three bases, and the Humans repeatedly send their units to them. If they manage to get 20 of their units into the canyons, then the mission ends in defeat. Managing this part of the mission is fairly easy, but it does require your attention each time a Human convoy moves into range of one of your bases.

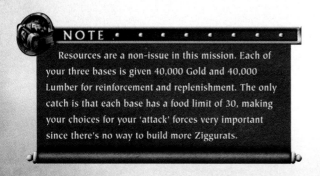

> **NOTE**
>
> Resources are a non-issue in this mission. Each of your three bases is given 40,000 Gold and 40,000 Lumber for reinforcement and replenishment. The only catch is that each base has a food limit of 30, making your choices for your 'attack' forces very important since there's no way to build more Ziggurats.

HOTKEY YOUR FORCES

Survey the situation as soon as the mission begins. Take a look at all three bases and hotkey each of the three forces so that you can jump between them quickly. The Human caravans start coming at your bases immediately. These attacks require your attention, so jump back to whichever base has encountered Humans as soon as you hear the warnings.

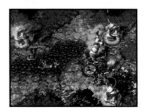

STOP THE HUMANS

The Alliance sends caravans in waves at each of the three bases, attempting to get at least 20 Humans past your guards and into the canyons beyond. Destroying these caravans is actually easy, but the difficult part is making sure that your guards successfully identify and attack all of the Humans in the caravans.

Quickly switch your attention to the area that has a caravan approaching it. If you are not 'there' paying attention to what's happening, a few Humans will easily sneak past to the Escape Routes. The caravans sometimes consist of civilians as well as military units. Your Undead units automatically zero in on the military foes, but the civilians and their ponies can go unnoticed and can slip past your defenses to freedom. For this reason, we suggest that each base's defense force is hot-keyed so that you can move quickly to the base in crisis and squash any Humans that try to sneak by.

You can also create a few extra Ghouls in each base and position them right in front of the Escape Route circles to better defend these areas. This is extra insurance, but it takes precious units away from the

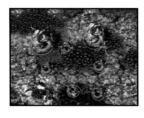

attack forces that you need to destroy the nine Human Camps. All of your Heroes start the mission with Goblin Land Mines! Place the Goblin Land Mines in a line leading away from the Escape Route Circle to get a solid backup defense. This ensures that as many as nine enemy units that have slipped past your defenses won't make it all the way!

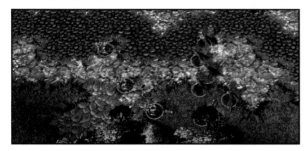

DESTROY THE BASES WITH ARTHAS

The plan we've laid out sets the Human Camps 1, 6, and 8 as the responsibility of Arthas and his troops. Arthas is a very powerful Hero, and he can single-handedly take out an enemy base if he's used properly. Still, it's best to have an attack force with him to support his efforts. Build a force that includes Arthas, two Abominations, and four or five Ghouls.

DESTROY THE PALADIN'S ALTARS

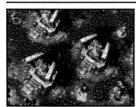

The second objective in this mission is to destroy the three Altars that produce Paladins in the Circle of Holy Light. To do this, use Kel'Thuzad on a series of two suicide missions to the Circle of Holy Light in the center of the map. Send Kel'Thuzad to this central Human base and cast his Death and Decay spell on the three Altars of Kings in the center of the base. After three 'suicide' trips by Kel'Thuzad (he can travel alone), the Altars will be destroyed and the Paladins will no longer be able to resurrect themselves once you've killed them. From this point, you can set about killing the Paladins one by one.

When the Paladins are permanently dead, they will no longer 'drop' into the camps when you move in to attack them, thus making the attack on each camp much easier. Of course, this tactic takes some time, but if you're having difficulties handling the Paladins, this not only takes care of the Paladins, but also satisfies a Required Quest!

Camp 1

Camp 1 is a lightly defended Human encampment. Remember that you need to eliminate only the Farms to satisfy the criteria of 'destroying' the camps. When you send your units into Camp 1, have the Abominations and Ghouls concentrate exclusively on the Farms one at a time. Initially, Paladins drop in from the Circle of Holy Light (the Paladin base in the center of the map) to help defend the camp. However, a concentrated attack on the Farms will have them razed in no time.

Camp 6

Camp 6 is better defended, but if you run your Ghouls directly to the Farms and attack aggressively, you can achieve the objective quickly. Arthas starts with a Book of the Dead in his inventory, and although it may be tempting to use in Camp 6, we recommend waiting until you reach Camp 8 before using it. Remember, only the Farms must be destroyed; you don't have to raze every building or even fight

the enemy units. Since you essentially have an unlimited amount of resources, simply throw everything at the Farms and don't worry about the enemy units.

Camp 8

This is the last base that Arthas is responsible for, and it's very well defended with Arcane Towers, Cannon Towers, and plenty of enemy units (not to mention the Paladins that drop in from the Circle of Holy Light). Still, the same principle applies— sprint toward the site with a group of Ghouls and a few Abominations, then target the

three Farms aggressively. As soon as a few enemies fall, use the Book of the Dead to get some more help, then finish off the Farms and Arthas' responsibilities for this mission.

DESTROY THE BASES WITH SYLVANAS

The tactics for Sylvanas are similar to those used for Arthas, with one big exception. In Sylvanas' case, you use her Banshees to Possess the most powerful enemy units that you face (specifically Knights), then use those newly-acquired units to attack the Farms in each camp. We suggest an attack force of four Ghouls and four to eight Banshees. Make sure that all of your Banshees have

enough Mana to Possess when you take them into battle. We recommend that you turn off Autocasting of Curse to conserve Mana.

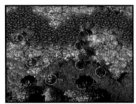

Camp 2

When the attack force is ready (you don't need to bring Sylvanas; you can actually just leave her at the base to

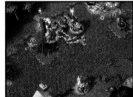

defend it), move to Camp 2 and send your Ghouls to attack one of the three Farms. A Paladin and two Knights eventually drop in. Use Possession to 'turn' the Knights to your side, then Possess any other units that are relatively healthy. When your supplemented force overwhelms the Farms, return to your base.

TIP

Be on the lookout for a pair of Knights just outside your base. They are excellent specimens for your Banshees to Possess.

Camp 3

Camp 3 is another quite manageable task; however, it is defended by a Cannon Tower. Charge the camp and be

ready to Possess the Knights that drop in. With these powerful opposition units on your side, you can crush the three Farms with relative ease.

Camp 5

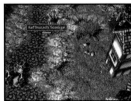

Camp 5 is actually the least-defended of the three that Sylvanas is responsible for attacking. Move in using the previously noted tactics and destroy it posthaste!

DESTROY THE BASES WITH KEL'THUZAD

Kel'Thuzad has access to Necromancers. These ghastly units can Raise Dead and create armies of Skeleton Warriors

that can overwhelm enemy defenses. Build an attack force of six Necromancers, six Ghouls, and Kel'Thuzad, then storm the nearby Camp 4.

> **TIP**
>
> During the mission, Kel'Thuzad must eliminate the caravans that come his way. Set your Necromancers to Autocast Raise Dead to perpetuate a constant generation of Skeletal Warriors with each failed caravan attempt on Kel'Thuzad's Escape Route. As soon as they are raised, send them to Camp 4 to attack one of the Farms. By the time you are ready to focus Kel'Thuzad's forces, Camp 4 will be significantly damaged, or possibly even destroyed!
>
>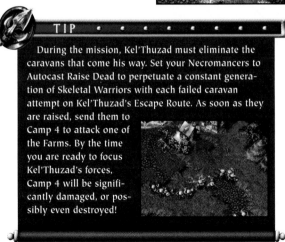

Camp 4

Send Ghouls and Necromancers into Camp 4, but this time instead of attacking the Farms immediately, concentrate on the lesser defensive units. Try to kill three or four

of them first before moving on the Farms. By creating three or four corpses, you'll enable the Necromancers to raise up eight Skeleton Warriors to help in the attack. As more units fall in battle, the Necromancers continue to create more and more warriors! Often there is a snowball effect that results in a quick victory.

Camp 7

Camp 7 is also poorly defended, and the standard attack group with Necromancers and Ghouls can defeat it quickly.

Camp 9

This is the toughest base of all, so you may want to join the forces of all of your bases to attack it with your total might (although this is not necessary). Again, concentrate only on the Farms, not the enemy units or structures. When you've destroyed the Paladin Altars and all nine camps, the mission ends victoriously!

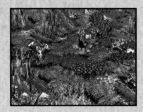

MAP EXTRAS

There are plenty of goodies to be had on the map, some of them are defended by enemy units, others are guarded by Creeps, and still more are simply hidden in crates that are tucked below groups of trees. Refer to our map to see what's where, and then make your own decisions as to whether or not it's worth going after them.

CHAPTER TWO

THE FLIGHT FROM LORDAERON

The next morning, on the palace grounds, King Arthas and his majordomo, Kel'Thuzad, discuss the Lich King's dire warnings. Arthas' power is rapidly decreasing, and it's not clear why. Unable to maintain control of his own troops, he is ambushed and must flee his own city.

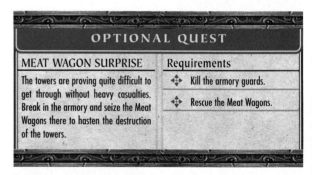

REQUIRED QUEST

THE KING'S EXIT	Requirements
With the Dreadlords' forces closing in, Arthas must make a quick retreat from the city.	✥ Bring Arthas to the city exit.
	✥ Arthas must survive.

OPTIONAL QUEST

MEAT WAGON SURPRISE	Requirements
The towers are proving quite difficult to get through without heavy casualties. Break in the armory and seize the Meat Wagons there to hasten the destruction of the towers.	✥ Kill the armory guards.
	✥ Rescue the Meat Wagons.

MAP SECRETS LEGEND

Most of the hidden items on this map are not essential. Indeed, if you try to get all of them, you won't even have enough room in your backpack. Here's what's out there:

	Circlet of Nobility		Rune of Greater Resurrection
	Claws of Attack +3		Rune of Healing (7)
	Minor Replenishment Potion		Rune of Mana (5)
	Orb of Venom		Rune of the Revenant (2)
	Pendant of Energy		Rune of Shielding
	Potion of Healing		Scroll of Protection
	Potion of Mana		Staff of Negation
	Ring of Protection +2		Staff of Reanimation
	Rod of Necromancy		Tome of Strength
	Rune of Greater Healing		

Legend:
- ⊞ Floor Switch
- ◯ Gold Coin +50
- RN Reinforcements
- //// Barricade
- ━━ Gate

Map labels: EXIT, Enemy Crypt, Enemy Crypt, Tomb of Relics, Meat Wagons, Boots of Quel'Thalas +6, START

THE PATH TO VICTORY

Like all missions that don't involve resource gathering or unit production/upgrading, this one is all about managing what you are given. Fortunately, there are plenty of reinforcements along the way, but you must still be very careful with what you are given to make sure Arthas escapes with his life.

The key to this mission is getting the Staff of Reanimation early on. With this item, you can selectively reanimate tough enemy units (like Abominations) to fight on your side, thus making your job much easier. When combined with Arthas' Animate Dead skill, the Staff of Reanimation can create a second attack group to lead the way and absorb much of the initial damage in tough battles.

GET YOUR BEARINGS

The mission starts with four Ghouls thrashing Arthas. Not to worry, Arthas can take them all down before they damage him too severely. Hack through the Elven Door to the north and get the Necromancer and Ghoul reinforcements that are waiting for you. Once the reinforcements are in

place, move north through the Elven Gate and defeat the Necromancer inside. A victory yields a **Scroll of Protection**.

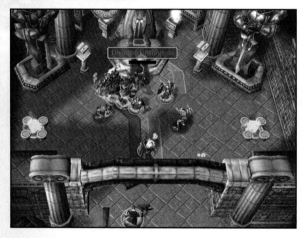

STAFF OF REANIMATION

While it's possible to move north toward your ultimate goal, we recommend first heading south to grab the **Staff of Reanimation** from the Abomination that holds it. This item makes your life much easier for the rest of the mission. The area around the staff has plenty of enemies, so set your Necromancers to Autocast Raise Dead to keep your numbers up and give the enemy fodder to hack at. The enemies in the tightly grouped houses in the south keep you on your toes, but the **Ring of Protection +2** and the **Rune of Mana** make it all worthwhile.

ZENEDAR AND REINFORCEMENTS

Follow the easternmost path that leads north to confront the Dreadlord, Zenedar, and his minions. Destroy him, then break through the gates to get some Crypt Fiends to join your ranks.

> **TIP** • • • • • • • • •
>
> Remember that Arthas' Death Coil *heals* your Undead units! This is very important in this mission because some of your core units occasionally become heavily damaged, and a shot of Death Coil completely replenishes their health. Using this ability carefully ensures that none of your most critical units is lost.

FOUNTAIN OF MANA

Before moving your troops to the Fountain of Mana in the lower central area (see our map), you may want to move north to pick up the **Claws of Attack +3**. It's a difficult fight, but there's also a **Rune of Healing** to help the situation. Once you're at the Fountain of Mana, replenish before moving north through the gate and hitting the floor switch inside.

Two Crypt Fiends are poised for attack just beyond the barricade. Crush them using some of the Skeleton Warriors and Skeletal Mages that your Necromancers have created, then proceed to the west to acquire two Ghouls, a **Staff of Negation**, and **50 Gold**.

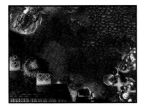 

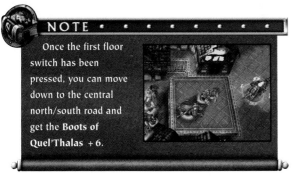

> **NOTE**
>
> Once the first floor switch has been pressed, you can move down to the central north/south road and get the **Boots of Quel'Thalas +6**.

MEAT WAGON SURPRISE

As you pass the barricade and move north, you receive the Meat Wagon Surprise quest. Directly north through the gate is a Dreadlord and two guards. Take them out, keeping a close eye on your units' health while making sure Death Coil is at the ready to heal them should they incur too much damage.

OPTIONAL QUEST
Meat Wagon Surprise
- Kill the armory guards
- Rescue the Meat Wagons

There's another floor switch that gives you access to the Meat Wagon and their Nerubian defenses, but before attacking them, break down the gate to the south of the floor switch to reveal another Abomination to help your cause. Move your troops onto the large platform, which eventually rises to take you up to the Meat Wagons. It's a tough fight against the Nerubian defenses, but once they're history, the Meat Wagons are yours.

CLAIM THE ORB OF VENOM

With your Meat Wagons ready for action, bust through the door to the east and use your latest acquisition to blast the two

Ziggurats inside. Once this is done, do NOT move them into the room, or the Meat Wagons will be lost forever. Instead, bring your other troops into the room to deal with the Crypt Fiends that show up.

Once the room is clear, continue north to claim the nearby **Orb of Venom** and **Circlet of Nobility**.

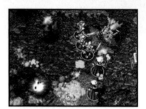

TIP

Since there's a Fountain of Mana in the vicinity, this is a great place to use the corpses that have collected inside the Meat Wagons. Unload the crumpled bodies and have your Necromancers create an army of Skeleton Warriors and Skeletal Mages, then send them north to fight in your name.

SKELETAL MINIONS

Since you have a pair of Meat Wagons and two Necromancers, you have the ability to quickly raise an attack group of Skeleton Warriors and Skeletal Mages. After you claim the Orb of Venom, use your Necromancers to create groups of skeletal minions to attack the various enemies. If you don't mind waiting for Mana to replenish, you can clear out the rest of the map using this technique!

FOUNTAIN OF HEALTH

Although not necessary, you can turn right when you reach the Orb of Venom and move around to a Fountain of Health. You can also pick up a **Rune of the Revenant** (creates an Ice Revenant) and a **Rod of Necromancy** if you're interested. (The latter is hidden behind the Fountain of Health; the path to it is just to the right of the Fountain.)

REINFORCEMENTS

Move your troops up and around to the north (following the western edge of the map), but beware of the enemies that lie in wait for you. When you reach the Nerubian Ziggurats, you discover two Ghouls in cages to the right. Always be on high alert for enemy Crypt Fiends that continually funnel up to nag you from behind.

THE CITY GATES

You're almost there! As you move into a large chamber with a **Rune of Shielding**, more reinforcements pitch in as you

join a large battle. When the dust settles, group the new units with your existing attack force, then break through the City Gates and proceed north.

A fierce mob of enemies greets you as you enter the gates, but the huge pile of corpses nearby allows your Necromancers and Arthas to quickly raise a formidable attack force of Skeletal Mages and Skeleton Warriors. Move past the enemies to the right and take out the Dreadlord that stands in your way, then continue your march north along the roadway.

BLOODFEAST AND THE EXIT

Obliterate the enemy structures around the gates, then destroy Bloodfeast. This huge, 3000-hit point beast is guarding the path north, along with some Abominations! Dispatch him, being careful to heal your units with Death Coil, then blast through the City Gate to finish the mission!

CHAPTER THREE

THE DARK LADY

Moment's later, in Tirisfal Glades, King Arthas and his Banshee escorts stop to regain their strength. Arthas is deceived by Sylvanas, and she attempts to poison him, leaving him paralyzed and in agony. However, Kel'Thuzad comes to his rescue. Two days later, at her base camp in the newly formed Plaguelands, Sylvanas ponders her newfound freedom and her future as one of the cursed Undead.

THE PATH TO VICTORY

The main goal of this mission is to destroy Varimathras' red Undead base in the northeast corner of the map, but there are two optional quests that segue perfectly into the final attack on the enemy base. You can gather an entire army of Ogres by using the Banshee's Possession ability, then round up even more siege by Possessing some of the other Creeps on the map, as well as some of Varimathras' troops that attack your base.

REQUIRED QUEST

VARIMATHRAS	Requirement
Varimathras has been dispatched here to lure Sylvanas to the three Dreadlords' cause. Sylvanas has her own plans for Arthas and will take Lordaeron for herself without the help of these pathetic Demons. Destroy Varimathras and his Undead army.	⊹ Destroy the red Undead base.

OPTIONAL QUESTS

OGRE WARLORD	Requirement
Mug'thol the Warlord is preparing his Ogres for battle in the hills. Find Mug'thol and possess his soul so that his war preparations are not wasted on the wrong enemy.	⊹ Possess the warlord Ogre Mug'thol.

BANDIT LORD	Requirements
With Lordaeron in ashes, the few remaining Humans have turned on each other. The ruthless Bandit Lord in this region could prove to be an invaluable asset. Find this Bandit Lord and Possess him to further bolster your forces.	⊹ Possess Blackthorn the Bandit Lord.

MAP SECRETS LEGEND

This map has its share of goodies on it, and unlike some of the other maps (like the secret Human mission), you actually have enough time to gather them! Here's what's available:

Claws of Attack +6		Rune of Healing
Gold Coins		Scroll of the Beast
Healing Salve (2)		Scroll of Healing
Lesser Scroll of Replenishment		Skull Shield
Mantle of Intelligence +3		Spider Ring
Manual of Health		Staff of Negation
Ring of Protection +3		

Goblin Merchant   Gold Mine   Mercenary Camp

The key to victory in this mission is to defend your base properly while Sylvanas and her group are away gathering Ogres and such. If the main base is secure from enemy attacks, then you can move freely around the map and prepare for the big battle. This mission is very unique, however, because it allows you to put together a group of attackers that include Bandits, Forest Trolls, Ogres, Murlocs, Gnolls, and Undead all in one massive attack force!

There are some significant attacks on your base, so take the time to set up its defenses properly.

151

SCOURGE CAMPAIGN   3   THE DARK LADY

BOLSTER DEFENSES

Before venturing out into the countryside, you need to bolster the defenses in your base and upgrade your units concurrently. We suggest building several Obsidian Statues and a group of 10 Ghouls while your Acolytes build more Ziggurats to increase your population maximum. You also need plenty of Banshees. Create at least a dozen of them and be sure to turn off their Autocast for Curse so that they don't waste their Mana by casting Curse on enemies. Ultimately, you want *all* of your Banshees to Possess other units (mostly Ogres).

POSSESS THE OGRE WARLORD

One of the optional quests involves Possessing the Ogre Warlord that lives on the western edge of the map. There are two ways of going about this. First, you can move Banshees in toward the Ogre Warlord bit by bit, Possessing all the Ogres you encounter, or you can attempt to run one Banshee straight in to Possess the Ogre Warlord first, which turns *all* of the other Ogres to your side immediately. However, this second method (getting to the Ogre Warlord first) is nearly impossible because of a Rock Barrier that divides the Warlord from the rest of his minions. Either way, it's important not to attack the Ogres and destroy any of them. Instead, use your Banshees to individually Possess them. In the end, you'll wind up with a large force of very tough Ogres on your side! There's also a

Mercenary Camp in the northern area of the map that sells Ogres, giving you a way to replenish these groups if they fall in battle.

MERCENARY CAMP 1

Here are the units available in Mercenary Camp 1 (see our map). (Gold/Lumber/Food)

- **Forest Troll** (120/10/2) – Axe-throwing Troll.
- **Ogre Brute** (120/0/4) – The standard brute of the Ogre Legion.
- **Ogre Woundmaster** (240/0/5) – A large, brutal warrior.
- **Ogre War Mage** (255/40/4) – A spellcasting warrior of the Ogre Legion. Can cast Bloodlust.

POSSESS THE GNOLLS AND SECURE GOLD MINE

There are two groups of Gnolls behind your base in the southwest corner of the map. Send a group of Banshees down (you need about 10 of them) to Possess all of these Gnolls and convert them into your advance scout group. When this is complete, you'll have another source of gold just waiting for you to Haunt!

OBTAIN OTHER NEW TROOPS (BANDIT LORD QUEST)

You likely have a sizable force of Ogres, Gnolls, and Undead units at this point. You could probably even move against Varimathras' base now. Still, there are plenty of other units to commandeer for your army, including the Bandit Lord (optional quest) in the central portion of the map. As with the Ogre Warlord, you need only capture the Bandit Lord to secure the use of all his troops. Send a few Banshees into his camp to Possess him quickly.

During the acquisition of enemy units through Possession, Varimathras continues to launch attacks on your base. We suggest using the Gnolls and a few Ogres that you've acquired to defend your base while your other units are out conquering the map. Keep a few Obsidian Statues (set to automatically heal your units) nearby to keep them healthy during attacks.

Once the Bandit Lord is yours, a cut-scene plays. Afterwards, you have a large group of Human units at your disposal! There are also bands of Murlocs and Forest Trolls that can join in if you choose to obtain them.

MERCENARY CAMP 2

Note that the contents of both Mercenary Camps change when you complete each optional quest. Mercenary Camps 1 & 2 both have all seven units you can hire when Blackthorn and Mug'thol are possessed.

- **Forest Troll** (120/10/2) — Axe-throwing Troll.
- **Ogre Brute** (120/0/4) — The standard brute of the Ogre Legion.
- **Ogre Woundmaster** (240/0/5) — A large, brutal warrior.
- **Ogre War Mage** (255/40/4) — A spellcasting warrior of the Ogre Legion. Can cast Bloodlust.
- **Assassin** (200/30/3) — Medium ranged unit that fires envenomed bolts.
- **Enforcer** (170/20/3) — Light melee unit with Evasion.
- **Renegade Wizard** (255/50/4) — Medium ranged unit that can cast Purge and Lightning Shield.

DESTROY PURPLE BASE (OPTIONAL)

It's time to take your powerful army out for a test drive, and attack the purple Undead base. Group your units into four or five attack forces. The particulars of this are up to you, but we recommend keeping at least one Obsidian Statue in each group so that they can heal as the battle progresses.

This base is no match for your troops, but you may still want to bring along some Banshees to Possess a few of the tougher enemies, such as Necromancers and Abominations (neither of which can be created in your base).

DESTROY VARIMATHRAS' BASE

With four or five groups of mixed units that you've gathered from around the map (and created yourself), bring the full strength of your army down on Varimathras' base. Move in and set each group against an enemy structure—don't even concern yourself with the enemy units. Using this tactic, you can destroy enemy structures easily with minimal casualties. The base quickly folds, and the mission ends once Varimathras has been defeated.

The Banshee's powerful Possess skill makes your troops almost unstoppable as the mission progresses. Continue Possessing enemies as they attack your base, and build five killer attack groups from them.

CHAPTER FOUR

THE RETURN TO NORTHREND

Three weeks later, King Arthas' ragged fleet drops anchor off the icy southern coasts of Northrend. As soon as Arthas lands, the Blood Elves inform him of their intent to recapture the land. Anub'arak, a Crypt Lord, offers his help.

MAP SECRETS LEGEND

There's a wealth of hidden items to collect, including some that you probably won't ever find unless you use this guide! Here's what's available:

	Claws of Attack +9
	Gold +250 (2)
	Health Stone
	Horn of the Clouds
	Healing Salve
	Lesser Scroll of Replenishment
	Lumber +250
	Mana Stone
	Pendant of Energy
	Ring of Protection +2
	Ring of Protection +4
	Rune of Mana (2)
	Scroll of Mana
	Scroll of Protection
	Sobi Mask
	Tome of Agility
	Tome of Intelligence (2)
	Tome of Strength

REQUIRED QUESTS

THE LANDING	Requirement
The Blood Elves are heavily encamped all around the shores of Northrend. You must lay siege to their island stronghold farther off the coast and claim its resources for your own.	✥ Destroy the Blood Elves' island stronghold.

BREAKTHROUGH	Requirement
Now that you have sufficient resources, you need only break through the pass to Azjol'nerub. Its guardians are vicious Dragonspawn that care for nothing but slaughter and bloodshed. Slay them, and the way through the pass will be clear.	✥ Slay the Dragonspawn guardians.

OPTIONAL QUEST

DRAGON HOARD	Requirement
The ancient Dragon, Sapphiron, lies within the nearby caves. There are rumors that he guards a wondrous trove of powerful items. Slay the Dragon and take the loot.	✥ Slay the Dragon Sapphiron.

THE PATH TO VICTORY

This mission progresses in stages. The first stage requires you to capture the Blood Elf base just to the north of your starting position. The catch is that you have virtually no resources, nor the ability to replace any units that you may lose early on. Consequently, the attack against the first Blood Elf base must be handled carefully.

Once the base is secured, you receive a pair of optional quests, as well as one required quest that sends you out to slay the Dragonspawn guardians. This mission draws on all of your skills and truly tests your tactical prowess as you battle Blood Elf, Naga, and various Creeps to achieve victory.

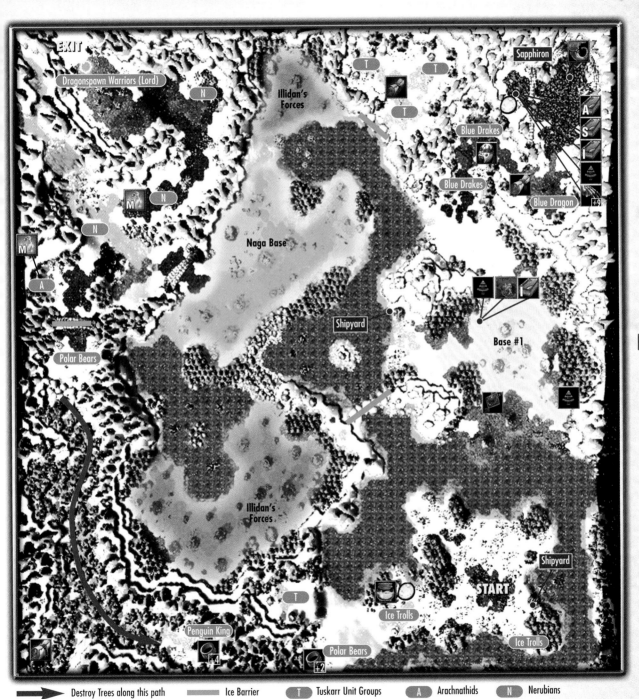

EXIT

Dragonspawn Warriors (Lord)

N

Illidan's Forces

T

T

Sapphiron

T

Blue Drakes

A

S

I

Blue Drakes

Blue Dragon

+9

M

N

N

Naga Base

I

M

A

Shipyard

Base #1

Polar Bears

Illidan's Forces

Shipyard

START

T

Ice Trolls

Penguin King

Polar Bears

Ice Trolls

+4

+2

Destroy Trees along this path   **Ice Barrier**   **T** Tuskarr Unit Groups   **A** Arachnathids   **N** Nerubians

EXPLORE THE STARTING LOCATION

The small pseudo-island where your forces begin has several groups of Creeps on it, including Tuskarrs, Polar Bears, and Ice Trolls. We recommend that you move carefully around the area, eliminating the Creeps while using great care not to subject your troops to any unnecessary damage. There are several items worth picking up, like a **Ring of Protection +2**, **Gold**, and a **Healing Salve**.

CAPTURE BASE #1

Once you've cleared out the starting location, group your Battleship and Frigates into one fleet, and the Transports into a separate one, then load all of your units into the Transports. If you have some extra Gold, purchase another

Battleship or another two Frigates for the upcoming battle. Remember, you only get one shot at winning this fight, so do it right from the start!

Before moving the Transports north, move the group of Battleships and Frigates up to the Blood Elf defenses for Base #1 to attack the towers, starting with the Cannon Tower. As soon as Blood Elf ground troops start showing up, move your Transports up and drop off your attack force to join the battle. The Blood Elf units concentrate on the Frigates as you blast through them. Once the Towers on the coast are down, move from structure to structure, destroying everything in your path. When the base has been totally obiterated, a short cinematic plays, after which you have already started construction on a base for your own use!

UPGRADE AND FORTIFY

Once you're into Base #1, expect attack waves of Naga from the east and Blood Elves from the southeast. You need a large attack force to succeed in this mission, so build plenty of Ziggurats. These structures serve two functions by providing defensive Nerubian and Spirit Towers, as well as allowing you to build up to the limit of 100 Food.

Build the defensive towers in pairs or triplets so that they can work symbiotically.

Build a Crypt to produce Ghouls, then produce a force of eight Ghouls strictly dedicated to harvesting lumber. Build every structure available to you, and start producing Obsidian Statues, Banshees, Necromancers, Abominations, and Meat Wagons. Also upgrade the tech trees to the maximum. During this time, simply remain in your base and let

your Acolytes and Ghouls harvest resources while your structures upgrade and create new units.

NOTE

If you lack sufficient lumber to build a Crypt, dig into the **Bundle of Lumber** in a barrel near your base (see our map).

SLAY SAPPHIRON (OPTIONAL)

A narrow path northeast of your base leads to the Dragon Sapphiron and two rather tough, magic-immune level 10 Blue Dragons. Along the way you must fight three groups of aerial units, but none is resistant to magic, so Death Coil is a very effective weapon. Your Crypt Fiends' Web ability brings them down long enough for your troops to vanquish them quickly.

This is a very tough battle because all of your enemies are completely immune to magic. Thus, many of your troops are not effective against these units. The way to defeat them is to form a large group of Crypt Fiends with two Obsidian Statues (set to Autocast Essence of Blight), and one large group of Abominations with two Obsidian Statues (also set to Autocast Essence of Blight).

Blue Dragon Whelp
Level 3

By doing this, your Crypt Fiends bring down the Dragons with Web (which should also be set to Autocast) so that your Abominations can crush them! Concentrate your attacks on the Dragons one at a time, and be prepared to lose some of your units, because these beasts are *very* tough. If you follow the above instructions, then the Obsidian Statues should help to heal your units as the battle progresses, thus limiting your losses.

When the battle is over, a Frost Wyrm (Sapphiron) joins your ranks, and you also get **Tomes of Agility**, **Strength**, and **Intelligence**, along with **Gold**, **Lumber**, and **Claws of Attack +9**—a bounty worth fighting for!

DESTROY NAGA BASE

By this time, you are likely running a little low on gold, so secure another source of the yellow metal. The Naga base is the most accessible source of gold, and since you must ultimately move your troops through the Naga base to get to the

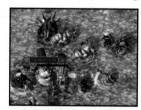

Dragonspawn anyway, it stands to reason that you should destroy it now. Use two Transports and a Battleship and Frigate to move your troops to the coast of the Naga base.

Move in with two attack groups, one led by Anub'arak and the other by Arthas. Be sure to include two Obsidian Statues per group, with one Statue set to replenish Mana and the other to restore Health. When you're ready, storm the Naga base and concentrate first and only on the Tidal Guardians, before attacking the Naga buildings that produce units. Use one of your groups to handle the Naga units, while the other goes after structures.

Once the Naga base is subdued, move an Acolyte in to Haunt the Gold Mine and harvest it dry. There should be at least 9,000 Gold left in it—more than enough for you to finish this mission.

OTHER BONUSES

There are several nonessential areas on this map, including the Tuskarr-controlled area in the north. If you want to pick up some extra experience and a **Lesser Scroll of Replenishment**, then move up and clear that area out. There

are several groups of Polar Bears, Nerubians (complete with Ziggurats, which methodically pump out more units), and even Arachnathids, in the west.

DEFEAT THE DRAGONSPAWN GUARDIANS

The Dragonspawn await you in the northwest corner of the map. Along the path to them you must first fight some Arachnathids, then more Nerubians, and finally, just outside the exit, a powerful army of Dragonspawn! This includes a Blue Dragonspawn Lord (level 10), two Blue Dragonspawn Warriors (level 5), and four Blue Drakes (level 6). Bring every unit you have for this fight, because all of the Dragonspawn must perish to claim victory. Arthas' Animate Dead is very handy once a few of the Dragonspawn Warriors have fallen—they make quick work of their former brethren once raised to fight on your side.

When the Dragonspawn are dead, victory is yours. If you haven't fully explored the map and want to go after every last item, then do it *before* you destroy the Dragonspawn, because once you complete this task, the mission is over.

THE PENGUIN KING

There is one secret area of the map that few will find without reading this guide. As you move south, an earthquake shakes things up, revealing a very long path that extends all the way down the western edge of the map! This path splits to the left and right. The left path is a short one. At the dead end is a **Scroll of Mana** that is hidden among the trees. The right path leads to the Penguin King, who drops a **Ring of Protection +4** if you pay him a visit.

CHAPTER FIVE

DREADLORD'S FALL

At that same moment, back in the Plaguelands, Sylvanas and her loyal minions plan their next surgical strike against the Dreadlords' power. Varimathras and Sylvanas note that Garithos and his army have been subjugated by Detheroc, and his forces are susceptible to the Banshee's Possession ability.

THE PATH TO VICTORY

This is a tricky mission with some objectives not yet seen in the Warcraft III realm. As the mission begins, you have seven (count 'em) minutes to destroy one of the two of Garithos' or Detheroc's bases. During this period, the units and structures for *both* bases are 'asleep' and do not mount a significant defense against you. After the seven minutes expires, any remaining enemy forces launch a significant attack on your base. If you choose not to attack either of the two bases, your base will surely be destroyed—you simply cannot withstand an attack by both forces at once.

Immediately decide which base to destroy (*disable* is actually a better choice of words) during the first seven minutes of the mission. Only by seriously damaging one of the two enemy bases will you be able to withstand the attack from the other one after the seven-minute window has closed. Once this time is over, it's up to you to build up a significant force that can destroy the *second* base as well. When the two bases are both destroyed, victory will be at hand.

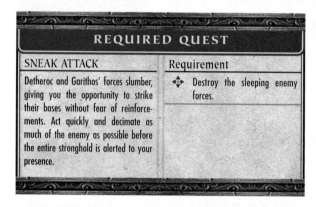

REQUIRED QUEST

SNEAK ATTACK	Requirement
Detheroc and Garithos' forces slumber, giving you the opportunity to strike their bases without fear of reinforcements. Act quickly and decimate as much of the enemy as possible before the entire stronghold is alerted to your presence.	⬦ Destroy the sleeping enemy forces.

MAP SECRETS LEGEND

There are only a few hidden items to find in this mission, which is not surprising when you consider the fact that there's a time limit on a portion of the proceedings. If you're still curious about the loot, here's what's available:

🔲	Pendant of Mana	🔲	Ring of Regeneration
🔲	Potion of Greater Healing	🔲	Rune of Lesser Healing
🔲	Potion of Greater Mana		

THE SEVEN-MINUTE SOLUTION

If you choose to attack the Human base, you can Possess a Human Peasant or two and use them to build the entire Human tech tree, giving you access to Siege Engines (which are great for assaulting buildings). We have found, however, that the Human base is more difficult to defeat than Detheroc's Undead base within the time limit.

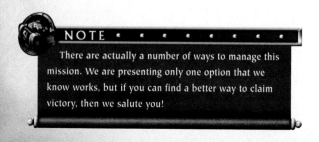

NOTE • • • • • • •

There are actually a number of ways to manage this mission. We are presenting only one option that we know works, but if you can find a better way to claim victory, then we salute you!

TIP • • • • • • •

If you like the idea of building the Human tech tree, but don't want to attack the Humans, simply send one Banshee to a sleeping Human Peasant, Possess it, then move it up to your base and start building the Human tech tree for yourself! It's certainly a unique opportunity to have access to both the Human and Undead units and structures in the same base.

H	Fountain of Health		Goblin Laboratory		Goblin Merchant		Gold Mine		Marketplace

We suggest that you group all of your units together with the exception of the Banshees, then move that force directly toward the opening of Detheroc's base. Use three of your Banshees to Possess the two Mortar Teams and the Footman

you pass along the way. Group the Mortar Teams together into a single group and have them target specific buildings inside Detheroc's base.

As your units enter the sleepy town, take the time to set the waypoints from your Crypt and your Temple of the

Damned directly to Sylvanas, so that all new units created during the seven minutes head right to Sylvanas, thus eliminating an entire level of micromanagement during this crucial time.

When your attack group gets inside Detheroc's base, only nearby enemies actually 'wake up' and attack you. This is a huge advantage for your units. Have your main attack force deal with Detheroc (concentrate on him so that he goes down quickly, leaving your forces to switch to building attacks) while your Mortar Team attacks key buildings, such as Crypts, Temples of the Damned, and Slaughterhouses. Essentially, every enemy structure capable of producing a unit must be destroyed in less than seven minutes.

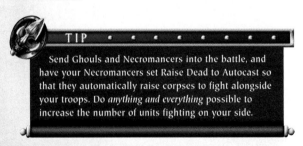

TIP

Send Ghouls and Necromancers into the battle, and have your Necromancers set Raise Dead to Autocast so that they automatically raise corpses to fight alongside your troops. Do *anything and everything* possible to increase the number of units fighting on your side.

Enemy forces are asleep.

Sweep through the base, concentrating only on enemy units and buildings that can produce units (especially the Altar of Darkness). As the seven-minute timeframe comes to a close, you should

be nearly finished, and in this case close *is* good enough—you don't need to completely destroy the base, just sufficiently cripple it. Remember, if you've put your unit production waypoints on Sylvanas, then a large number of new units (Ghouls and Necromancers) have arrived since the start of the mission. Hotkey these new units so that you have proper control over them.

STEM THE TIDE

When the seven minutes expires, you receive a verbal warning that the remaining base will be coming after you with a vengeance. As soon as you hear this, pull *all* of your units together into a tight

bunch and use the one Scroll of Town Portal you have to zip everyone back to defend the base in a hurry. If you've done your job, you will receive no attackers from Detheroc's base, and only Garithos and his men will attack you.

Continue to produce units and use all of your special abilities to defeat Garithos as quickly as possible. Once he falls, you can concentrate on the units he brought with him. Expect to lose several units, along with a structure or two in the battle, but when it's over, you'll be left standing with at least a handful of units ready to defend your base in the future.

EXPLORE THE MAP (OPTIONAL)

If you're inclined to seek out power-ups around the map, there's both a Goblin Laboratory and a Mercenary Camp where you can purchase some nice goodies (details follow). Also note that there's a Marketplace *and* a Goblin Merchant for those hard-to-find items. If you're interested in some other items, check out the Sasquatch camps, and take a look at our map to see where one or two other items are tucked away.

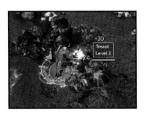

MERCENARY CAMP

Here are the units available in Mercenary Camp (see our map). (Gold/Lumber/Food)

- **Rogue** (120/0/2) – Light melee unit with Shadowmeld.
- **Assassin** (200/30/3) – Medium ranged unit that fires Envenomed Bolts and can Shadowmeld.
- **Kobold Geomancer** (205/30/2) – A light ranged unit that casts Slow and Abolish Magic.
- **Forest Troll High Priest** (245/40/4) – A high priest of healing magic. Hurls fiery missiles. Can cast Abolish Magic and Inner Fire.

GOBLIN LABORATORY

Here are the units available in Goblin Laboratory (see our map). (Gold/Lumber/Food)

- **Reveal** (50/0/0) – Reveals an area of the map, detects invisible units, and lasts six seconds.
- **Goblin Sapper** (215/100/2) – An explosive team of Goblin Sappers. They explode in spectacular fashion; very effective against buildings.
- **Goblin Zeppelin** (240/60/0) – A flying air-transport unit.
- **Goblin Shredder** (375/100/4) – A medium melee unit made of iron. The Shredder is exceptional at harvesting large quantities of lumber in a short period of time.

DESTROY GARITHOS' BASE

After destroying Detheroc's base, you need only stay put, defend your own base, and upgrade your units and structures. Once you've built a Boneyard, you can then put together an attack force of six or seven Frost Wyrms.

Between a conventional force of Ghouls, Necromancers, Abominations, and Heroes, as well as an aerial force of Frost Wyrms, Garithos' base won't last long at all!

Move your troops down and attack the base one structure at a time, laying waste to every building in your path. It takes a few minutes, but Garithos is unable to survive a large wave of Frost Wyrms supported by ground troops, so victory will be yours.

COUNTERPOINT

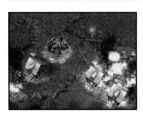

Some of the staff at Blizzard feel very strongly that attacking the Human base first is the better route to take, at least in part because your Banshees can Possess a Peasant or two who can then build the Human structures and units in your base for you to control! If you successfully do this, then you can build Siege Engines, which are *extremely* effective at demolishing enemy buildings.

CHAPTER SIX

NEW POWER IN LORDAERON

The next day, on the outskirts of Lordaeron's capital city, Sylvanas and her allies prepare to lay siege to Balnazzar's formidable defenses.

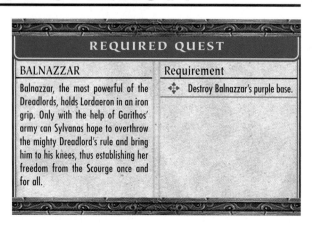

REQUIRED QUEST

BALNAZZAR	Requirement
Balnazzar, the most powerful of the Dreadlords, holds Lordaeron in an iron grip. Only with the help of Garithos' army can Sylvanas hope to overthrow the mighty Dreadlord's rule and bring him to his knees, thus establishing her freedom from the Scourge once and for all.	⬥ Destroy Balnazzar's purple base.

OPTIONAL QUEST

RONFORGE DWARVES	Requirement
Unlike the rest of Garithos' troops, the Dwarven contingent seems to have gone astray during the march to Lordaeron. If they could be located, their assistance in laying siege to the city would be invaluable.	⬥ Locate the missing Dwarves.

THE PATH TO VICTORY

As one would expect so late in the game, this mission is a real challenge. Indeed, it requires a large amount of resources, time, and well-managed tactics to defeat Balnazzar and his base. You have control over both Garithos' and Sylvanas' bases, and as a bonus you also have the Hero Varimathras at your disposal (in Sylvanas' base).

The first thing you must do is upgrade your units and build a significant defensive force in both bases. After that, take Garithos up to free the Dwarven units in the northeast corner of the map. liberating these units provides access to Mortar Teams and Siege Engines, both of which are critical to your success in this mission.

MAP SECRETS LEGEND

This map has several killer items, including the Crown of Kings and the Ring of the Archmagi, but they are tough to get, especially considering the task at hand (defeating Balnazzar).

🔹	Amulet of Recall	🔹	Rune of Healing
🔹	Belt of Giant Strength +6	🔹	Rune of Speed
🔹	Crown of Kings +5	🔹	Runed Bracers
🔹	Diamond of Summoning	🔹	Scroll of Animate Dead
🔹	Mask of Death	🔹	Scroll of the Beast
🔹	Ring of the Archmagi	🔹	Talisman of Evasion

Destroy Hut to get Talisman of Evasion

Sylvanas' Base

Dragons

Kobolds

Dwarven Reinforcements

Rock Golems

RN

Kobolds

Demon Gate

H

Dreadlord Insurgents' Base

Sp

Banshees

Sasquatch

H

Balnazzar's Base

Stash #1*

H

Stash #2*

Flesh Golem

Dreadlord Loyalists' Base

Dreadlord Insurgents' Base

Garithos' Base

Stash #3*

 Fountain of Health

 Goblin Merchant

Gold Mine

Rock Chunks (Destroyable Rock Barrier)

RN Reinforcements

* **Stash #1 contains:** Diamond of Summoning, Mask of Death
* **Stash #2 contains:** Ring of the Archmagi, Crown of Kings +5
* **Stash #3 contains:** Scroll of Restoration, Kelen's Dagger of Escape, Hood of Cunning

UPGRADE AND BOLSTER

Both Garithos and Sylvanas are the target of Balnazzar's attack waves, featuring Balnazzar himself and a cadre of Demons. Unfortunately, the Dreadlord Insurgents (green) attack Garithos' base in the south, and the Dreadlord Loyalists (yellow) attack Sylvanas' base from the south. Because of all of these repeated attacks, you need to build a force of Knights and Towers in Garithos' base, and separate defense groups in your Undead base.

While you're building for defense, be sure to also upgrade both tech trees as quickly as you can. Generally speaking, you won't be attacked at both bases simultaneously, so you can concentrate on defending the attack that's currently underway. If one of the two bases starts to *lose* a battle, then you can use Town Portal scrolls (which can be purchased in the Arcane Vault/Tomb of Relics) to quickly transport either Garithos or Sylvanas and their groups to each other's bases.

TIP

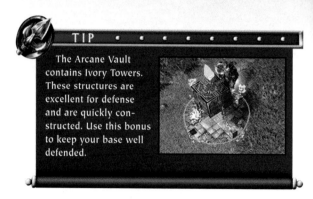

The Arcane Vault contains Ivory Towers. These structures are excellent for defense and are quickly constructed. Use this bonus to keep your base well defended.

FREE THE DWARVES

Shortly after the mission begins, you receive an optional quest to free the Dwarven units trapped in the northeastern region of the map. Freeing these units is critical because it enables your Human Peasants to build Workshops and a Gryphon Aviary, thus giving you access to Siege Engines and Gryphon Riders. Take a group of six Knights and Garithos up the path (past the Fountain of Health) to face the Kobolds and Rock Golems guarding the path.

The Creeps that you find en route to the Dwarven camp are entirely manageable for Garithos and six Knights. Be sure to use Garithos' Holy Light to heal any Knights that take too much damage and you'll complete this task without losing any troops. When you get to the Rock Chunks, attack them and a cut-scene will play. You then receive an entire group of Riflemen, Mortar Teams, and Siege Engines. Group these units into their own team and move your men back to the main base.

OTHER ITEMS ON THE MAP

There are several items on the map, but most of them require some bloodshed to obtain them. To the west of Garithos' base, a Flesh Golem and his minions guard a Lordaeron Stash containing a **Ring of the Archmagi** and a **Crown of Kings +5**. There are two more Stashes to the south of Sylvanas' base. One holds a **Diamond of Summoning** and a **Mask of Death**, but it's guarded by some rather nasty and possessive (if you get our meaning) Banshees. The Stash in the southwest corner is loaded with

even more items (see our map). There are also a few other items patrolled by Sasquatch, Dragons, and Revenants (see our map). Whether or not you decide to pursue these items is entirely your choice. If you feel that a particular item will make destroying Balnazzar's base any easier, then go get it!

TIP

Both Goblin Merchants contain key items, such as Healing Wards, that can improve your chances in a close battle. If you can get to them, we recommend picking up Healing Wards for your ultimate battle with Balnazzar's forces.

MORE GOLD

There's a Gold Mine to the north of Garithos' base that can make rebuilding your attack groups much faster. Send a Peasant up there to build a Town Hall (once the Kobolds have been dispatched).

Likewise, Sylvanas can get more gold by crushing the base directly to the south of her location. This base is the least-defended of those occupied by the enemy, and the Gold Mine has at least 17,000 Gold for you to spend. It's also important to note that there's a Goblin Merchant (with Healing Wards) just to the south of this base, so destroying the base also provides easy access to this shop.

DESTROY BALNAZZAR'S BASE

The title of this section is deceiving, because destroying this base isn't something you're going to do in just one shot. You must attack it in waves. Expect to build and rebuild attack forces several times before you've finally achieved total decimation. Start by building two attack groups in Sylvanas' base; one for Sylvanas and one for Varimathras. Both of these can be balanced forces, composed of a variety of Undead units. Be sure, however, to include a pair of Obsidian Statues in each group with one set to replenish Mana and the other to replenish Health. We also recommend building a small group of Frost Wyrms as a third group. These flying units are extremely effective at destroying enemy structures, so having a few greatly increases your chances of victory.

Move this attack force down into Balnazzar's base with the intention of destroying any Ziggurats, along with any structures that produce units—specifically the Boneyards (Balnazzar's Frost

Wyrms are a huge thorn in your side). The main structure on your 'must destroy' list is the Demon Gate. With the first wave, try to destroy all the buildings up to and including the Demon Gate, and don't become frustrated when Balnazzar stops your attack dead in its tracks after that.

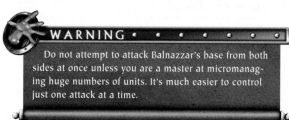

WARNING

Do not attempt to attack Balnazzar's base from both sides at once unless you are a master at micromanaging huge numbers of units. It's much easier to control just one attack at a time.

When Sylvanas' attack force is completely obliterated (and it will be), a good chunk of Balnazzar's base will also be destroyed, including his Demon Gate. Queue up Undead units to create another attack force and, while that's happening, take two groups from Garithos' base to attack the eastern side of Balnazzar's base. Gather one group of Riflemen, Knights, and Garithos, and another group of Mortar Teams and Siege Tanks, then send them into Balnazzar's base. Use the Siege Tanks to attack enemy structures one at a time, while Garithos and his men deal exclusively with the enemy units that will quickly respond to the attack. Again, concentrate on destroying buildings that produce Balnazzar's units: Crypts, Temples of the Damned, Slaughterhouses, Boneyards (especially), and the Altar of Darkness.

Once Garithos' attack has failed, you should have dented Balnazzar's base significantly on both sides. Balnazzar does not rebuild structures that you destroy, so by eliminating his means of reproducing units, you reduce his capacity to create defenses to your attacks. Resume rebuilding attack groups in both of your bases once again. When they're ready to go, run your attacks again (one at a time) into the purple base. If you manage your troops properly, you can defeat the base with three waves (six distinct attacks) on the base. It may take you more than this, but it's possible to do it in six attacks.

WARNING

Never leave either of your bases completely undefended. While it may be tempting to throw *everything* you've got at Balnazzar, don't give in to those temptations, or you'll end up with a completely destroyed base. The Dreadlord Loyalists and Insurgents both continue to attack your bases throughout the mission, so keep your bases supported with a defensive garrison.

INTO THE SHADOW WEB CAVERNS

At that same moment in Northrend, King Arthas and Anub'arak march into the dark, forgotten halls of Azjol-Nerub.

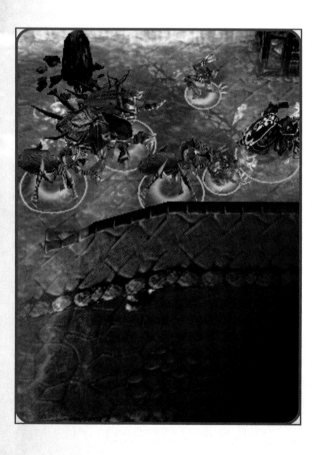

REQUIRED QUEST

THE OLD KINGDOM	Requirements
The shortcut requires passage through the Old Kingdom. Locate the entrance to this realm.	✥ Locate the entrance to the Old Kingdom Lock. ✥ Kill Baelgun. ✥ Bring Blood Key to the Circle of Power. ✥ Arthas and Anub'arak must survive.

OPTIONAL QUEST

FIND THE GOLD STASHES	Requirement
Gold Coins have been hidden throughout these underground chambers. Find them to increase your gold coffers. This is useful the next time you require gold to sustain and build your forces.	✥ Find the five Gold Stashes.

THE PATH TO VICTORY

The three Chapter 7 missions are short mini-missions which, together, amount to one large mission. Your goal in this portion is strictly to make your way through the maze and defeat Baelgun to obtain the Blood Key. There are several levers that must be operated, along with a few secret doorways, but the path is entirely linear. The most important thing in this mission is to keep both of your Heroes alive—your entire group for that matter. Use Arthas' Death Coil to heal them as they take damage.

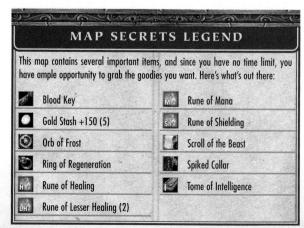

MAP SECRETS LEGEND

This map contains several important items, and since you have no time limit, you have ample opportunity to grab the goodies you want. Here's what's out there:

Blood Key		Rune of Mana	
Gold Stash +150 (5)		Rune of Shielding	
Orb of Frost		Scroll of the Beast	
Ring of Regeneration		Spiked Collar	
Rune of Healing		Tome of Intelligence	
Rune of Lesser Healing (2)			

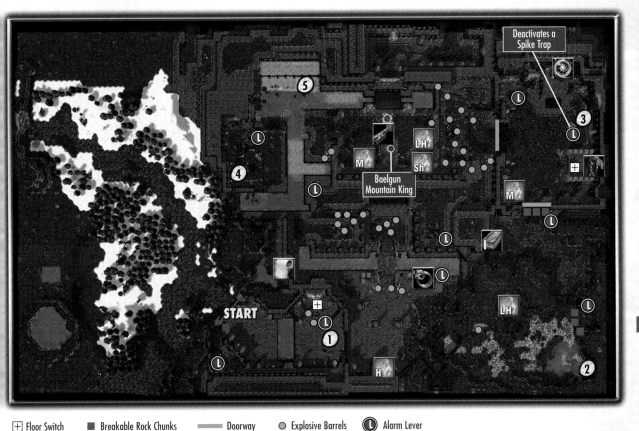

Deactivates a
Spike Trap

Baelgun
Mountain King

START

⊞ Floor Switch   ▪ Breakable Rock Chunks   ▬ Doorway   ● Explosive Barrels   Ⓛ Alarm Lever

THE FIRST GOLD STASH

As the mission begins, you quickly find a sunken area of the floor that's impassible. There are two ways to get around it. You can destroy the Rock Chunks by the entrance, then move down the path and hit the lever (see our map). Alternatively, you can use one of your Meat Wagons to detonate the Exploding Barrels by the other lever. Either way, the floor will rise up and you'll be able to take out the Riflemen, then move to the floor switch to open the door. You can also pick up the first of five **Gold Stashes**.

Gold Coins

THE BRIDGE EXPLODES

When you move into the next area, the bridge goes up in flames, leaving you no obvious direct route to Baelgun. Destroy the enemies in this room, then approach the Rock Chunks that conceal a lever. Engage the lever, and pick up the **Ring of Regeneration**, then detonate the Exploding Barrels. The ensuing explosion opens up a pathway into a cavern beyond.

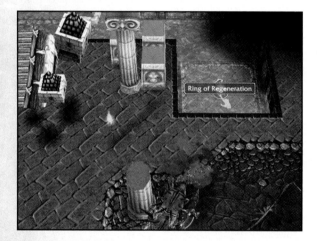

GOLD STASH 2

Move into the caverns and destroy all enemies. You face some Humans and a few Nerubians. There are plenty of Egg Sacks in this area, but none of them houses any items—it's still fun to destroy them. The second **Gold Stash** is located in the far southeast corner of the map, right there in the open.

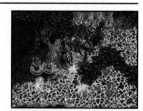

Destroy the ridge of Rock Chunks to reveal another lever. Hit this one to open a previously unseen door, and enter the storage room beyond.

GOLD STASH 3

There are several items in the storage room, including an **Orb of Frost** in the Nerubian Vault on the far end, and a **Spiked**

Collar behind a gate. Move through the room and destroy all of the Barrels and Crates to find the third **Gold Stash**.

Move up to the northwest corner of the room and hit the lever, providing access to the Nerubian Vault, as well as inviting a pair of Nerubians down for a fight. Take them out then get the Orb of Frost from the Vault. Hit the second lever to deactivate the spike trap, then blast through the

door to get the Spiked Collar (by stepping on the floor switch inside). A door on the west wall then automatically slides open, and several Riflemen enter and start shooting.

EXPLOSIVES ROOM

The room where the Riflemen emerge from is absolutely *full* of Exploding Barrels. Use your Meat Wagon to land *one* shot on some of the Barrels to detonate the entire batch, killing all of the nearby Human Riflemen.

BLOW THEM UP REAL GOOD

Move through the room, and hit the lever to the south. This raises the floor and allows you to move across to the western side of the map. Move your Meat Wagon along the newly raised area, then have it land one key shot on the Exploding Barrels on the platform above. Again, this one shot kills all of the enemies in the area quickly and easily.

GOLD STASH 4

Engage the next lever, and the floor raises up, allowing access to a room with some Nerubians fighting Human Riflemen. Prevent your troops from entering the fight, so they can pick up the fourth **Gold Stash** first while the warring factions beat each other up. Kill off any remaining enemies, then hit the next lever and move up to the waterfall in the north.

GOLD STASH 5

The last **Gold Stash** is tucked away in the waterfall, but it is still accessible with either Arthas or Anub'arak. There are just a few more Riflemen to eliminate before you move into Baelgun's chamber. Take the time to heal your units by lingering near the Fountain of Restoration before you confront Baelgun.

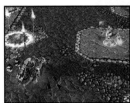

BAELGUN

The Mountain King's room contains several power-ups. Be sure to obtain this item before the fight with Baelgun—he's very tough, so you'll need every advantage you can get. There's a **Rune of Mana**, a **Rune of Lesser Healing**, and a **Rune of Shielding**. Activate the Rune of Shielding, then begin your attack on Baelgun. As your troops incur damage, use Arthas' Death Coil to heal them, then have one of your Heroes touch the Rune of Healing to provide a little extra

health boost for your forces. When Baelgun falls, you get the **Blood Key**. Pick it up and walk through the doorway to end this part of the mission.

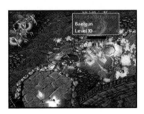

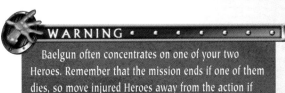

> **WARNING**
>
> Baelgun often concentrates on one of your two Heroes. Remember that the mission ends if one of them dies, so move injured Heroes away from the action if they start to get low on health.

THE FORGOTTEN ONES

Moments later, within the Inner Kingdom, Anub'arak warns Arthas that whatever scared the Dwarves still lurks down here within the Inner Kingdom.

REQUIRED QUEST

LOCATE THE EXIT	Requirements
The shortcut requires passage through the Old Kingdom. Locate the exit to the Old Kingdom.	✦ Locate the exit from the Old Kingdom.
	✦ Arthas and Anub'arak must survive.

OPTIONAL QUESTS

FIND THE GOLD STASHES	Requirement
Gold Coins have been hidden throughout these underground chambers. Find them for an increase of your Gold supplies. This would be useful the next time you require Gold to sustain and build your forces.	✦ Find the five Gold Stashes.

RESCUE THE CRYPT FIENDS	Requirement
The rebel Spiders captured several Crypt Fiends! They're being held in a nearby chamber. Release them, and they will be yours to command.	✦ Find and release the Crypt Fiends.

MAP SECRETS LEGEND

Here's a rundown of the many useful items you can find hidden throughout this map:

🔲 Belt of Giant Strength +6		Ⓗ Rune of Healing	
⬤ Gold Stash +150 (3)		Ⓛ Rune of Lesser Healing	
🔲 Manual of Health		Ⓜ Rune of Mana	
🔲 Medallion of Courage		Ⓢ Rune of Shielding (3)	
🔲 Ring of Protection +3		Ⓡ Rune of Restoration (2)	
Ⓓ Rune of Dispel Magic		🔲 Runed Bracers	
Ⓖ Rune of Greater Healing (5)		🔲 Tome of Intelligence	
Ⓖ Rune of Greater Mana (4)			

THE PATH TO VICTORY

As in the mission before (and the one that follows), your job is to get your troops through the map and to the exit in one piece. There are two optional quests—one to find the Gold Stashes and another to free some Crypt Fiends from bondage—which are easily satisfied while en route to the exit. The challenge with this mission is to keep your group of warriors alive and healthy. Hence, you must ration Arthas' Death Coil, using it to heal your damaged units rather than as a weapon against the Nerubians.

Spider Crabs

Arachnathids

Breeding Grounds **Breeding Grounds**

Breeding Grounds **Breeding Grounds**

Nerubians

Nerubians

Tentacles

Faceless Ones

Faceless Ones

Forgotten One (Boss)

START

RN Reinforcements ■ Breakable Rock Chunks ▬ Gate ▬ Rolling Stone Door L Lever ◯ Gold +150 (Stash)

DISABLE THE TOWERS

A long corridor comes into view before you, but as Anub'arak tells you, it is lined with dangerous defensive towers that will rip your troops to shreds in seconds. To disable the towers, you must hit two levers that cause water to flow into the tower chambers, disabling them. The first one is under some Rock Chunks to the left. Destroy the rocks, then hit the lever to make the left side of the corridor safe.

The second lever is down the walkway on the right, and it's guarded by three Nerubians that can summon Skeletal Warriors, so keep a close eye on the health of all of your troops. Hit this one and the right-hand row of towers becomes submerged. On the way out, pick up the **Gold Coin** to trigger the first optional quest.

After you flood the towers and pick up the first Gold Coin, you can cross the bridge and destroy the Icy Gate. Now continue north into a room where some Nerubians are holding a Crypt Fiend captive. When you rescue this Crypt Fiend, you will receive the optional quest to rescue all the other captive Crypt Fiends. Destroy the crate lying on the floor next to the rescued Crypt Fiend, and you can pick up your second Gold Coin.

SPIDER CRABS

Move your troops north, onto a large platform. When the entire group is on the platform, it drops down into the water, where you must do battle with a group of Spider Crabs, including a Spider Crab Behemoth that yields a **Ring of Protection +3**. Destroy the crabs, and then head east.

ARACHNATHIDS

There's a **Belt of Giant Strength +6** in the next room on a floor switch. As you might expect, grabbing this item activates the switch, this time unleashing a large group of Arachnathids. The good news is that Anub'arak's Locust Swarm coupled with Carrion Beetles can help you to quickly reduce these enemies to dust. Defeating them gives you **Runed Braces** to add to one of your Hero's inventories.

FREE THE CRYPT FIENDS

Hack away at the rolling door to the south, then enter the next room where three Crypt Fiends are being held captive by Nerubians. Destroy these enemies and add the Crypt Fiend reinforcements to your collective. Move on to the Rolling Stone Door that leads north (see our map). Break through it and then heal up your troops at the Fountain of Health.

As you encircle the Fountain of Health, Anub'arak mentions the Egg Sacks that dot the room. Move through the room and destroy the Egg Sacks to retrieve the third **Gold Stash**.

BREEDING GROUNDS

The next room (to the east) is full of Egg Sacks, small Nerubians, and a giant Nerubian Queen. Enemies continually pour out of the four Breeding Ground rooms (see our map) until you close their doors by hitting the four levers (one for each door). You can then destroy the Nerubian Queen and eradicate the Egg Sacks to earn a **Medallion of Courage**, a **Manual of Health**, and the fourth **Gold Stash**.

After you've retrieved the fourth Gold Stash, destroy the Iron Gate to the east, and head through the hallway until you come to a room with more hostile Nerubians. Just south of the door will be a few crates lying on the ground. Destroy the topmost crate to retrieve the fifth and final Gold Stash. Smash the other crates lying around the room in order to gain access to a **Rune of Lesser Healing** and a **Tome of Intelligence +2**. Now you can break down the Iron Gate to the west and move onto the next room.

> ### TIP
> Anub'arak's Locust Swarm is an excellent weapon when your troops are surrounded by a seemingly overwhelming group of enemies. It can make a huge difference in battle, so be sure that the spell is ready to go before going into a dangerous area.

THE TENTACLES AND FACELESS ONES

There's a mob of Tentacles supported by Faceless Ones inside the next room. The Tentacles are immune to Death Coil, but Locust Swarm helps to kill them more quickly than fighting them alone. Keep an eye on the health of your units during this fight, and don't worry if Carrions take damage because they can always be replaced.

As you venture further into the room, you confront more Tentacles and even a Faceless One Deathbringer (and his minions). Destroy these units to free the last imprisoned Crypt Fiends, thus satisfying the second optional quest!

THE FORGOTTEN ONE (BOSS)

The Forgotten One awaits through the next doorway to the east. This giant blob can stick Tentacles up through the ground. The Forgotten One has a total of 4000 hit points, so make sure that both of your Heroes have full Mana and can use all of their abilities before you go in. Attack the Forgotten One immediately, sending Carrion Beetles directly at it, as well as your newly acquired Crypt Fiends. There are plenty of Runes all around the Forgotten One, including Mana, Healing, and Shielding. Use these right from the start to increase your chances of victory, and be sure to use Anub'arak's Locust Swarm to help with the Tentacles. Once the Forgotten One is all but forgotten, the second part of this mission is complete!

ASCENT TO THE UPPER KINGDOM

Moments later, at the entrance to the Upper Kingdom, there is a massive quake and Arthas is separated from the rest of the group. He must find a way out of these passages alone!

REQUIRED QUEST

ESCAPE THE CAVERNS	Requirements
The caverns are collapsing. You must survive the traps and make it to the surface.	✛ Escape before the caverns collapse.
	✛ Arthas must survive.

OPTIONAL QUEST

FIND THE GOLD STASHES	Requirement
Gold Coins have been hidden throughout these underground chambers. Find them for an increase of your gold coffers. This would be useful the next time you require gold to sustain and build your forces.	✛ Find the three Gold Stashes.

THE PATH TO VICTORY

This mission is all about avoiding the various traps that have been set to stop Arthas. There is only one path, so there's no confusion about where you must move, but you need to concentrate on the timing of many of the traps so that you don't get hit. Although there is a 10-minute time limit, don't rush your effort! A typical hit from a trap takes 250 hit points off of Arthas, and can kill him in just a few seconds!

MAP SECRETS LEGEND

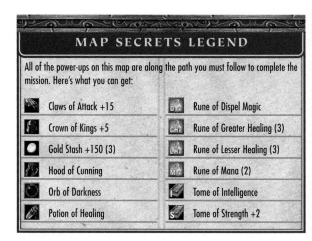

All of the power-ups on this map are along the path you must follow to complete the mission. Here's what you can get:

Claws of Attack +15		D	Rune of Dispel Magic
Crown of Kings +5		GH	Rune of Greater Healing (3)
Gold Stash +150 (3)		LH	Rune of Lesser Healing (3)
Hood of Cunning		M	Rune of Mana (2)
Orb of Darkness			Tome of Intelligence
Potion of Healing		S	Tome of Strength +2

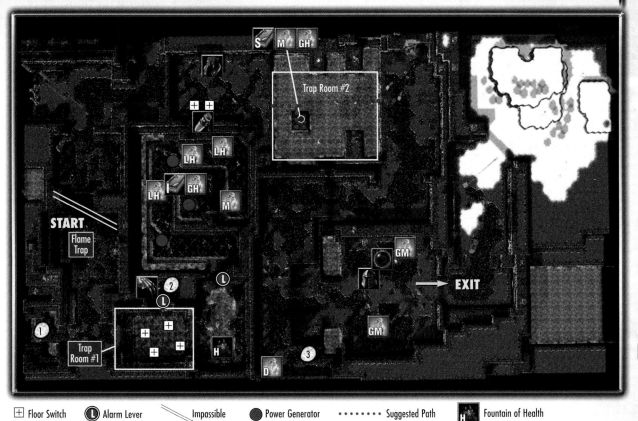

⊞ Floor Switch　　Ⓛ Alarm Lever　　╲╲ Impassible　　● Power Generator　　•••••••• Suggested Path　　H Fountain of Health

THE FIRE TRAP AND GOLD STASH 1

You have just 10 minutes to get through this level, so move quickly. The first trap is a flame trap with six jets of flame (three on either side) shooting from adjacent walls. If you watch, you'll notice

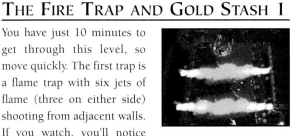

that there's a pattern that allows you to move through the trap without taking a hit. Try to time this up and be sure to stay exactly in the *middle* of the jets of flame! Just past the trap, move to the west to find the first of three **Gold Stashes**. This triggers the optional quest.

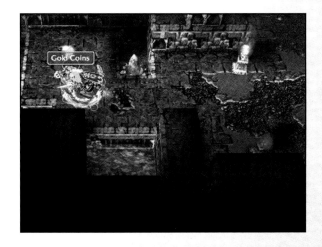

TRAP ROOM #1 AND THE SECOND GOLD STASH

Hit the lever to open the door to the trap room. There are four switches on the floor of this room that you must step on while avoiding the flame jets from the floor. Again,

there's a pattern, and if you time it properly, you can move through without taking a hit. That said, you may want to save before taking your first stab at it.

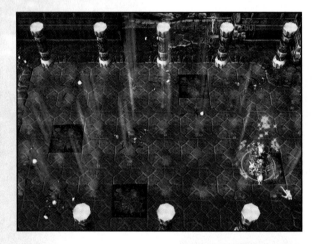

There's another lever at the top of Trap #1 room that leads to the second **Gold Stash** and an Arachnathid that yields a **Claws of Attack +15** when destroyed.

THE FOUNTAIN OF HEALTH AND POWER GENERATOR 1

Through the next room is a Fountain of Health. Replenish yourself, but don't spend too much time there because the clock is ticking! There's another Lever to the north of the Fountain. Hit it and move

into the area beyond. Expect an immediate attack, but remember that Death Coil stops each of these enemies (Darkfinders) cold. Move through to the Power Generator, then destroy it to allow passage north.

POWER GENERATOR 2

Move up to the next Power Generator and waste it. You'll be getting rained on from above and more Darkfinders show up, but fortunately many of them give up **Runes of Lesser Healing** when they perish.

POWER GENERATOR 3 AND THE FACELESS MAGE

As you move through the area around the pedestal that holds the Faceless Mage, you receive relentless beating from Faceless Darkfinders and the Mage's spells. Approach the Mage and kill him right away. Two Death Coils will do the job, so make sure you have at least enough Mana to hit

the Mage twice. Once the enemies are gone, destroy the third Power Generator and pick up the **Rune of Greater Healing**, and **Tome of Intelligence** left behind.

THE HOOD OF CUNNING

Once the Power Generator is destroyed, a shimmering blue bridge comes into view that you can cross over. A few more Faceless Ones await your arrival on the other side, and you'll see two floor switches before you. You must hit both switches *at the same time* to get the **Hood of Cunning** on the platform above. To do this, drop an item from your inventory on one switch, then stand on the other! Grab the Hood, retrieve your inventory item, then head east.

TRAP ROOM #2

The next room is a maddening maze of platforms that constantly move up and down and rarely line up for you to

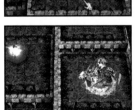

move across them. Still, there is a way to get across that requires just a little patience (see our map). If you have time to spare, you can pick up some of the items around this area, but since Anub'arak awaits you on the other side, we suggest you get a move on. Just wait and watch for the platforms to line up (they do eventually), then make your move.

THE THIRD GOLD STASH

The third **Gold Stash** lies at the end of the long hallway ahead. Move quickly down the hall (Rock Chunks disintegrate in front of you), then dispatch the enemies as quickly as possibly and head

for the very southernmost portion of the hallway. There's a crate there with a **Dispel Magic Rune** (which you need if you're cursed) and a crate with the last **Gold Stash** inside!

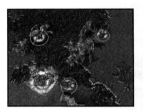

THE FINAL STRETCH!

Proceed into the next room and attack the enemies inside. You must defeat the guardians of the gate to win this mission. Your foes are four Unbroken Darkhunters (level 2), one Faceless One Terror (level 8), two Unbroken Darkweavers (level 5), and a Faceless One Annihilator (level 10).

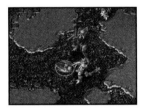

There are a couple of fantastic items in this last room, including the **Orb of Darkness** and a pair of **Runes** (**Greater Healing** and **Mana**). Once you defeat the host of enemies and pass through the gate, you proceed to Chapter 8.

CHAPTER EIGHT

A SYMPHONY OF FROST AND FLAME

Moments later, at the Scourge stronghold, King Arthas and Anub'arak make their final plans to defend the Lich King's Throne Chamber.

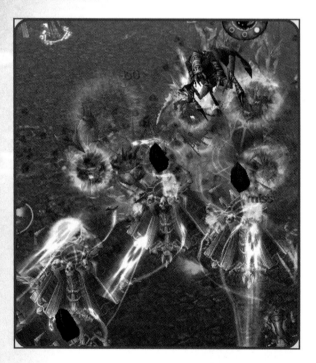

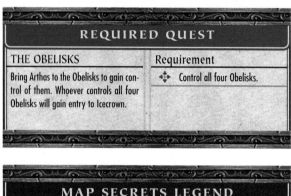

REQUIRED QUEST

THE OBELISKS	Requirement
Bring Arthas to the Obelisks to gain control of them. Whoever controls all four Obelisks will gain entry to Icecrown.	✛ Control all four Obelisks.

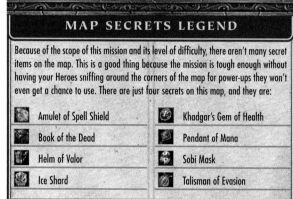

MAP SECRETS LEGEND

Because of the scope of this mission and its level of difficulty, there aren't many secret items on the map. This is a good thing because the mission is tough enough without having your Heroes sniffing around the corners of the map for power-ups they won't even get a chance to use. There are just four secrets on this map, and they are:

	Amulet of Spell Shield		Khadgar's Gem of Health
	Book of the Dead		Pendant of Mana
	Helm of Valor		Sobi Mask
	Ice Shard		Talisman of Evasion

THE PATH TO VICTORY

This is the final mission of the main campaign, so expect the most significant challenge you've experienced thus far in *Warcraft III: The Frozen Throne.* The goal is control all four of the Icecrown Obelisks

at the same time—no small feat. Illidan almost immediately captures the northern Obelisk (Obelisk 3 on our map), and there isn't anything you can do about it. The other three Obelisks, however, can be claimed by your forces early if you're willing to go out and fight the Ice Revenants that guard them.

Ultimately, this mission is about controlling the Obelisks and nothing else. You must secure enough gold and lumber to completely upgrade your tech tree and build several groups of high-end units. You do not attack any of the three main enemy bases (Kael'thas, Lady Vashj, and Illidan); instead, you must concentrate only on the tactical strategies necessary to secure all four of the Obelisks. To take control of an Obelisk, Arthas (and only Arthas) must remain on the Circle of Power in front of it for one minute. Once an Obelisk is in your possession, Illidan has to personally take it back from you (also by standing on the circle for one minute).

Kael'thas'
Blood Elf
Base

Illidan's
Naga Base

③

Icecrown

④

②

①

Polar Bears

START

Build Base
Here

Lady Vashj's
Naga Base

Sacrificial
Skulls

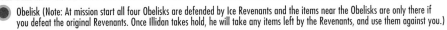

Obelisk (Note: At mission start all four Obelisks are defended by Ice Revenants and the items near the Obelisks are only there if you defeat the original Revenants. Once Illidan takes hold, he will take any items left by the Revenants, and use them against you.)

 Gold Mine

CLAIM THE NEARBY BASE

You start with a sizable force. Break it up into two groups so that your Meat Wagons do not rush into battle and get destroyed immediately. Send the group with Arthas, the Ghouls, and Crypt Fiends into the nearby Naga base to destroy its units while the Meat Wagons follow behind and lay waste to the Tidal Guardian. The base falls quickly, so be sure to have both Arthas and Anub'arak pick up one each of the Sacrificial Skulls that were near your starting position.

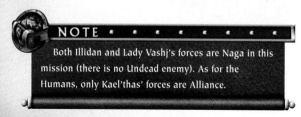

NOTE • • • • • • •

Both Illidan and Lady Vashj's forces are Naga in this mission (there is no Undead enemy). As for the Humans, only Kael'thas' forces are Alliance.

BUILD LIKE THE WIND!

Once you've cleared the base, you must work very quickly to build your base and upgrade. You have enough resources to start haunting the Gold Mine, begin construction of the

Necropolis, and get a pair of Ziggurats underway. While you are doing this, you'll notice that Illidan takes the northern Obelisk (Obelisk 3 on our map). Don't worry—this one is out of reach at this early stage in the mission.

Your base is attacked by Lady Vashj's Naga on the eastern edge and by Kael'thas' forces from the north. Fortunately, these attacks are most often composed of small groups of enemies, and only occasionally do Vashj and Kael actually accompany the attack groups. Build up a row of Spirit Towers to defend both areas—you must have the Ziggurats in place anyway to get your Food limit up to 100.

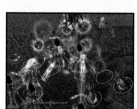

READY ATTACK/DEFENSE FORCES

You must ultimately amass two groups. The defensive group is a force led by Anub'arak that contains Abominations, Crypt Fiends, Necromancers, and a pair of Obsidian Statues. The offensive group is headed by Arthas and is comprised of one Abomination, two Obsidian Statues, and six Frost Wyrms (fully upgraded). If left alone, Illidan will capture all four of the Obelisks in 16-18 minutes (of real time). Therefore, you obviously won't be able to build up your tech tree to the necessary level before your adversary claims victory.

The answer to this conundrum is to build up in stages. Get your base moving, build a Crypt, and upgrade through the

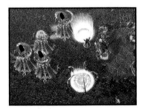

first cycle, then take your troops to either Obelisk 1 or Obelisk 4. Frankly, we think you'll have better luck with Obelisk 1 because it's farther from Kael'thas' base. Move Arthas, Anub'arak, and a full group of units (primarily the units you started with) and make your way toward one of these two Obelisks.

ATTACK OBELISK 1

The Obelisk area is guarded by Revenants, all of which are fairly tough. If you have Banshees ready and upgraded, then you can Possess the lesser Revenants while Arthas and his troops destroy the larger Ice Revenants. Either way, the

Revenants *will* fall. Move Arthas onto the Circle of Power; as soon as you do this—the timer starts showing only 30 seconds before the Obelisk falls under your control.

NOTE

Once an Obelisk is taken, both Vashj and Kael's forces cease to target your main base. Instead, they throw all their attacks on your expansion base, so you should not leave many defensive forces in your main base after you have an Obelisk. There may still be a couple of small attacks against your main base, however, so it's important to keep one or two units and some Ziggurats there.

DEFEND THE OBELISK AND UPGRADE

Once you hold one of the four Obelisks, Illidan *cannot* win the game. At this point, it's best to just let your foe capture the other three Obelisks (for now) while you fully concentrate on upgrading your tech tree to the max. As you might expect, Illidan wants to get his hands on this fourth Obelisk, so this is a good time to use a Sacrificial Skull to create an area of Blight near the Obelisk so that you can

build some Spirit and Nerubian Towers to help with defenses. Also have an Acolyte move over and Haunt the nearby Gold Mine. This gives you all the extra gold you need in this mission.

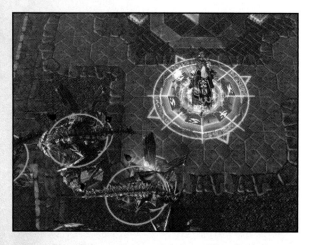

Split Arthas off from the group and send him back to your base (to help with the base's defense) and feed more units into Anub'arak's group to make it stronger and better balanced. Anub'arak does well with two Obsidian Statues, one set to Autocast Essence of Blight (to automatically heal units) and the other set to Spirit Touch to keep all the units in the group topped up with Mana. Add two or three Necromancers with Raise Dead set to Autocast and you'll

have a solid defensive force that can handle most attacks (especially with some Towers in defense). When Illidan comes to attack, use your full strength, including Impale,

Locust Swarm, and Carrion Beetles to help with the battles. With a few Spirit Towers, this fully upgraded defensive group led by Anub'arak should be reasonably self-sufficient, requiring only occasional reinforcements.

BUILD ATTACK FORCE

Once you've got Anub'arak set up as the defensive line at the Obelisk, build Arthas' attack group. This takes some time because you must fend off several attacks on your base, and you still have some upgrading to do. Aim to build one Abomination, two Obsidian Statues, and six Frost Wyrms. As with Anub'arak's group, set the Statues up with one replenishing Mana and the other restoring Health.

GO GET 'EM, TIGER!

When your troops are fully upgraded and you have the two forces described earlier (Anub'arak's defensive force and Arthas' group of Frost Wyrms), move them BOTH toward Obelisk 2 and attack the Naga defenses that Illidan has constructed there. These two groups outmatch the Naga you encounter. Use all of your Heroes' abilities to make the battles as one-sided as possible.

COUNTERPOINT

While the strategy we've laid out can work, you must be very precise and manage your units perfectly to get results. Another good plan is to wipe out Lady Vashj's base in the southeast corner of the map first, before you move out to the other Obelisks. Once she's been destroyed, she can't attack you with her Naga and her powerful Tornado spell.

With Lady Vashj out of the picture, you may also consider taking out Kael's base, as well! Having Kael and Lady Vashj off your back will allow you to fight Illidan without any distractions.

NOTE

Yes, you've left Obelisk 1 undefended (except for a few Spirit Towers), but you need to have *both* groups of units together to sweep the Naga defenses at the other three Obelisks. Remember what Sun Tzu said about having overwhelming numerical superiority before attacking. You can be almost positive that Illidan will retake Obelisk 1 by the time you get to Obelisk 4, but you can reclaim it with ease in a few minutes.

Place Arthas on the Circle of Power and assume control of Obelisk 2, then immediately advance toward Obelisk 3 and destroy the base there in the same manner.

Once Obelisk 3 is yours, move on to Obelisk 4 and do the same. At this point, Illidan will likely recapture one of the Obelisks. When you see this happen, send your troops straight over there and destroy him. You should then have time to

place Arthas on the last one or two remaining Circles of Power. When all four Obelisks are under your control, victory is yours. Congratulations!

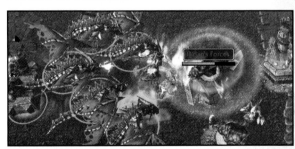

BONUS CAMPAIGN:
THE FOUNDING OF DUROTAR

This Campaign, which reintroduces the Orcs to the game, is an exciting departure for the Warcraft series, because it's not a mission-based strategy game. Indeed, it is instead an RPG-style game with one large map, multiple quests, and several subsidiary maps that you access from the main map. In some ways, it's more like Diablo® II than Warcraft® III. The main map contains some elite items, as well as a 'stash' also like Diablo II, that you can use to store these items as you acquire them!

In the months following the Battle of Mount Hyjal, Warchief Thrall led the Horde back into the central Barrens of Kalimdor. Freed at last from generations of Demonic corruption, the Orcs looked forward to building a new homeland for themselves in Kalimdor. They settled in a harsh, rugged land near the Barrens' eastern shore. Thrall named the new nation Durotar—in honor of his heroic father.

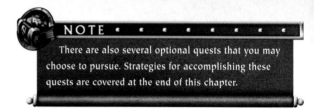

NOTE

There are also several optional quests that you may choose to pursue. Strategies for accomplishing these quests are covered at the end of this chapter.

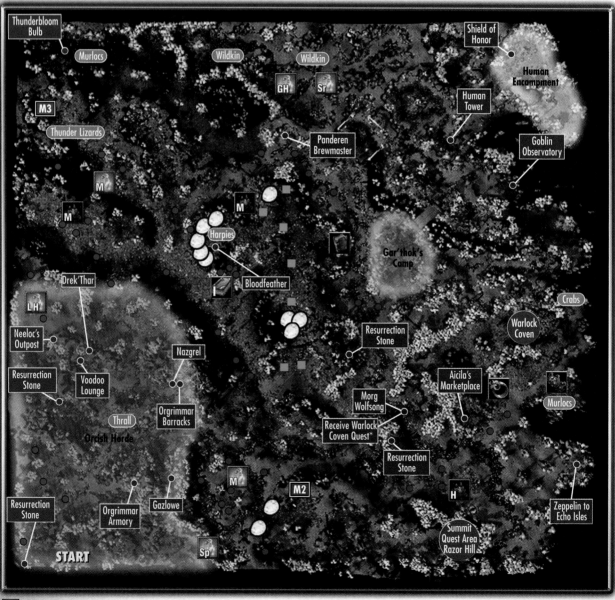

Thunderbloom Bulb

Murlocs

Wildkin

Wildkin

Shield of Honor

Human Encampment

GH

Sr

Human Tower

M3

Thunder Lizards

Panderen Brewmaster

Goblin Observatory

M

M

M

Harpies

Bloodfeather

Gar'thok's Camp

Crabs

Drek'Thar

LH

Resurrection Stone

Warlock Coven

Neeloc's Outpost

Nazgrel

Aicila's Marketplace

Murlocs

Resurrection Stone

Voodoo Lounge

Morg Wolfsong

Thrall

Orgrimmar Barracks

Receive Warlock Coven Quest*

Orcish Horde

Resurrection Stone

Zeppelin to Echo Isles

M

M2

H

Resurrection Stone

Orgrimmar Armory

Gazlowe

Summit Quest Area Razor Hill

START

Sp

| M | Gateway to Other Map | ● Group of Creeps | ■ Harpies | ➜ To Bloodfeather | ◯ Gold Coin +50 |

*Warlock Coven Quest Completion: Shaman Claws, Potion of Mana, Gold +50, Tome of Intelligence

BONUS CAMPAIGN | I | THE FOUNDING OF DUROTAR

MAP SECRETS LEGEND

H	Fountain of Health	**MR**	Rune of Mana
M	Fountain of Mana	**SP**	Rune of Speed
	Gloves of Haste	**SR**	Rune of Spirits
	Ring of Regeneration		Tome of Experience
GH	Rune of Greater Healing		Tome of Intelligence
LH	Rune of Lesser Healing		

QUEST: DYING WISH

	Requirement
For the sake of honor, you must complete Mogrin's final task. Seek out the city of Orgrimmar and deliver Mogrin's Report to the Orc warchief, Thrall.	❖ Deliver Mogrin's Report to Thrall.

DELIVER MOGRIN'S REPORT TO THRALL

This first quest is a short exploration of the immediate area, designed to give you a feel for Rexxar and Misha. Move to the southwest corner of the map to find a **Resurrection Stone**—this is where Rexxar respawns if killed. Move through the area and eradicate the Razormanes and other Creeps.

There are some **Gauntlets of Ogre Strength +3** for you to grab after defeating the Razormane Brute. Once you hit the Orc Horde's base, the quest ends, then you meet up with Thrall and are accepted into his outpost. You gain several new quests at this time, thus adding to your tasks.

NOTE

Try splitting up your Heroes into separate groups to more efficiently complete quests. For example, you can leave the Pandaren Brewmaster in town to talk to Thrall to complete quests. This eliminates the need to move your troops all the way across the map each time you must report back.

QUEST: EARNING YOUR KEEP

FOUR QUESTS FOR EARNING YOUR KEEP

❖ Solve Gazlowe's problem.		❖ Complete Nazgrel's task.
❖ Complete Drek'Thar's task.		❖ Return to Thrall.

To repay Thrall's hospitality, you have offered your services to the warchief. Fortunately, there is plenty of work for someone with your talents. Talk to Nazgrel, Drek'Thar, and Gazlowe, and help them complete their tasks. Note that these tasks can be approached in *any* order. We actually present the strategy in an order that isn't reflected by the quest's task list—our method suggests a more logical way to complete these tasks. That said, feel free to approach the quests in any order you wish, referencing this guide whenever necessary. Thrall has given you the services of Rokhan, a Shadow Hunter Hero that will make your quests far more interesting!

REXXAR'S STASH

There are all kinds of items available to Rexxar as he moves through these quests, but fortunately he is not limited to just his own personal storage space! Thrall has, in fact, given Rexxar a special Stash that contains 6 spaces to store excess items!

SEAL THE TUNNEL (SOLVE GAZLOWE'S PROBLEM)

Requirements
❖ Enter the Goblin tunnels beneath Orgrimmar.
❖ Destroy the Support Columns.
❖ Report your success to Gazlowe.

Gazlowe's efforts to secure a reliable water source for Orgrimmar have hit a snag. The Goblin mining teams have accidentally tunneled into a Kobold den. This opening must be sealed before the Kobolds cause any serious damage.

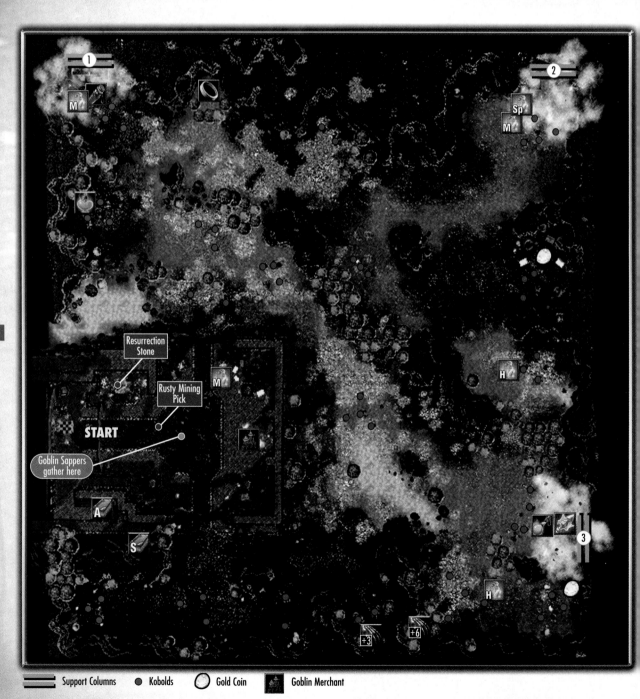

Resurrection Stone

Rusty Mining Pick

START

Goblin Sappers gather here

Support Columns   Kobolds   Gold Coin   Goblin Merchant

MAP SECRETS LEGEND

Anti Magic Potion		**H** Rune of Healing	
Claws of Attack +3		**M** Rune of Mana	
Claws of Attack +6		**Sp** Rune of Speed	
Minor Replenishment Potion		Staff of Negation	
Potion of Clarity		**A** Tome of Agility	
Ring of Superiority		**S** Tome of Strength	

Within the tunnels below Orgrimmar, the Goblins have dug deep into the ground in search of water for the Orc's new home. Though the Goblins are master diggers, they have little regard for the repercussions of turning so much soil.

ENTER THE GOBLIN TUNNELS BENEATH ORGRIMMAR

This portion of the mission is a snap. After you receive the quest, the entrance to the Goblin Tunnels appears in the east. Make your way over to the Goblin Tunnel entrance, keeping an eye out for Centaur along the way—there are *plenty* of them for you to fight, so Rexxar will likely level-up soon. Pick up the pair of Gold Coins (+50) outside the tunnel, then enter to reveal a new map.

DESTROY THE SUPPORT COLUMNS

As you enter the tunnels, a group of Goblin Sappers come under your control. There's also a Goblin Merchant where you can purchase items, although at this point you likely won't have enough gold to afford much of anything.

Head for the northwest corner of the map, toward Support Column 1 (see our map). There are several Kobold groups to fight along the way, so we recommend leaving the Goblin Sappers behind and just using Rokhan and Rexxar to manage these battles. Use Rexxar's Misha (a permanent summoned creature) and Quilbeast (a temporary summoned creature) to round out your ranks while Rokhan uses Healing Wave to keep Rexxar healthy.

Once the Kobolds have been destroyed, move the Sappers up and have one of them use their Kaboom ability to destroy the first Support Column.

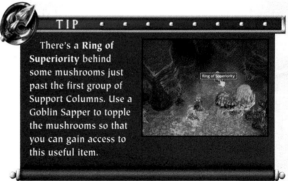

TIP

There's a **Ring of Superiority** behind some mushrooms just past the first group of Support Columns. Use a Goblin Sapper to topple the mushrooms so that you can gain access to this useful item.

Proceed to the northeast corner of the map for another tough battle against a large group of Kobolds. Use Rokhan's Serpent Ward and Healing Wave to even the odds, and keep an eye on Rexxar's health. Once the Kobolds are gone, bring in yet another Sapper and destroy the second Support Column.

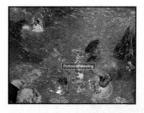

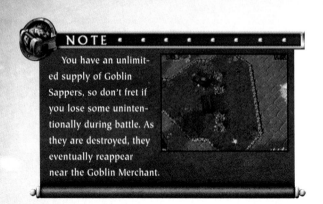

Tome of Strength. You can also get some **Claws of Attack +6** in the south, which are hidden nicely behind some mushrooms (see our map).

Now move your troops down to the third Support Column and destroy it in a similar matter. Beware that some of the Kobolds you eliminated on your way up to the first Support Column may now have returned! Use whatever it takes to clear out the guys in front of the third Support Column, then destroy it with a Sapper. Once finished, you can return to Gazlowe or think about clearing out the rest of the map.

SWEEP THE MAP

There are plenty of other areas that you can explore to find extra items (see our map), so feel free to snoop around and pick up any you might find. There are a few key items, including some that are hidden behind mushrooms. There is one in particular near the start point that requires you to destroy a large number of mushrooms with Sappers in order to open up the corridor that leads to a

RETURN TO GAZLOWE

Just like it says, move back up to the main map and return to Gazlowe! You receive **Runed Gauntlets** and an **Arcane Scroll** as a 'thank you' for your efforts.

THUNDER HERB (COMPLETE DREK'THAR'S TASK)

Requirements
✦ Collect six Shimmerweed herbs.
✦ Return to Drek'Thar.

Drek'Thar has sent you to Thunder Ridge to collect six Shimmerweed herbs for a potion he is brewing. The normally docile Thunder Lizards have shown unprecedented hostility lately, making your fighting abilities a necessity for the herbs' retrieval.

QUEST SOLUTION

To complete this mission, you must get up to Thunder Ridge. The entrance, in the northwest corner of the map, is heavily guarded by a large group of Thunder Lizards, but you have to deal with some Centaur first. Once in Thunder Ridge, even more battle is necessary before you can claim all six herbs.

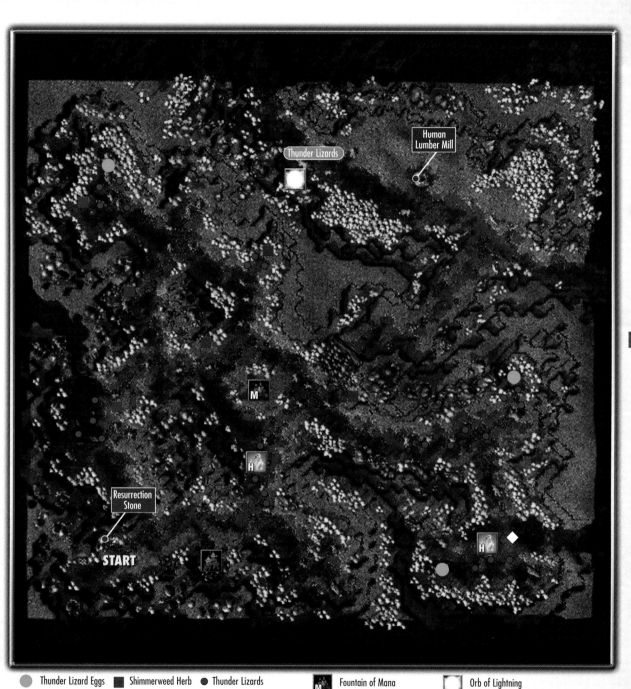

Thunder Lizards

Human Lumber Mill

M

H

Resurrection Stone

START

H

BONUS CAMPAIGN | I THE FOUNDING OF DUROTAR

● Thunder Lizard Eggs ■ Shimmerweed Herb ● Thunder Lizards

◇ Random Item (Many of the items in the Bonus Campaign are dropped randomly, making it impossible for us to show you exactly what you'll obtain in certain areas of the map. This is a great feature because it means that multiple trips across the main map will often not be in vain; you may get different items each time you pass through an area!)

M Fountain of Mana

Goblin Merchant

☐ Orb of Lightning

H Rune of Healing

MOVE TO THE THUNDER RIDGE ENTRANCE

Eliminate the Centaur and Thunder Lizards between you and the entrance to Thunder Ridge, stopping along the way to take advantage of the Fountain of Mana. Once the area has been swept of foes, take the plunge to Thunder Ridge.

FIND SIX SHIMMERWEED

This map contains the Shimmerweed needed to solve the quest. There really isn't a particular sequence in which to collect these, so we suggest that you create Misha, a Quilbeast, and make sure Rokhan's Mana is full (so that he can use Healing Wave and Serpent Wards), then move out and battle the Thunder Lizards for the Shimmerweed Herbs (see our map). There's a Fountain of Mana and a Goblin Merchant to assist your efforts.

> **NOTE**
>
> There are more than six Shimmerweed locations on the map, but once you obtain six, the remaining weeds disappear. You won't have trouble finding the requisite six Shimmerweed.

This map is teeming with Thunder Lizards. Sweep through and destroy them all if you want to quickly ramp up your Heroes' levels. When you have the six Shimmerweeds and you're done exploring, you can return to Drek'Thar to receive the **Enchanted Vial** as a reward.

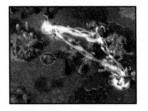

> **NOTE**
>
> You may be wondering why the northeast corner of this map is yet unexplored. Not to worry, you gain the ability to destroy the trees that block your way into this area later in the campaign.

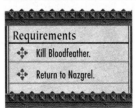

Enchanted Vial

HARPY THREAT (COMPLETE NAZGREL'S ASSIGNMENT)

Requirements
✦ Kill Bloodfeather.
✦ Return to Nazgrel.

Nazgrel has informed you that the vile Harpies are ransacking the Horde's supply caravans. He wants you to put an end to their threat by killing the Harpy leader, Bloodfeather.

QUEST SOLUTION

This quest requires you to move through a long and narrow area, destroying Harpies the entire way. You eventually come to Bloodfeather—your ultimate goal. Destroy her to complete the quest.

DESTROY BLOODFEATHER

To get to Bloodfeather, you must move your troops up through a long, narrow gauntlet that's defended by a bevy of Harpies. It sounds dangerous, but you can defeat these creatures quite easily as long as you keep a Quilbeast active.

Destroy the Harpy buildings to uncover a **Tome of Experience** and some **Gold**. Don't worry about the treasure

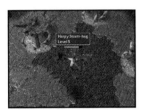

surrounding Bloodfeather until she's dead! Just concentrate on finishing her off first, and have Rokhan's Healing Wave ready to go for Rexxar (who takes the brunt of Bloodfeather's attacks).

Once Bloodfeather is history, return for your reward—an item from the Orgrimmar Armory! You may choose an **Arcanite Shield**, **Bladebane Armor**, or **Firehand Gauntlets**.

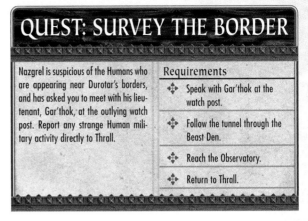

QUEST: SURVEY THE BORDER

Nazgrel is suspicious of the Humans who are appearing near Durotar's borders, and has asked you to meet with his lieutenant, Gar'thok, at the outlying watch post. Report any strange Human military activity directly to Thrall.

Requirements

- Speak with Gar'thok at the watch post.
- Follow the tunnel through the Beast Den.
- Reach the Observatory.
- Return to Thrall.

QUEST SOLUTION

This quest is actually a larger over-quest that has smaller sub-quests associated with it. Much like the 'Earning Your Keep' quest, you'll complete it when the smaller quests within it are satisfied.

SPEAK WITH GAR'THOK AT THE WATCH POST

To get to Gar'thok, follow the path through the northern portion of the map. Along the way, you'll fight Murlocs, Centaur, and even Harpies.

FOLLOW THE TUNNEL THROUGH THE BEAST DEN

Move through the Beast Den. Technically, you need only move across this map, but since you can complete an optional quest by simply defeating all of the Quillboars, it pays to sweep the area completely.

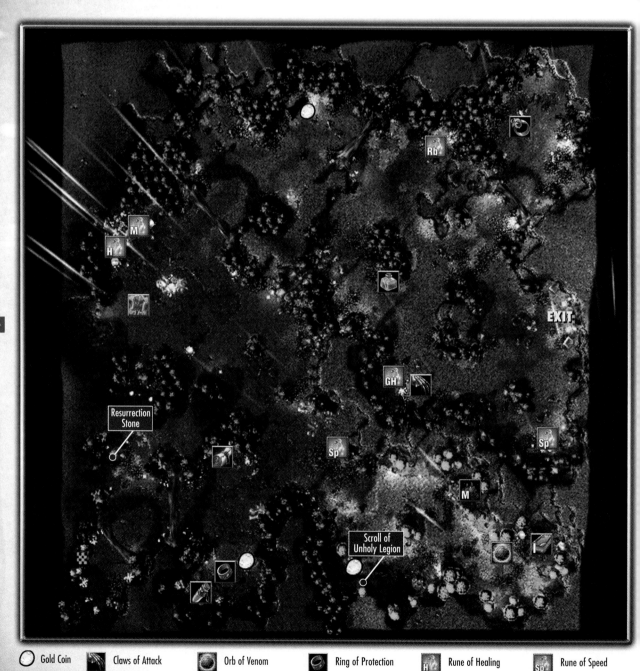

EXIT

Resurrection Stone

Scroll of Unholy Legion

	Gold Coin			Claws of Attack			Orb of Venom			Ring of Protection	H	Rune of Healing
												Sp	Rune of Speed
M	Fountain of Mana			Potion of Greater Mana			Ring of Regeneration	M	Rune of Mana			Scroll of Mana
	Healing Wards			Potion of Healing		GH	Rune of Greater Healing	Rb	Rune of Rebirth	I	Tome of Intelligence

SLAY THE QUILLBOARS QUEST

Within the Beast Den is yet another optional quest, the Slay the Quillboars quest. To meet this challenge, you must slay *all* of the Quillboars on the map. Complete this task while working on other quests! There are 50 Quillboars in total. Hunt them all down, and you earn one bonus skill point per Hero!

REACH THE OBSERVATORY AND RETURN TO THRALL

At this point, you just need to run up to the nearby Goblin Observatory. Now check off the final item on your list and get your troops back to Thrall for further instruction!

PROTECT THE BORDER

Thrall has ordered you to return to the watch post with Nazgrel and maintain surveillance on the Humans. Thrall

does not wish the situation to escalate out of control, but if the Humans attack, then they are to be neutralized.

QUEST SOLUTION

There are several things that need to be done in this quest. First, get to the watch post, then track and slaughter the Humans before returning to Thrall.

TRACK THE HUMANS TO THEIR BASE

Start off by heading to the north. When you discover some Orc and Human corpses, a cut-scene ensues. Following this brief interlude, get ready to fight some Humans. Pull out all the stops and lay waste to the Alliance forces!

SLAUGHTER THE HUMAN ENCAMPMENT

Continue north, following the string of Human units, until you reach the Human encampment. Destroy it quickly with

Rexxar's Stampede skill (if you have it). A combination of the Serpent Ward, Healing Wave, and Rexxar's Quilbeast (along with Misha to round out your troops) also works quite well.

RETURN TO THRALL

Return to Thrall once again, and the quest is complete.

QUEST: WARN THE TROLLS

The Human fleet poses a serious threat to the Darkspear Trolls on the Echo Isles. Thrall asks that you warn them of the immediate danger posed by the reckless Humans.

Requirements

- ✦ Take the Zeppelin to the Echo Isles.
- ✦ Meet up with Vol'jin.

MAP SECRETS LEGEND

H Fountain of Health		**H** Rune of Healing	
M Fountain of Mana		**Rb** Rune of Rebirth	
Goblin Merchant		**Rs** Rune of Restoration	
Healing Salve		**Sh** Rune of Shielding	
Mantle of Intelligence		**Sp** Rune of Speed	
Potion of Greater Mana		Runed Bracers	
Potion of Healing		Scroll of Healing	
Robe of the Magi		Scroll of Regeneration	
GM Rune of Greater Mana		Tome of Experience	

QUEST SOLUTION

This quest actually leads to additional quests on the Echo Isles (see our map). You must fight your way across the main map to the Zeppelin on the eastern edge. This vehicle transports you to the Echo Isles map, where you'll fight your way to Vol'jin.

TAKE THE ZEPPELIN TO THE ECHO ISLES

Again, this task involves merely traversing the map. While you *can* simply run your units over to the Zeppelin, it's more fun to fight the enemies in your way. Razormanes, Centaur, and Crabs all stand between Thrall and the Zeppelin, so hack your way through them to gain valuable experience for your two Heroes.

MEET UP WITH VOL'JIN

Vol'jin's location is identified on our Echo Isles map. Once you've touched the Resurrection Stone and have secured the Fountain of Health, head toward Vol'jin.

There are plenty of Revenants to fight as you work your way through the map. The path is fairly linear, making the enemies in front of you an obstacle rather than a distraction. Still, with the well-honed abilities of your Heroes, you can make it through without losing a single unit. Eventually you confront the Deathlords, who are considerably tougher to fight. Concentrate on one of them at a time, and be sure to have Rokhan's Healing Wave ready to go! Defeat these deadly foes to claim the **Crown of the Deathlord**, then follow the path we've charted on the map to face Vol'jin.

SINK THE FLEET

Requirements

- ✦ Destroy the Human Battleships (five total).
- ✦ Return to Vol'jin.

Before the Darkspear tribe can safely evacuate the Echo Isles, the Human Battleships bombarding its villages must be destroyed. Lead the Troll Batriders in a strike against the Human navy.

QUEST SOLUTION

There are five Battleships to destroy. Sink the fleet, then return to Vol'jin to complete the quest. The key to victory is to avoid biting off more than you can chew, which is to say that it's best to attack the Battleships one at a time.

DESTROY THE HUMAN BATTLESHIPS

Gather all of your units into a single group around the Fountain of Health, then move north and attack the first Battleship when everyone is healthy and ready for war.

Expect plenty of targets, ranging from Riflemen to Gryphon Riders to Human Frigates, but remember that your specific task is to destroy the Battleships only!

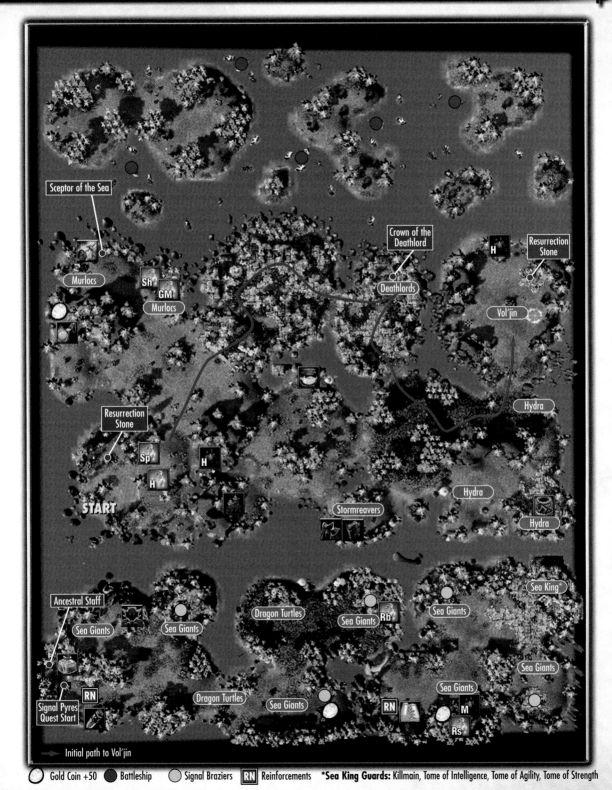

Sceptor of the Sea

Crown of the Deathlord

Resurrection Stone

H

Murlocs

Sh

GM

Murlocs

Deathlords

Vol'jin

Resurrection Stone

Sp

H

H

Hydra

Hydra

START

Stormreavers

Hydra

Sea King*

Ancestral Staff

Sea Giants

Sea Giants

Dragon Turtles

Sea Giants

Rb

Sea Giants

Sea Giants

Signal Pyres Quest Start

RN

Dragon Turtles

Sea Giants

RN

Sea Giants

M

Rs

→ Initial path to Vol'jin

⬭ Gold Coin +50   ⬤ Battleship   ⬤ Signal Braziers   **RN** Reinforcements   *Sea King Guards: Killmain, Tome of Intelligence, Tome of Agility, Tome of Strength

When the first Battleship finds its watery grave, move your group back to the Fountain of Health right away to heal up. If you lost any Batriders, they will be replenished over time. Once your troops are healthy, move out and attack the next Battleship, returning once again to the Fountain of Health when the job's done. If you engage these ships in this manner, you will have great success. The furthest Battleship (near the western edge of the map) is heavily defended, so

concentrate your entire group's fire on the Battleship alone when your troops arrive! In fact, continually reaffirm your units' target as the Battleship. Use Healing Wave as many times as you can during this final battle. You will likely lose most of your Batriders, but you can always return to the Fountain of Health once the Battleship sinks.

RETURN TO VOL'JIN

Head back to Vol'gin to receive the next quest. You get an **Ancestral Staff** and a **Potion of Greater Mana** as a reward for completing this quest.

QUEST: THE SIGNAL PYRES

Now that the Human fleet has been driven back, the Darkspear tribe is ready to set sail for the mainland. Five Signal Braziers have been placed across the island, and you must light each one to signal the evacuations commencement.

Requirements

- Light the Signal Braziers (five total).
- Return to Thrall.

QUEST SOLUTION

You must ignite five Braziers. All five are very well guarded by Sea Giants, Dragon Turtles, and other foes. Move across the map, fighting your way to each Brazier.

LIGHT THE SIGNAL BRAZIERS

This area of the map is heavily populated with Sea Giants and Dragon Turtles. These are all manageable enemies, especially if you use your Heroes' abilities during the fights. Traverse the map, destroying the guards and lighting the Braziers one at a time.

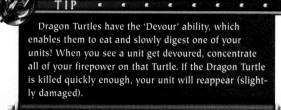

TIP

Dragon Turtles have the 'Devour' ability, which enables them to eat and slowly digest one of your units! When you see a unit get devoured, concentrate all of your firepower on that Turtle. If the Dragon Turtle is killed quickly enough, your unit will reappear (slightly damaged).

The Sea King is on the eastern edge of the map, just before the fifth Brazier. He's a tough customer with 1750 hit points and a group of Sea Giants guarding him, but you can destroy him with your newly acquired reinforcements. When he dies, you get the three **Tomes** that surround his throne. He also drops the **Killmaim**, an incredible item that

 increases the attack damage of your Hero by 20, and also causes life-stealing to occur with each attack! Vanquish the Sea King and light the final Brazier.

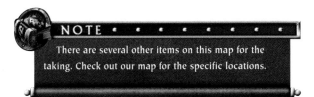

> **NOTE**
> There are several other items on this map for the taking. Check out our map for the specific locations.

QUEST: THE SUMMIT

The Humans have offered to meet with the Orc warchief, but you are suspicious of their motives. Go to the meeting in Thrall's place and sniff out any traps to protect Thrall from harm.	Requirement
	✥ Travel to Razor Hill.

QUEST SOLUTION

You must get to the Summit Quest area (see our map), then fight the Humans to the death. Unfortunately, there are plenty of Centaur between you and Razor Hill!

TRAVEL TO RAZOR HILL

This path is well traveled by now. Use every trick you have to hack through the enemies along the way, but be sure that Stampede is available to Rexxar when he gets there. Once you arrive at Razor Hill, you soon learn that you walked into a trap, and you must destroy all of the Human assassins. Use Stampede to crush the enemy quickly!

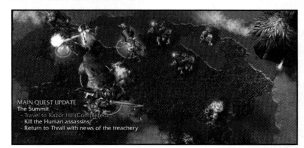

MAIN QUEST UPDATE
The Summit
- Travel to Razor Hill Complete
- Kill the Human assassins
- Return to Thrall with news of the treachery

> **NOTE**
> The following quests are optional and can be done in almost any order.

OPTIONAL QUEST: STRANGE BREW

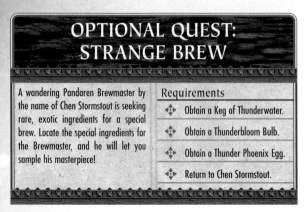

A wandering Pandaren Brewmaster by the name of Chen Stormstout is seeking rare, exotic ingredients for a special brew. Locate the special ingredients for the Brewmaster, and he will let you sample his masterpiece!

Requirements
- Obtain a Keg of Thunderwater.
- Obtain a Thunderbloom Bulb.
- Obtain a Thunder Phoenix Egg.
- Return to Chen Stormstout.

QUEST SOLUTION

The brew ingredients are all over the map, making your task a real challenge. This challenge is well worth the effort, however, because it adds Chen to your party!

OBTAIN A KEG OF THUNDERWATER

This is available in Aicila's Marketplace in the southeast corner of the map. Of course, there are plenty of enemies to deal with along the way. Note that the cost of this item is 1000 Gold.

OBTAIN A THUNDERBLOOM BULB

This item can be found in the northwest corner of the map. Watch out for those Murlocs!

OBTAIN A THUNDER PHOENIX EGG

This ingredient is located in the northeast corner of the map, but you'll have to roast the flock of Phoenix first.

RETURN TO CHEN

Chen is so happy when you return with all of the fixin's that he joins your party!

OPTIONAL QUEST: WARLOCK COVEN

A group of renegade Orc Warlocks—still loyal to the Burning Legion—has ambushed a caravan of Shaman and stolen their Sacred Relic. Avenge the fallen Shaman by destroying the Warlocks' secret coven and recovering the stolen artifact.

Requirements
- Slay the Warlock Coven.
- Recover the Sacred Relic.
- Return to Morg Wolfsong.

QUEST SOLUTION

Your goal is to destroy the Warlock Coven. This is tough, unless you use your abilities carefully (especially Healing Wave). Both Stampede and Voodoo Spirits turn this battle in your favor quickly.

SLAY THE WARLOCK COVEN

Move your troops to the Warlock Coven (see our map) and destroy them. They are difficult to put away because they raise the dead to fight against you. Still, you should emerge victorious with your Serpent Wards, Misha, and the Pandaren Brewmaster on your side.

GRAB THE RELIC AND RETURN TO MORG

When the battle's over, the Relic drops. Pick it up and return to Morg for several items, including a **Tome of Intelligence**, **Shaman Claws**, a **Potion of Mana**, and **Gold**.

OPTIONAL QUEST: THUNDER LIZARDS

	Requirements
Investigate Thunder Ridge with Drek'Thar to determine what has agitated the Thunder Lizards and caused them to migrate out of the valley.	✛ Discover the cause of the Lizard migration.
	✛ Destroy the rampaging Thunder Lizards.
	✛ Report the Human sighting to Thrall.

DISCOVER THE CAUSE OF THE LIZARD MIGRATION

Move your troops into the northeast portion of the map to discover the root of the problem: Humans.

DESTROY THE RAMPAGING THUNDER LIZARDS (50 TOTAL)

Here comes the fun part! Now you must move through the map and destroy 50 Thunder Lizards! When the mission is complete, you get the Thunderlizard Diamond from one of the slain Lizards.

OPTIONAL QUEST: COLLECT LIZARD EGGS

	Requirement
Drek'Thar would like the chance to study the Thunder Lizard's ecology. Collect three Thunder Lizard eggs for the benefit of science.	✛ Collect Thunder Lizard Eggs (three total).

QUEST SOLUTION

As you're patrolling the map for the Thunder Lizard Quest, you can pick up the three Lizard Eggs along the way to complete this optional challenge. It's a good idea to set upon this quest right away, as it saves time later.

GATHER THE EGGS

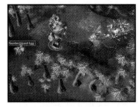

The three Eggs are marked on our map. They are easy to pick up as you move through the map to eradicate the 50 enraged Thunder Lizards. Completing the quest yields **Drek'Thar's Spellbook**, an item that grants the ability to portal to your home town. It also reduces spell damage by one-third and increases the Hero's Mana by 75.

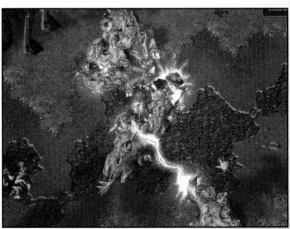

For generations, mighty warriors have heeded your command and
battled for control of Azeroth. Now it's your turn. Descend into the
World of Warcraft™ and join thousands of adventurers in an online
world of myth, magic and legendary chaos.

Your definition of epic adventure is about to be shattered...

COMING SOON

THE MOST UNREALISTIC RACING GAME EVER.

Heavily armed renegade racing
on 29 interplanetary tracks.

The Blizzard classic. Now on
Nintendo Game Boy® Advance.